Guide to
Wild Foods
and Useful
Plar

Guide to Wild Foods and Useful Plants

Christopher Nyerges

Foreword by Ed Begley, Jr.

CHICAGO
REVIEW
PRESS

Library of Congress Cataloging-in-Publication Data

Nyerges, Christopher
    Guide to wild foods and useful plants / Christopher Nyerges.—
1st ed.
        p.   cm.
    ISBN 1-55652-344-0
    1. Wild plants, Edible. 2. Plants, Useful. 3. Medicinal plants.
4. Wild foods. I. Title.
QK98.5.A1N94   1999
581.6′3-dc21   98-49812
                                                     CIP

All photographs taken by Christopher Nyerges unless otherwise noted.

Cover photographs: toyon berries (top), nasturtiums in flower (bottom), prickly pear cactus and nasturtiums (middle inset).

Cover design: Barb Rohm

Questions, comments, and authenticated reports (as requested in the text) should be sent to the author in care of the publisher.

©1999 by Christopher Nyerges
All rights reserved
First edition
Published by Chicago Review Press, Incorporated
814 North Franklin Street
Chicago, Illinois 60610
ISBN 1-55652-344-0
Printed in the United States of America
5 4 3 2 1

Contents

Foreword

Most children entering grade school these days can identify, by sight, hundreds of name brands. Hold up a flash card with three red diamonds and, though some will mispronounce, most will know we're talking about Mitsubishi. Display the next card with a rainbow apple, and they understand we're pitching a computer, not an edible addition to their lunch sack. And show any child on the planet twin arches painted gold . . . I don't think I need to go on. These same children can identify two or three plants, at best.

How did we get to this place as a society?

Not so long ago, we maintained a connection to the soil and the earth. We realized our place in the natural world and sought to maintain a balance with it. Some cultures still do, but their numbers drop precipitously every year. Is this the direction we should be headed? Is dirt just a place to put a house, an apartment complex, or a high-rise? What is the value of "idle land," when we could be erecting factories to employ hundreds, indeed thousands, of people?

Though we all labor under the illusion that we get our paychecks from these same factories, we do not. Though we feel snug in our homes and apartments, they are not the ultimate source of our security. All the many species that inhabit the planet get their real paycheck from the "idle" field, the "unused" forest, the "unmined" oceans, which supply the air, the soil, the water, the very elements we need for survival. We now have more shopping malls than high schools in this country. I'm certainly not suggesting we do away with either, but we need to strike a balance between the worlds of commerce and education. We need to educate our children about the web of life that supports us all. Christopher Nyerges's book offers such an education.

Though I have great admiration for Christopher and those who can live a truly spartan existence, I live in a home and always will. I work in a movie factory and probably always will. But we must all learn more about the plants and animals that share our home and revere them for the incredible job they do of keeping our world in balance.

I have learned what little I know about the many plants that surround us in California very late in life by walking in the hills with Christopher Nyerges and from reading and rereading an early version of his book *Guide to Wild Foods and Useful Plants*. I suggest readers do both.

—*Ed Begley, Jr., actor and environmentalist*

Acknowledgments

I'd like to especially thank Ernest and Geraldine Hogeboom and Richard White for their original support of the wild food outings and with this book. Also, I thank Dr. Leonid Enari who offered suggestions throughout this project. Proceeds from this book help support the School of Self-Reliance's educational activities, such as the wild food outings and various youth programs in the Angeles National Forest and throughout southern California.

—*Christopher Nyerges*

Introduction

When we allow our minds to reflect on the broad expanse of human experience in past millennia, we can see that most peoples were intimately involved with the plant kingdom. Knowledge of and interaction with plants was simply part of The Way. Today, though we've created vast amounts of material abundance, we seem to have lost our way in our technological wilderness. We have forgotten our roots. Our consumer-oriented capitalistic way of thinking and living has lulled many of us into believing that we are above all that, and we show our scorn for unwanted nature by attacking wild plants with poisons, weed whackers, and hoes. How far we've drifted.

The original concept for this book was an emergency survival manual. Someone who was lost, stranded, or otherwise without the conveniences of modern civilization could pick up this book and identify plants for making meals, medicine, and tools. Of course, it is far better to learn such skills as a normal part of everyday life, and not just as something to do in an emergency.

I have collected the information and used the techniques described in *Guide to Wild Foods and Useful Plants* for 30 years. My goal in writing this book is to educate and to instill appreciation for the floral wealth that continues to grow everywhere. We hope that by reading this book you will gain a heightened sense of responsibility to be a keeper of the flame, to strive to learn and use the ancient skills of self-reliance.

This book is written so that it can be easily used in the field or at home. The photographs, illustrations, and descriptions of the various parts of the plant should make identification easy. In addition, a comprehensive glossary defines the terms you'll come across as you read this book. We welcome authenticated reports from readers to add to this book in future editions (see copyright page for instructions).

Each listing is organized first by how to identify the plant covering each part of the plant so that you can accurately recognize it in the field. I discuss the various uses of the plant—the edible, medicinal, and the useful properties. I then indicate if there are any detrimental properties. I also explain where you are most likely to find the plant. Some listings contain nutritional and/or chemical composition information. In some entries, you'll see descriptions of the lore or the signature of the plant. Lore, which originally meant teaching, is a story where some aspect of the plant can be used to convey a lesson or teaching. Lore can be a metaphor, or literal.

camphor leaf

The signature of a plant refers to the Doctrine of Signatures, whereby each plant contains a clue as to its value or use. The classic example is the walnut. The inner edible meat resembles the human brain, and this meat is good brain food. The hard shell resembles the skull. The fleshy outer layer is a good dye and has been used to dye hair.

Signatures are usually not so simple to see and interpret. You might note function, color of leaves and fruits, interaction with other plants or fauna, aromas, or another characteristic. Though we have only scratched the surface, a whole world of meaning awaits those who use analogy and explore these signatures in depth.

We suggest you thumb through this book and look at all the photographs and illustrations. Then when you find a plant, you can begin by comparing its leaf or fruit to the pictorial keys on pages 1–8. Though there are many, many other plants that you might find in your area, we have included those plants that we actually use, those that are easy to recognize, and those that are common to many regions.

There are no shortcuts to learning the art of plant identification and uses. There are no rules of thumb to determine if a plant is edible or poisonous. You will need to devote a certain amount of time to studying and using these individual plants, and you will need to observe these plants in the field. Study and fieldwork are a sine qua non. You cannot and will not learn how to identify a plant and its uses simply by reading about it.

Collecting Useful Plants

When you find a plant that you want to use, always reflect on the fact that this living floral-being is allowing you to use its leaves or fruits or bark. Feel thankful. Don't uproot plants if you only need some leaves. Pinch off what you need carefully. We have observed that our careful pinching of leaves actually extends the life of the plants, causing them to produce two to three times as much leaf and fruit as they would have without our interaction. This phenomenon has been described in an article I wrote in the January/February 1998 issue of *The Wild Foods Forum* entitled "Passive Agriculture."

Move around. Pick a little here, a little there. Don't strip a single plant bare. Also observe the relative abundance of the plant. If there are few in the area, perhaps it would be best not to pick from that plant at all. If you're collecting various roots, always leave a few so that the plants continue to grow.

When we collect from the wild, we make the effort to return something back to the plant. In the old days, bits of tobacco would be left at the base of the plant because tobacco is both a fertilizer and a sacred plant to many Native American cultures. We may put tobacco or mulch under the plant, or we may just breathe on it so that it can inhale our carbon monoxide. It is certainly possible for large numbers of us to utilize the foods and herbs of the wild without exploiting and ruining the wild. Preservation requires careful attention to the details of each plant and insistence that your actions be part of a solution, not part of the problem. Carelessly harvesting wild plants can lead to denuded, unsightly areas, and an imbalance between us and our environment.

Of course, for perspective, that is exactly what we've done to the earth in the name of civilization and agriculture and earning a living. Like it or not, modern agriculture (and its related activities of raising animals, logging, and even mining) represents the single greatest cause of environmental destruction throughout the world. Few complain about this because we have accepted it as a necessary evil. So it might seem like a drop in the bucket to be concerned about how you collect "weeds" in a vacant lot when millions of acres are routinely being devastated. Don't be discouraged. Your thinking and your subsequent actions can have profound effects. Do the right thing.

rosemary

There was a natural area where I carefully collected willow for years, as well as an assortment of wild herbs. I always conscientiously picked and pruned and regarded myself as the caretaker of that willow forest. One day, bulldozers came in and leveled it all. Was I upset? Discouraged? Of course, though I accepted the fact that some things were beyond my control. I still gained insight and knowledge and strength by the way in which I chose to interact with that once-beautiful willow forest. It revealed secrets to me, and there was balance and equity between us.

chicory flowers

We hope you find this book useful. Let the skills of past generations come alive as you discover the wild foods and herbs that thrive everywhere. Let the plants be your friends.

Pictorial Key to Leaf Shapes

How to Use This Key

Determine which shape(s) on these pages most closely resembles the plant in question, then refer to the alphabetical listings for more information. This book includes common edible, medicinal, and some poisonous plants. (Not all plants encountered throughout the United States are listed in this book.)

How to Read the Scales

The numbers next to each plant are to be interpreted as follows: ×¼ means that the drawing is ¼ the plant's size; ×1 means that the drawing is the actual size of the plant; ×4 means that the drawing is four times larger than the actual plant.

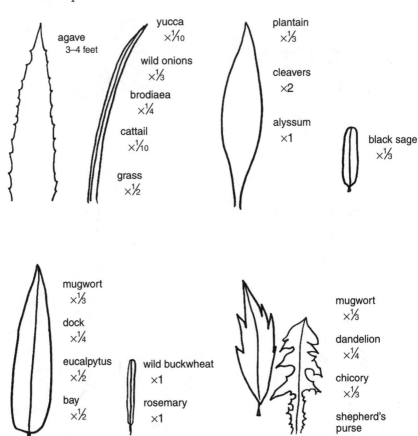

agave
3–4 feet

yucca
×¹⁄₁₀

wild onions
×⅓

brodiaea
×¼

cattail
×¹⁄₁₀

grass
×½

plantain
×⅓

cleavers
×2

alyssum
×1

black sage
×⅓

mugwort
×⅓

dock
×¼

eucalpytus
×½

bay
×½

wild buckwheat
×1

rosemary
×1

mugwort
×⅓

dandelion
×¼

chicory
×⅓

shepherd's purse
×½

1

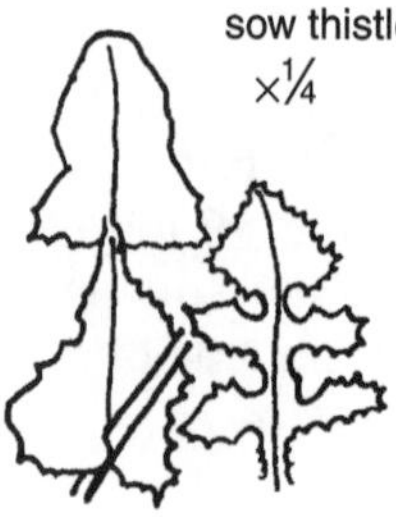

sow thistle $\times\frac{1}{4}$

prickly lettuce $\times\frac{1}{4}$

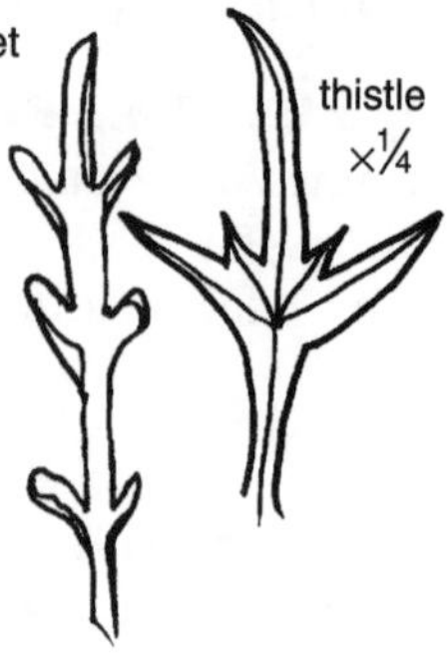

sea rocket $\times\frac{1}{3}$

thistle $\times\frac{1}{4}$

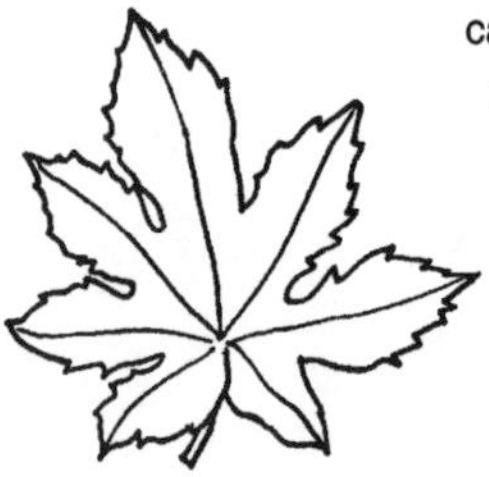

castor bean $\times\frac{1}{10}$

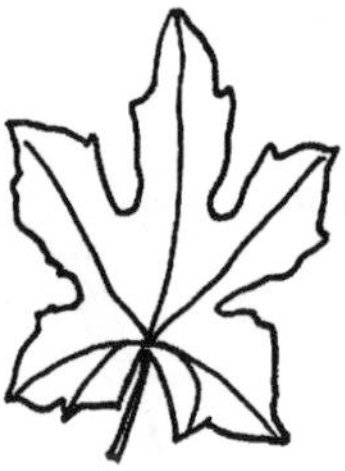

wild cucumber $\times\frac{1}{4}$

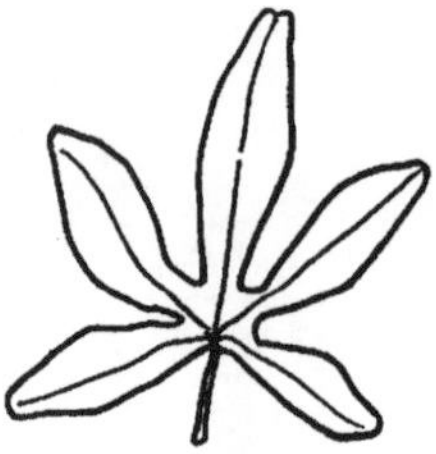

passionflower $\times\frac{1}{4}$

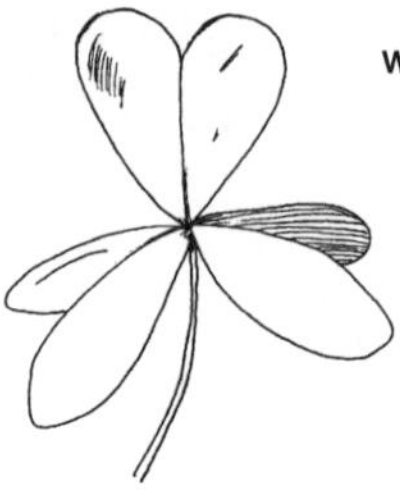

wood sorrel $\times\frac{1}{2}$

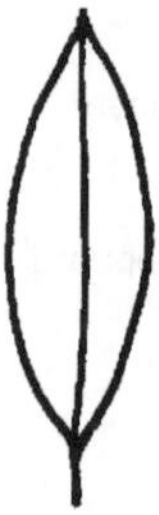

milkweed $\times\frac{1}{4}$

toyon $\times\frac{1}{3}$

white sage $\times\frac{1}{3}$

yerba santa $\times\frac{1}{3}$

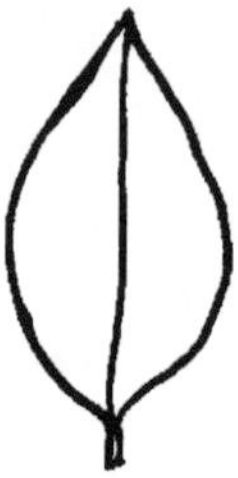

camphor $\times\frac{1}{3}$

coffee berry $\times\frac{1}{2}$

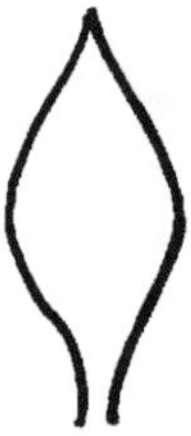

miner's lettuce $\times\frac{1}{3}$

lamb's quarter $\times\frac{1}{2}$

amaranth $\times\frac{1}{2}$

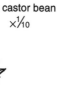

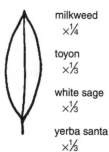

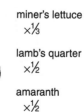

epazote
×⅓

jimsonweed
×¼

lamb's quarter
×½

nightshade
×⅓

oak
×½

milkweed
×⅓

tree tobacco
×⅓

chickweed
×1

plantain
×¼

nettle
×½

water
hyacinth
×⅓

nettle
×⅓

yerba santa
×¼

purslane
×1

nasturtium
×⅓

miner's lettuce
×½

mallow
×⅓

horehound
×1

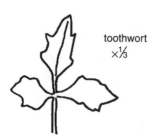

toothwort
×⅓

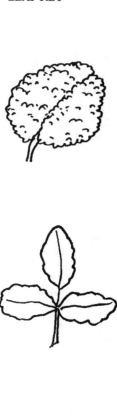

poison oak
×⅓

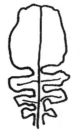

mustard
×⅓

currants and
gooseberries
×1

watercress
×⅓

carob
×⅕

rose
elder
×⅕

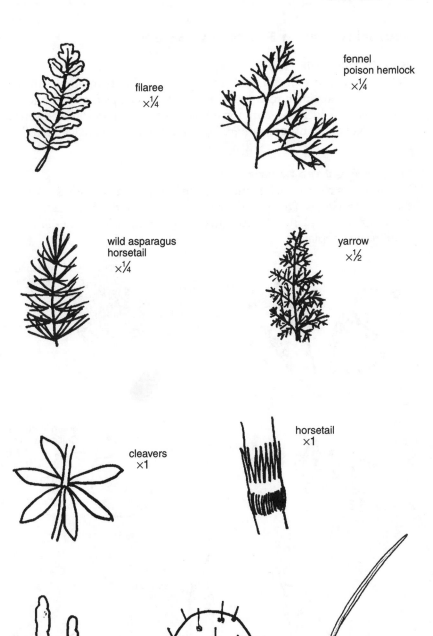

filaree
×¼

fennel
poison hemlock
×¼

wild asparagus
horsetail
×¼

yarrow
×½

cleavers
×1

horsetail
×1

glasswort
×1

prickly pear
×⅟₁₀

pinyon
Russian thistle
×1

Pictorial Key to Fruits and Seeds

How to Use This Key
Determine which shape(s) on these pages most closely resembles the plant in question, then refer to the alphabetical listings for more information. This book includes common edible, medicinal, and some poisonous plants. (Not all plants encountered in the United States are listed in this book.)

How to Read the Scales
The numbers next to each plant are to be interpreted as follows: ×¼ means that the drawing is ¼ the plant's size; ×1 means that the drawing is the actual size of the plant; ×4 means that the drawing is four times larger than the actual plant.

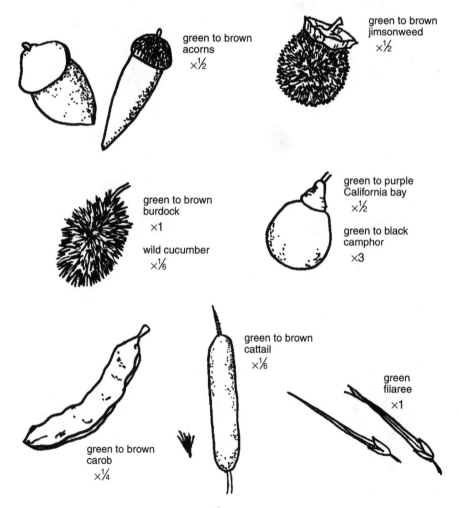

green to brown
acorns
×½

green to brown
jimsonweed
×½

green to brown
burdock
×1

wild cucumber
×⅙

green to purple
California bay
×½

green to black
camphor
×3

green to brown
cattail
×⅙

green
filaree
×1

green to brown
carob
×¼

green to red or
orange
currants and
gooseberries
×1

wild buckwheat
×1

pinyon
×1

black seed
amaranth
brodiaea
epazote
lamb's quarter
miner's lettuce
mustard
purslane
watercress
wild onion
×1

brown seed
alyssum, sweet
buckwheat, wild
chickweed
grass
mugwort
mustard
nettle
plantain
sea rocket
tree tobacco
×1

seed cluster
black sage
chia
horehound
×½

yellow
poison oak
×1

tan
nasturtium
×1

green
mallow
×1

dark brown
dock
×2

green
cleavers
×2

light brown
fennel
×1

cattail
chicory
dandelion
milkweed
prickly lettuce
sow thistle
thistle
×2

green to
orange
rose
×1

green to
brown
castor bean
×1

green to dark purple
coffee berry
×1

green to red or purple
elder
×3

green to orange-red
toyon
×2

green to dark purple
Western black nightshade
×1

green to red
wild asparagus
×2

agave
yucca
×1

shepherd's
purse
×2

mustard
green
toothwort
watercress
wood sorrel
×1

sea rocket
×2

various shapes
eucalyptus
×1

green, ripening to yellow,
red, or purple
prickly pear cactus
×¼

orange
passionflower
×1

Agave (Agave spp.)

Agave Family (Agavaceae)

Common Names Century plant, mescal, maguey

Most Prominent Characteristics

Overall Shape and Size The base of the mature plant is an approximately four- to five-foot diameter rosette (circular cluster). The flower stalk reaches up to 20 feet tall upon maturity. The leaves grow to approximately three to four feet in length on the mature plant.

A patch of agave plants. Note the birdhouse openings on the dead flower stalks.

Leaves The strong, tapered, evergreen, spine-tipped leaves have toothed margins (edges).

Flowers When the plant is 10 to 20 years old, a flower stalk shoots up from the center of the rosette. The flower stalk, which reaches a height of 10 to 20 feet, is clustered at intervals with small, bright-yellow flowers. These clusters of edible, thick, fleshy flowers are spaced along the stalk so that they appear almost like steps (such as those used to climb telephone poles).

Beneficial Properties

Edible Properties The center bud, or caudex (fleshy, cabbage-size center of the plant from which the leaves radiate), available year-round, is edible—preferably steamed, roasted, or boiled. In the past, the Apache, Hopi, Havasupai, Kaibab, and other southwestern Native Americans prepared the buds by digging firepits and building a large fire. When the fire died down to a bed of hot coals, the Native Americans put in the buds, covered them with fresh vegetation and a layer of soil, and let them steam for two days. The steamed buds were then simply peeled and eaten or mashed, formed into cakes, and sun-dried for later use. (This dried product also makes a nourishing beverage when crumbled finely into water.) The unique (but somewhat bland) taste of the agave buds has been described as a combination of turnip, squash, and pineapple.

The flowers can be boiled and eaten or dried and later steeped into teas. The seeds, also nutritious, can be ground into flour. John Watkins of Harbor City, California, reports that during a trip to Mexico City in August 1979, he was served Agave flowers. "The women boiled the flowers and mashed them into patties," Watkins said. "They seasoned the patties with their herbs. (I don't know what herbs were used.) Then the women sautéed them. They were delicious."

9

A sweet water can be obtained directly from the agave plant. When you observe the mature plant, which has not yet flowered, you'll note that there is a solid center cylindrical spike from which each leaf unfolds. To obtain water, cut off approximately the top half of this center spike, making a horizontal cut. Next cut off a one-inch piece, which will be used later as a cap. Then use a sharp knife to hollow out a bowl into the spike and place the cap over the bowl. Within a few hours, a sweet water will seep into the

peeling off the paperlike epidermal layer from the agave leaf

bowl and you can drink it as is. It is mildly sweet, and is called *aguamiel* (sweet water in Spanish). Water will continue to seep into the bowl for up to a month, depending on the size of the plant.

When allowed to sit for about two weeks, the sugar content of aguamiel naturally ferments, producing pulque, legally classified as a wine due to its approximately 12 percent alcohol content. Tequila can be made by distilling this liquid.

Medicinal Uses A juice made by boiling the caudex can be used directly on the skin to heal infections and fresh wounds.

Other Uses The stringy fibers of the leaves can be extracted and used in much the same way as yucca fiber: 1. Pound the fresh leaves until only the fiber remains; 2. Separate the fiber separated into strips; 3. Join the strips; 4. Twirl strips into twine; and 5. Weave twine into items such as sandals, mats, or rope.

The peeled skin of the agave leaves can be used as paper. You make the paper by cutting a large rectangle from the broadest section of the leaf. Carefully and slowly peel back the rectangle from one corner. If you peel carefully, and if the leaf has no imperfections, you should be able to get a large piece of this agave paper.

At the Museum of Natural History in Mexico City, John Watkins reported seeing photocopies of early Spanish reports written on agave parchment. He was told by the curator that many of the reports that went to Spain from this part of the world were written on this parchment.

If you experiment with this, you'll note that as the skin dries, the paper tends to curl into a small tube. To prevent this, the fresh paper must be stretched and kept flattened between two boards. To prevent the paper from becoming brittle, rub glycerin over it as soon as it is peeled. This causes the paper to retain water.

The pulp of the agave leaves can be mixed with water and vigorously beaten or mixed. This results in a soapy lather that can be used for washing your skin, hair, or clothing. Considering that the fresh agave juice sometimes causes a poison-oak-like rash, it would be wise to use this soap only with clothing (unless you're absolutely certain the juice doesn't affect your skin). Thoroughly rinse your clothing in fresh water before drying and wearing.

The large agave leaves make an excellent roofing material for emergency shelters. They're waterproof, and can actually be used like shingles.

Agave has long been one of the most important plants of the desert Native Americans. In fact, it was the cultivation of agave that made it possible for the Hohokam Native Americans to flourish in the deserts of southern Arizona from around A.D. 1100 to 1300. Although archaeologists had long known of the foraging practices of the desert Native Americans, it was not until 1988 that they confirmed that the Hohokams once had 102,000 agave plants under cultivation. A survey by four archaeologists (Paul and Suzanne Fish of the Arizona State Museum, Charles Miksicek, and John Madsen) showed evidence of dams, terraces, and rock piles where 1,200 acres of agave were under cultivation. This desert plant provided a significant amount of the Hohokams' food, water, fiber, and construction material.

Even in death, agave is useful. When the large flower stalk dies and dries, it can be 20 feet long and up to a foot and a half at the base. Cut two- to three-foot sections of these dead stalks, hollow them out, put on a bottom, and attach a leather strap and you'll have created an attractive and useful quiver (a carrying case). The wider sections can be hollowed out and covered with skins for a drum.

Detrimental Properties

Be careful when gathering agave leaves. The fresh juice can cause a rash the equivalent of that caused by poison oak. (See Poison Oak for treatment.) Thus, long sleeves and gloves are advisable during the harvest.

One species, A. lecheguilla, found in western Texas, southern New Mexico, and northern Mexico, has caused liver damage and photo-sensitization poisoning in grazing sheep, goats, and horses. Poisoning occurs with this species most often during drought years.

Where Found

The plant is commonly found in dry, desert-like canyon areas and in the upper half of alluvial fans.

Growing Cycle

Agave is a perennial that flowers once after 10 or 20 years and then dies. Numerous babies are typically found around the base of the dying adult.

Alyssum (Alyssum maritimum)

Mustard Family (Cruciferae)
Common Names Sweet
alyssum, lobularia maritima

Most Prominent Characteristics

Overall Shape and Size This plant grows in low clumps, usually just a few inches tall, rarely over a foot tall. The plant is mildly aromatic.

Cassius Clay, Christopher Nyerges's canine friend, next to sweet allysum

Stalks and Stems The weak and branching stems lay on the ground and reach possibly a foot in length. The main, somewhat fibrous, stem appears to be five sided in the cross section and is about one-tenth of an inch thick.

Leaves The linear- to lance-shaped leaves are from ½ to 1½ inches long and approximately ⅛ to 3/16 inches wide, tapering to a point at both ends. Leaves are alternately arranged, but some appear almost opposite. Although the leaf surface appears to be hairless, careful observation through a 10× magnifying glass reveals that both the upper and lower surfaces of the leaf are scattered with fine white hairs.

Flowers The white, sometimes lavender, flowers have the typical mustard family characteristics, that is, four petals, four sepals, six stamens (four long, two short), and one pistil. Each individual flower is about ⅛ inch across, and each cluster measures about ¾ inch across. The six yellow anthers are somewhat noticeable. The flowers, formed in racemes, bloom all year if there is enough moisture—provided, of course, they're not in a climate where they are covered with snow.

Fruit The fruit is a two-celled pod, often referred to as a pouch.

Seeds The small, approximately 1/16 inch diameter tan or yellowish-brown seeds are formed singly in round-shaped pods along the stalk. They are without albumin. From my observations, the pods seem rather ephemeral, and seeds do not always develop.

Roots There is a small, slender, somewhat fibrous tap root. The color is off-white to tan. It is slightly larger in diameter than the lower part of the mature (above-ground) stem.

Beneficial Properties

Edible Properties The blossoms, leaves, and tender stems are all good additions to your salad bowl. Entire flower clusters can be picked and eaten raw. Adding ¼ to ½ cup of the flowers to your salads imparts a mildly hot, watercress-like flavor. The flowers, leaves, and tender sections of the stems can also be mixed into cooked foods, such as omelettes, soups, stews, and vegetable dishes.

Because of the mildly hot flavor and the tediousness of gathering the flowers and leaves, alyssum is used mainly as a seasoning in salads and other dishes where a watercress spiciness is desired.

A tender flowering sprig can even be served with meals, in the same way you'd serve a sprig of watercress, parsley, or cilantro.

Medicinal Uses We'd appreciate authenticated reports from readers.

Other Uses The attractive, mildly aromatic plant is great for flower gardens and for simply planting and allowing to go wild in your yard.

Detrimental Properties

We'd appreciate authenticated reports from readers.

Where Found

Aside from the commercial varieties that grace many gardens, wild alyssums are common along many hiking trails. Being low growing, it is well known in the western United States as both a flowering ground cover and a weed; it generally grows as an annual ornamental in the rest of the United States.

Growing Cycle

Alyssum is an annual in the eastern states, whereas it is almost perennial in California, considered a weed in gardens. The plant seems to be readily available year-round in warmer climates where there is no snow. It dies back somewhat in the heat of the summer and early autumn.

Lore and Signature

Alyssum comes from the Greek, "a" meaning *without* and "lussa" meaning *madness*, since it was anciently used as an antidote for hydrophobia.

The four petals are arranged in such a way as to suggest the form of a cross (as with most members of the mustard family). Particularly interesting is the member of this family called rose of Jericho (or resurrection plant).

Amaranth
(Amaranthus retroflexus)
Amaranth Family
(Amaranthaceae)
Common Names Pigweed,
redroot

amaranth

Most Prominent
Characteristics

Overall Shape and Size
Amaranth, introduced from tropical America, is an annual herb
reaching from one foot to three
feet tall.

Stalks and Stems The root and lower part of the stalks are red.

Leaves The underside of the young, lower leaves is purple. The oval-
shaped (ovate) leaves are alternately arranged on the stems, are pinnately
veined, have wavy margins, and are glossy green.

Flowers The small, green, inconspicuous flowers are in bristly dense
spikes. When dead, they give the plant an unkempt, weedy appearance.
Numerous small black seeds develop after the flowers mature.

Beneficial Properties

Edible Properties The leaves and tender stems can be eaten raw in
salads (the flavor is pleasant and mild) or lightly cooked. To cook, chop
the greens, add onions, bring to a heat, season, and sit down to a delicious, better-than-spinach meal.

The seeds can also be used for food. Gather them when the plant is
fully mature. Rub the seed clusters between the hands to free the seeds
from their husks. Then winnow if there is a breeze, or, if the air is too
calm, slowly pour the seeds out of the hand and blow the chaff away. The
whole seeds can be added to bread products or ground and used as flour.
The young stems also make a tasty vegetable when lightly steamed,
cooked, or sautéed.

One hundred grams, about ½ cup, of amaranth leaf has between 267
and 448 milligrams of calcium, between 411 and 617 milligrams of potassium, between 53 and 80 milligrams of vitamin C, 4,300 micrograms of
beta carotene, and 1,300 micrograms of niacin. This volume of leaf contains about 35 calories. (The variations listed here depend on whose
analysis you are reading.)

One hundred grams of the seed contains about 358 calories, 247 milligrams of calcium, 500 milligrams of phosphorus, and 52.5 milligrams of potassium.

Medicinal Uses The leaves of amaranth are a recognized astringent. Made into tea, it is used for abnormally excessive menstruation, diarrhea, and dysentery.

Other Uses We'd appreciate authenticated reports from readers.

Detrimental Properties
We'd appreciate authenticated reports from readers.

Where Found
You'll find this ubiquitous friend in dry fields, cultivated fields, foothills, arroyos, vacant lots, orchards, front lawns, vegetable gardens, and even sidewalk cracks! For this reason, amaranth is unfortunately looked upon as a weed, and, thus, its many benefits are lost as it's hauled by the truck-load to the dump through spring and summer.

Growing Cycle
Amaranth is an annual. The large leaves are best gathered in the spring. The seeds are harvested in late summer and autumn as the plant matures and dies.

Black Sage (Salvia Mellifera)

Mint Family (Labiatae)

Most Prominent Characteristics

Overall Shape and Size This shrubby plant is one of those common species of Salvia characterized as belonging to chaparral. It grows from three to six feet high. The base of the flowering stalks is very leafy.

black sage

Leaves The simple leaves are narrowly oblong, one to two inches long, and ⅓ as wide. The leaf margin is crenulated. The upper leaf surface is rugulose (minutely wrinkled or creased), and the lower leaf surface is cinerous and minutely tomentose. The leaves are opposite and very aromatic.

Flowers The lilac-colored corolla (united petals) is about ½ inch long. Flowers appear in whorls arranged in a spike-like inflorescence. Closely situated under the upper whorls are oblong to ovate leafy bracts, each of which is sharply pointed.

Beneficial Properties

Edible Properties The dried or fresh leaves can be used for flavoring in soups and stews in much the same way that you'd use ordinary garden sage. The leaves can also be infused for a strong-tasting tea. They are best gathered when the plant is not flowering.

Medicinal Uses Drinking black sage tea is said to calm and strengthen the nerves, and it is used as a digestion aid after heavy meals. Some have claimed that slowly sipping the strong hot tea relieves headaches. (Also see White Sage).

Other Uses Ninety percent of California's famous sage honey comes from bees feeding on the nectar of black sage.

The dried and powdered leaves can be used as a herbicide because they contain an inhibitor. When the mature plant drops its leaves, those leaves tend to prevent all other plants besides black sage from growing around their base.

Detrimental Properties
We'd appreciate authenticated reports from readers.

Where Found
Black sage is found in chaparral and on grassy hillsides below 2,000 feet.

Growing Cycle
Black sage is a shrub whose flowers appear in spring and whose leaves are best gathered in winter.

Brodiaea
(Brodiaea capitata)
Lily Family (Liliaceae)
Common Names Blue dicks, wild onions

Photo by Doug Haipt

Christopher examines brodiaea flowers.

Most Prominent Characteristics

Overall Shape and Size
Brodiaea is a grasslike plant whose flower stalk rises from an edible underground corm to a height of up to 1½ feet.

Leaves The leaves are linear and grasslike, reaching an average length of about 10 inches. Sometimes the plant is leafless.

Flowers The flower stalk is from 1 to 1½ feet tall, erect, and topped by a headlike umbel of 4 to 10 purplish-blue flowers, with about 4 dark-purple bracts at the base of the umbel. Each flower is about ½ inch long. The flower consists of 3 purple sepals, 3 similar-looking petals, 6 stamens, and 1 pistil, a typical lily family pattern. The flower appears in the spring.

Roots The root is a thick, vertical, solid stem, similar in appearance to a bulb. Its diameter is approximately ½ to 1 inch, and it is covered in a brown papery sheath.

Beneficial Properties

Edible Properties The corms of brodiaea are very good raw or cooked, in salads, or as a snack. Those who dislike the chalky taste and slightly slimy texture of the raw corm prefer it cooked, although overcooking produces a rather flat flavor. Due to its blandness, the corm is a versatile food ingredient.

In order to get the corms out of the ground, you must carefully dig around and under the whole plant. A traditional digging stick works well. If you tug at the stalk to get the corm, the corm will almost invariably stay in the ground. When gathering, take only what you need and *know* you will use. Leave the small corms for reproduction.

Medicinal Uses We'd appreciate authenticated reports from readers.

Other Uses We'd appreciate authenticated reports from readers.

Detrimental Properties
We'd appreciate authenticated reports from readers.

Where Found
Brodiaea grows in open grassy places and hillsides. Preferring a somewhat dry soil, it is not uncommon in dry arroyos, vacant lots, and deserts.

Growing Cycle
This is a perennial herb, producing its flower stalks and flowers each spring from the corm.

Survival Tips: Insects

Insects (three-segmented animals of the arthropod phylum having three pairs of legs) are a practical and nutritious source of food.

The protein content of insects far surpasses that of our conventional meats. Termites are 40 percent protein and grasshoppers are 60 percent, compared to the 20 percent of either chicken or beef.

Tastewise, insects are surprisingly good—often merely bland. When mashed and added to soups, stews, rice dishes, or baked into bread, you hardly notice their presence. Prejudices against eating insects on the basis of being unclean, unpalatable, or not nutritious are entirely without basis.

To early Native Americans, a large grasshopper roasted on a stick was a delicacy. The wings, legs, and head of the grasshopper were removed before eating it. Grasshoppers, locusts, and cicadas fried in oil were considered a finer delicacy than the best meat or fish in ancient Greece and Rome. Fried grasshoppers, chopped finely, can be added to your favorite bread recipe for subtle flavor enhancement.

When hordes of locusts destroy acres of crops, farmers should be counting their blessings and rapidly collecting locusts. After all, the locusts are a much higher protein source than the grains they're devouring.

Large ants are good fried. They can also be ground into a paste and mixed into other foods. In rotting wood, you can find larvae of beetles and termites, which can be eaten roasted, boiled, or raw.

Small, white termite larvae, easily picked out of rotten logs, can be eaten raw or cooked. The flavor is bland. If you close your eyes and recall the texture and flavor of cottage cheese—a bit lumpy, a bit watery, somewhat bland—you get an idea of the texture and flavor of termite larvae.

In this world where famine breaths down our necks, how can we ignore the multiple sources of free and nutritious food offered all around us?

Burdock (Arctium minus and A. lappa)

Sunflower Family
(Compositae)

Common Names Gobo, great
burdock

Most Prominent Characteristics

Overall Shape and Size The first-year plant produces a rosette of rhubarb-type leaves; in ideal soil the second-year plant produces a stalk from six to nine feet tall.

Notice the burdock plant's resemblance to rhubarb.

Stalks and Stems The stout stalk of A. minus grows to six feet tall. A. lappa grows to nine feet.

Leaves The leaves are velvety smooth when young, becoming coarse with maturity. They are heart-shaped and resemble rhubarb. The leaves are conspicuously veined. The first-year leaves are large and up to two feet in length. In the second season, the plant sends up a flower stalk with similar, but smaller, leaves.

Flowers The purple to white flowers, compressed in burlike heads, bloom in July and August. In late summer and early fall, they dry and their tiny fruits become hitchhiker burs that stick to animals and clothing.

Fruit The seed containers are spiny-hooked burs that stick to socks and pants. This characteristic has enabled the plant to become spread far and wide wherever there are animals or people to which their dried fruits can cling for a ride.

Root Burdock's pithy root looks like an elongated carrot, except that it is white inside with a brownish-gray skin that is peeled away before eating.

Beneficial Properties

Edible Properties Burdock is a common food throughout the world. It is cultivated in Japan. The first-year roots are eaten once peeled. They are usually simmered in water until tender and cooked with other vegetables. Some people say the flavor resembles artichokes. In Russia, the roots are used as potato substitutes when potatoes aren't available. Roots can be peeled and sliced into thin pieces and sautéed or cooked with vegetables.

The Iroquois dried the roots of the first-year plants and used them in soup. They also cooked the large leaves as greens.

Leaves can be eaten once boiled; in some cases, two boilings are necessary, depending on your taste. Peeled leaf stems can be eaten raw or cooked. The erect flower stalks, collected before the flowers open, can be peeled of their bitter green skin and then dried or cooked.

The roots can also be roasted, ground, and percolated into a coffee substitute.

An analysis of the root (100 grams or ½ cup) shows 50 milligrams of calcium, 58 milligrams of phosphorus, and 180 milligrams of potassium.

Medicinal Uses The root acts as a diuretic and a diaphoretic. Herbalists claim that it is great as a blood-purifying agent for people with kidney diseases, skin disorders, and boils. The roots contain a high insulin content (27 percent to 45 percent), and the root is used in the making of fructose.

Tea of the roots is said to be useful in treating rheumatism. Herbalists all over the world use burdock—the roots and seeds are a soothing demulcent, tonic, and alterative (restorative to normal health) that soothe the entire system's mucous membrane.

Burdock leaf is the best herbal treatment for rattlesnake bites, according to Linda Sheer, who grew up in rural Kentucky. Two leaves are simmered in milk and given to the victim to drink. The burdock helps to counteract the effects of the venom. The body experiences both shock and calcium loss as a result of a rattlesnake bite. The lactose in the milk offsets the calcium loss and prevents or reduces shock.

The burs have been used to help keep wounds closed to promote healing, while the leaves (lightly crushed) laid over the wounds promote healing and eliminate airborne infectious particles. Though generally a veterinary practice, it's apparently been used on humans in dire emergencies.

Other Uses Observe the efficiency with which the seed pods attach themselves to your socks and pants. Look closely at the hooks on each spine of the bur. Compare these hooks with Velcro, that fastening device first so common on camping gear, such as packs and coats, and now found in countless other applications. Now ask yourself: do you believe Velcro is an invention of the human mind?

In fact, Velcro was invented by George de Mestral, a Swiss engineer. While walking his dog one day in 1948, some burs got stuck to his wool socks. He noted the tiny hooks at the end of each needle on the bur. He attempted to replicate nature by attaching velour to crocheted nylon. Velcro was born. It took 30 years for Velcro to be accepted and used in a broad array of applications.

Burdock burs can act as temporary pins to hold ripped clothing together or to substitute for a missing button.

Burdock is frequently collected and burned by farmers and gardeners in autumn. Three pounds of ashes contain 15 ounces of alkaline salts (which is as good as the highest grade potash).

The presence of a large amount of burdock on your land generally indicates that the soil has a low pH, is heavy in iron, and needs calcium.

Wrap fish and game in large burdock leaves and roast in the coals of a fire pit. Foods cooked this way are mildly seasoned by the leaves.

Last, but not least, burdock leaves make ideal toilet paper.

Detrimental Properties
We'd appreciate authenticated reports from readers.

Where Found
This plant is native to Europe and Asia. It is common throughout the United States, in pastures, orchards, around barns, and other moist areas rich in manure. A. minus is most common in the West.

Growing Cycle
This biennial produces large rosettes of leaves the first year and sends up its flowering stalk the second year.

Lore and Signature
For you to explore: First comes the leaves, second comes the stems. Also explore that bur which sticks with tenacity via the simplest of technologies.

Hard Times Survival Tip: Wood Bread

In times of famine and great scarcity, people resort to ingenious solutions. For those without the foresight or the ability to store up for the future or for those who lack garden space, the following advice may come in handy.

First, collect beech wood or another type of wood lacking in turpentine (wood that contains turpentine includes pines, firs, spruces, and other conifers). Chop the wood into chips, or better yet, shavings. Boil the shavings three or four times, stirring regularly.

Next, dry the wood and then reduce it to powder, or to as fine particles as possible. Then bake the wood in your oven three or four times and grind it as you would corn or wheat.

Wood prepared like this becomes a palatable spongy bread that acquires the aroma and flavor of corn, according to the *Emigrant's Handbook* from 1854. Leaven prepared for corn bread is best to use with this wood flour.

If the wood flour is boiled in water and left to stand, a thick, edible jelly results.

While some readers may think this tip is a joke, it is a viable survival skill should the need ever arise. We have abundant lessons from prison camps, countries impoverished by war, and economic depression illustrating that the ability to utilize every available resource to its fullest can be a prime survival skill.

California Bay (Umbellularia californica)

Laurel Family (Lauraceae)

Common Names Bay laurel, laurel tree

California bay nuts with dried bay leaves

Most Prominent Characteristics

Overall Shape and Size

California Bay is an amazingly versatile plant, reaching over 50 feet as a tree under ideal conditions, but also appearing as a shrub in dry chaparral areas.

Trunk and Bark The trunk, which often divides at the base, has a diameter of one to two feet—sometimes even larger. There is a dense crown of slender branches. The bark is smooth and gray-brown and becomes scaly and darker as the tree ages.

Leaves The evergreen leaves are leathery, lance shaped, arranged alternately on the branches. Crush a leaf in your hand and smell its unmistakable strong aroma. The leaves can be gathered year-round for their flavoring or medicinal uses.

Fruit The nutlike fruits, about an inch in diameter, are spherical to egg shaped. They begin green, then turn a purplish-brown color upon ripening in late summer through autumn.

Beneficial Properties

Edible Properties When fully ripe, the nutlike fruits are quite edible, though somewhat bitter if eaten raw (resembling slightly bitter walnuts). These fruits are made more palatable by drying and then roasting.

The dried leaves have long been used to flavor dishes, such as stews and soups, giving the meal a pleasant, refreshing flavor. This is not the same bay commonly sold in stores—that is, European bay (Lauris nobilis) of Turkey and the eastern Mediterranean region. California bay is distinctly more aromatic. A large spice company once ran an advertising campaign intended to discredit the growing popularity of the California bay over the European bay. The ad by Schilling Gourmet stated, in part, "There are many bay leaves you can buy that are beautifully green. As houseplants, they're gorgeous. As bay leaves, they're impostors, because they come from a common domestic plant. . . . Real bay leaves come from Turkey." This was somewhat amusing, as well as misleading. These native California bay trees can hardly be called domestic or houseplants. Furthermore, their fragrance is much stronger than the European bay. Schilling should simply add the California bay to their spice list and let the consumer choose.

Medicinal Uses Bay leaf tea is said to aid digestion and to relieve mild stomach pain. It also makes a zesty after-dinner drink (the perfect alternative to commercial seltzers).

Timothy Snider reaches up to collect California bay leaves.

California Native Americans reportedly placed a crushed leaf in one nostril to cure headaches.

Other Uses The tea can also be used as a disinfectant and pesticide. The dried leaves can be scattered in animal pens, coops, and sleeping quarters to repel fleas, in the cupboard to keep away insects, and suspended in flour and grain storage containers to repel various insects.

The finely grained wood of the tree is prized for cabinet work.

Detrimental Properties
Some claim that breathing the aroma of the leaves causes headaches, a direct contradiction to the Native American practice of using the leaves to get rid of headaches. I've both observed and been told of these conflicting effects from various individuals.

Where Found
California bay tree is found in dry, open areas, along canyon sides and ravines, and along streams. It is readily cultivated in southern California.

Growing Cycle
It is an evergreen tree, flowering and producing fruit annually.

California Coffee Berry and Cascara Sagrada (Rhamnus californica and R. purshiana)

Buckthorn Family
(Rhamnaceae)

California coffee berry tree with the ripe fruit

Most Prominent Characteristics

Overall Shape and Size Some botanists once believed that these were simply two varieties of the same plant; today, however, they're generally considered two distinct species. In fact, several varieties of the coffee berry have been recorded. The main difference between the two are their growing locales and their relative size—R. californica is virtually always found growing as a shrub, approximately 5 to 8 feet tall. R. purshiana, on the other hand, usually grows treelike, reaching a height of 8 to 30 feet.

Leaves R. californica is more attractive than many of the plants found in the dry and dusty territory of the chaparral. The leaves of this evergreen are brighter green than the surrounding vegetation, and several leaves on each plant are usually yellow (somewhat resembling a gardenia plant). Coffee berry's alternately arranged leaves are from 1 to 2½ inches long, narrowly oblong shaped, and with a margin of very small teeth or serrations.

Fruit The globose, two- to three-seeded fruits are usually ¼ to ½ inch in diameter. First green, they turn red, and finally black in midsummer. This is somewhat attractive since there are usually fruits of all colors on the plant.

Beneficial Properties

Edible Properties My interest in this southern California plant stemmed from the word *coffee* in its name. "Can you actually make coffee from it?" I often asked others who might know. The answer was always the same— No. It was only called "coffee" because the seeds slightly resemble true commercial coffee berries.

I not only accepted this answer for several years, but I even parroted this stock answer myself during my wild food outings when asked the same question. Imagine my consternation, then, when John Watkins of Harbor City, California, a regular participant on the wild food outings, drawled in his Southern accent, "No, sir, it's *not* called coffee berry just because the seeds *look* like coffee! Of course you can make coffee from these seeds." Holding a handful of the berries in his hand, he then proceeded to tell an enraptured audience (and a surprised Christopher) exactly how he does it.

He gathers up to one gallon of the fresh seeds and piles them in his yard until the fleshy part rots away, which makes it easier to get the seeds out. Then he thoroughly washes the seeds, dries them in a medium oven, grinds them coarse in the seed grinder, roasts them at 375° F to a deep brown, and then percolates them in a drip coffee maker. "The result," Watkins testified with all the Southern sincerity he could muster, "is identical to the taste, look, and smell of fresh coffee." He emphasized, "And I mean *identical!*"

I couldn't wait to try it! To hurry the process, I hand-cleaned the fresh picked fruits to remove the seeds, but otherwise I followed the rest of his instructions. The resulting beverage did taste remarkably like coffee, even though it had little of the aroma of coffee. An accurate description of the flavor would be either strong tea or weak coffee. Nevertheless, the long-held chaparral myth that you can't make coffee from this plant has been exploded by personal experience. The wisdom of the sage is certainly valid in this case: try to rediscover everything; know truth by your own direct experience.

Although the flesh of the small ripened berries appears appealing, they should only be consumed if you need a laxative, and even then, only consume two or three. (During my tentative experiments, I was able to eat the flesh of up to a dozen ripe fruits that I picked off the bush while hiking. I experienced very mild or no laxative effects.)

Medicinal Uses Of all the plant medicines used by Native Americans, cascara sagrada is possibly the best known. Its outer bark was used as a laxative; still today, in cases of chronic constipation it is regarded as one of the safest and best laxatives in the world. It is also said to act as a tonic, and reportedly improves the appetite. *The Dispensatory of the United States* states, "It often appears to restore tone to the relaxed bowel and in this way produces permanent beneficial effect."

Historians believe that California's early Spanish priests first learned of this plant from the Mendocino County Native Americans and that it was the priests who named the plant cascara sagrada, which means *sacred bark* in Spanish.

To use cascara sagrada as a laxative, the bark should be collected from the tree and aged for at least a year before being used. When the aged bark is soaked overnight, or boiled for about an hour, the water can be drunk as a laxative.

It is worthy to note that in the early part of this century, a minor industry developed around the many medicinal uses of this shrub. In the Pacific Northwest, the bark was being peeled to such an extent that no new bark would form. This soon destroyed so many trees that the entire industry almost died.

Both R. californica and the closely related R. purshiana have been referred to as cascara sagrada. Today, however, the name cascara sagrada is used most often to designate R. purshiana. Although both species can be used as a laxative, R. purshiana is preferred.

Other Uses We'd appreciate authenticated reports from readers.

Detrimental Properties
Someone not familiar with the laxative properties of these fruits might be tempted to nibble on several handfuls while hiking along the foothill trails. This

Photo by Dolores Lynn Nyerges

When roasted and ground, the California coffee berry can be prepared and enjoyed just like store-bought coffee.

could result in abdominal pains and diarrhea. One natural remedy would be to consume carob products. Better yet, never eat any fruits, nuts, or wild plants unless you've positively identified them as being safe foods.

Where Found
R. purshiana is found primarily along the Pacific Coast from northern California to Canada. The smaller R. californica is a relatively common shrub in the southern California chaparral.

Growing Cycle
The fruits of this plant mature around July. This can vary as much as a month earlier or later, depending on many factors, such as the amount of rain and heat. The optimum harvesting period lasts about one month. You know the fruits are mature and ready to pick when they are nearly black and when the flesh is readily removed from the seed simply by squeezing the fruit.

Camphor Tree (Cinnamomum camphora)
Laurel Family (Lauraceae)

camphor leaf

Most Prominent Characteristics

Overall Shape and Size Where the ornamental camphor trees have grown large and showy, one travels under a cooling, soothing, even awesome (and, in the wind, an exciting) canopy of green. Its dense, lush, glossy light-green foliage makes the camphor a tree of exceptional beauty. The camphor is a slow-to-moderate grower, reaching about 40 feet (as high as 50 feet under best conditions). Its sprawling base often lifts sidewalks and pushes cement curbings away as it expands, forming the foundation for the large, meandering branches and the full-leafed, round-topped crown.

Leaves The leaves, which have a pronounced camphor odor when crushed, are simple, ovate to elliptical in shape, pinnately veined (or three nerved), one to two inches wide, two to five inches long, and tapered to a point. The leaf blades are thin, glabrous, glossy green above and light green to grayish white below, and appear alternately on the branches. The yellowish-brown leaf buds (the youngest, newly emerging leaves) are enclosed by imbricate scales.

Flowers The inconspicuous, yellow-to-white flowers, arranged in axillary clusters (panicles), appear in May. The flowers have nine or fewer perfect stamens in three whorls and a row of imperfect stamens. The short-tubed perianth (corolla and calyx collectively) is in sixes, and the segments are nearly equal in length.

Fruit The flowers develop into single-seeded globose black berries (drupes), about ¼ inch in diameter, or approximately the size of a large pea. The peak season for the fruit is the fall, but you'll always find some fruit since there are some flowers at any given time of the year.

Beneficial Properties

Edible Properties According to the book *Herbal Highs*, camphor has at various times been misused for its physiological and psychological after-effects. Technically, it acts as a reflex stimulant by irritating the nerve endings. One gram of commercial camphor taken orally produces a pleasant, warm, tickling sensation on the skin, mental excitation, and the impulsion to heightened physical activity. But two grams brings on thought floods, ego loss, vomiting, amnesia, delirium, and convulsions, all lasting for about three hours with possible spontaneous recurrence several hours later. Thus, ingestion of camphor should be carefully regulated—if done at all!

Medicinal Uses Commercial camphor (used for medicinal and skin-protective purposes) is obtained by steaming the chipped root, branches, twigs, and leaves until they sweat or give off drops of camphor. The resultant distillant is processed to remove unwanted oil and water. Finally, in the form of white crystals, the camphor is purified into a liquid (camphor = $C_{10} H_{16} O$).

Camphor is used as a pain reliever (anodyne) and to expel intestinal worms. Oil of camphor is sometimes used as a heart stimulant. Spirits of camphor, a mixture of 10 parts camphor, 70 parts alcohol, and 20 parts water, is a mild antiseptic.

Camphor can also be safely applied to inflammations, bruises, and even sprains.

Camphor is used in traditional Chinese medicine as a diaphoretic, carminative, sedative, anthelmintic, and as an antirheumatic remedy. It's used on decaying and aching teeth. For bronchial congestion, one can boil camphor leaves in a tightly closed room and inhale the steam.

Other Uses Camphor is put into shoes to cure strongly perspiring feet. (Is it bad for feet to perspire?) It's used to protect clothing from insect attack, although this practice is sometimes said to weaken the fabric, making it more liable to tear.

Camphor leaves like the leaves of California Bay can be scattered in cupboards to repel insects (though it appears that their effectiveness is somewhat inferior to the bay leaves).

According to *The International Book of Wood*, in the Far East, the wood is highly prized and used in chests, trunks, wardrobes, and bookcases, owing to its reputation for repelling moths and other insects. Seamen's chests were formerly made from, or lined with, camphor wood because it was widely supposed to have preservative properties.

According to Eric Zammit, "I was told by a carpenter at Ogasawara lumberyard in Zushi, Japan, that sculptors of Buddhist images prefer to use camphor wood. I've also heard that silver will not tarnish in a camphor box. This has been confirmed by my friend Junko, who has been using a camphor-wood jewelry box I made for her a few years ago to store her collection of silver jewelry."

And not the least of its uses is the fact that the camphor tree makes great climbing for the youngsters. In the majestic upper boughs of camphor, surrounded by the lush aromatic foliage, who knows how many great dreams have been born?

Detrimental Properties
See the comments in the Edible Properties section.

Where Found

Camphor is native to China, Japan, and tropical Asia. During the Middle Ages, when Venice was a flourishing trade center, camphor was one of the commonest drug ingredients. It was, however, introduced into southern California as an ornamental tree, and is extensively planted in the northeast Los Angeles and Pasadena areas. It also grows in other warm climates.

Growing Cycle

See Flowers and Fruit for the growing cycle of this tree.

Survival Tip: Mosquitoes

The presence of mosquitoes can ruin an otherwise excellent cookout, hike, or camping trip if we don't know how to deal with them.

There are many commercial mosquito repellents on the market. Their effectiveness is often quite variable from day to day and from person to person. Commercial repellants come in sprays, creams, and sticks. I prefer the rub-on sticks because they won't leak into my backpack and because I dislike the oily creams.

Commercial repellents are like books of matches—they run out or we lose them when we need them most. This is why we must master the knowledge of plant uses.

If you find yourself in a mosquito-infested area with no commercial repellent, you can use certain plants to keep away these biting, blood-sucking insects. The leaves of laurel sumac (*Rhus laurina*), an evergreen shrub very common in chaparral, crushed by rubbing them between your hands, will leave your hands oily and sticky. Rub this oil on the exposed parts of your body. Mosquitoes dislike the strong aroma of the shrub and tend not to land, although they may still buzz around you. Native Americans would rub the leaves of laurel sumac over their bodies to mask their human aroma when hunting.

Geraldine Hogeboom from Delhi, California, suggests increasing the amount of raw apple cider vinegar in one's diet to reduce the incidence of mosquito bites.

First-aid kits should contain a product to relieve the pain of insect bites. If not, a baking soda paste applied to the bite makes a good remedy to relieve the itching. Vinegar will do the same.

The leaves of plantain (*Plantago* spp.) can be crushed and applied to bites to relieve pain. In her excellent book *Indian Herbalogy of North America*, Alma R. Hutchens says that the "juice of the [plantain] leaves will counteract the bite of poisonous insects." She suggests taking one tablespoon every hour and, at the same time, applying the bruised leaves to the wounds.

Carob
(Ceratonia siliqua)
Pea Family (Leguminosae)
Common Names St. John's
bread, Locust, Locusta

carob pods

Most Prominent Characteristics

Overall Shape and Size The
carob is a drought-resistant tree
once it is well established, since its
long roots reach deep for underground water. Allowed to grow
wild, carob grows as a shrub with
its branches to the ground. With
the lower branches removed, it grows at a moderate rate, forming a
dense, round-headed tree 20 to 40 feet tall.

Leaves The alternately arranged carob leaves are even-pinnately compound (compoundly divided into an even number of leaflets arranged
along a common axis, with 6 to 10 round, glossy, leathery leaflets, each
about 1½ inches long).

Flowers The small red flowers are arranged in short single racemes or in
clustered lateral racemes.

Fruit The carob fruit is a flattened, dark-brown, leathery pod (or legume),
about 1½ inches broad, 4 to 10 inches long, and rich in sugar. There are
both male and female carob trees; sweet-tasting pods are produced only
by the female and bisexual trees. The pods—which grow prolifically—
ripen, dry, and remain on the tree until shaken down by rain, wind, or
animals (or human climbers).

Beneficial Properties

Edible Properties Carob pods, once ripened, can be picked and eaten
with no preparation whatsoever (besides wiping off the dust). The pods
are very sweet and chewy, although carob has 60 percent fewer calories
per pound than chocolate and lacks the stimulants that are found in coffee
(caffeine), chocolate (theobromine), and tea (tannic acid).

The carob pods are 4 percent protein (4.5 grams of protein per 100
grams, 20.4 grams of protein per pound) and 76 percent carbohydrate. In
addition, carob pods contain substantial phosphorus (81 milligrams per 100
grams, 367 milligrams per pound) and are extremely rich in calcium (352
milligrams per 100 grams, 1,597 milligrams per pound). And carob contains
none of chocolate's oxalic acid, which interferes with the body's ability to
assimilate calcium. It is rich in A and B vitamins and many other minerals.

Although the odor of carob on the ground is offensive to some, the taste remains sweet and unobjectionable. If children were encouraged to eat carob instead of candy bars, there would soon be no more litter problems under the carob trees and, perhaps, fewer cavities in youthful mouths.

Years ago, some farsighted Seventh Day Adventists planted carob trees around and on the grounds of almost all the Pasadena public schools, apparently hoping that the students would gather and eat this free and nutritious food should there be another Depression and a scarcity of food. Pasadena school children take note!

Besides making a good snack, the carob pod (with seeds removed) can be ground into a fine powder and used in milk shakes or as a chocolate substitute in pastries and other baked items. The grinding can be done with a hand or electric mill, the final product being comparable to what health-food stores sell.

The sticky pulp of the pods is also fed to cattle and horses. A type of wine or liquor, popular in Syria, is also made from carob pods. The residue from this fermentation is then given to the pigs. The prodigal son in the Bible, hungry from famine and without money, looked in the pig's feed for carob husks to eat (Luke 15:16). These husks were not corn, as commonly believed.

The carob tree is subject to attack by the sulfur fungus (Polyporus sulfureus), a very colorful (and edible!) fungus appearing on the upper trunk during the rainy season. This shelf fungus (growing in horizontal layers, or shelves) is bright yellow on the bottom and layered in red, orange, and yellow on top. The tender outer layers are gathered, cut into bite-sized pieces, and boiled in chicken broth for 15 minutes. The broth is then drained and the fungus chunks are dipped in flour, eggs, and bread crumbs and then deep fried. Delicious!

Warning! Do not eat the Polyporus sulfureus fungus raw since this will result in vomiting. As a matter of fact, never eat any mushroom or fungus until you have made a positive identification. Some recommended mushroom manuals are:

Mushrooms of North America by Orson K. Miller

A Field Guide to Western Mushrooms by Alexander Smith

The Mushroom Handbook by Louis C. C. Krieger

Toadstools, Mushrooms, Fungi, Edible and Poisonous; One Thousand American Fungi; How to Select and Cook the Edible; How to Distinguish and Avoid the Poisonous, with Full Botanic Descriptions by Charles McIlvaine

Medicinal Uses   In a 1976 article in *Desert Magazine*, Marian Seddon writes:

Only lately have medical journals in North America and Europe begun advocating carob powder for the prevention and cure of human dysentery, especially in children. The pectin and lignin in the carob not only regulate digestion, they combine with harmful elements—even radioactive fallout—in digested foods and carry them out of the body.

Use pliers to squeeze open the carob pods and remove the hard seeds.

Other Uses The small, hard seeds inside the pods were once used as weights and provided the term *carat*, as in the weight of gold. They can be boiled in water to be softened and then strung into a necklace.

All in all, the carob is a beautiful friend to have around, offering shade in the summer's heat and year-round food to all who are willing to partake.

Detrimental Properties

I consider carob one of the best "survival foods," and the tree lives well and lives long with little care. Yet, it has its detractors.

In some residential neighborhoods where the trees line the streets, people have complained about the strong odor in the springtime when the trees are in flower. Some compare the odor to sweet manure. And the grand old trees, which are just starting to produce mighty crops of fruit, have the tendency to buckle sidewalks if they are planted too closely to walkways. Unfortunately, in most such cases city workers come in and cut down the tree.

Where Found

This lofty evergreen is native to the eastern Mediterranean region, where it is extensively cultivated for its edible fruit. In southern California, and particularly in Pasadena where there are 2,000 carob trees, carob has been commonly planted as an ornamental tree. You'll find this also in other southwestern states. The fact that the shallowly watered roots often break sidewalks, and the pods continually fall to the ground, should not, we feel, overshadow the much more beneficial aspects of this tree.

Growing Cycle

Carob is a drought-tolerant long-lived tree. It flowers in late spring and summer. The fruits begin to mature and turn brown from September through December.

Lore and Signature

In the New Testament, Mark says (1:16) that John the Baptist ate locusts and wild honey in the desert. Although many believe that these locusts were the insect relatives of grasshoppers, reliable sources indicate that they were more likely carob pods. In his *Natural History of the Bible*, author Thaddeus M. Harris says:

> It is well known that the insect locusts were eaten in the east. And commentators have exhausted their learning and ingenuity to prove that St. John ate these insects in the wilderness. But the origins of the word "locust" signifies also buds or pods of trees, as several learned men have proved. And everyone must suppose that the Baptist lived on a food which nature itself furnished to accommodate his palate.

Furthermore, Harris points out that locust insects are never eaten without some kind of careful preparations, such as roasting, drying in the sun, or salting and smoking, and concludes that this "doesn't seem an occupation worthy of the Baptist, whom scripture represents as sufficiently taken up in devout meditation and spiritual exercises." Finally, carob pods are often called locusta, and the tree is commonly called Saint John's Bread Tree.

POISON

Castor Bean
(Ricinus communis)
Spurge Family (Euphorbiaceae)

Nathaniel Schleimer stands next to a castor bush. *All* parts are toxic, especially the seeds.

Never chew unknown nuts or fruits is perhaps *the* cardinal rule for wild food gatherers. For that matter, never eat any wild plant until it has been positively identified as being edible. If followed, this rule would save 20 to 30 lives each year because people wouldn't sample the very attractive castor beans.

Most Prominent Characteristics

Overall Shape and Size This drought-defying plant is a large, multi-stalked, treelike shrub reaching to 10 feet tall.

Stalks and Stems The young branches are red and turn to purplish green or green when the plant is mature. The leaf's petiole (stalk) is attached on the underside of the leaf blade.

Leaves The ½- to 1-foot broad leaves consist of 7 to 11 sharp, palmate lobes.

Flowers Castor is monoecious; that is, it has male and female flowers on each plant, which form in terminal racemes. The uppermost red flowers on the plant are pistillate (female), and the lower yellow flowers are staminate (male).

Seeds The spiny, three-lobed fruits are actually capsules that contain three or more seeds. The seeds are flecked with oftentimes beautiful designs and are commonly strung together and sold as necklaces in Mexico and South America. The individual seeds vary in size from the size of the little fingernail to the thumbnail.

Beneficial Properties

Edible Properties *Poisonous!* People in the armed forces stationed in the Pacific have reportedly eaten one or two castor seeds as a laxative. However, there is potential danger in this practice and it is highly discouraged.

Medicinal Uses The castor bean is extensively planted in the United States for its oil. Since the poison from castor beans, called *ricin*, is insoluble in oil, commercial castor oil contains no ricin; however, ricin is heavily concentrated in the leftover pulp of the seed. Thus, commercial castor oil is safe to use (following manufacturers' instructions) as an occasional laxative, though there are far better ways to regulate fecal elimination.

Processed castor oil is sold as a skin conditioner. It is sometimes applied to protect against sunburn and chapping. I have found it to be the most effective remedy for chapped lips.

Writing in *Prevention Magazine* in March of 1973, Carol Wiekens of Commack, New York shares her experience with castor oil. She writes:

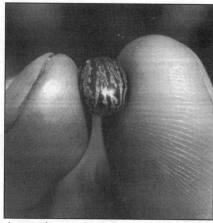

close up of a castor bean

> *Three years ago when I was reading a book about Edgar Cayce, I came across his advice on how to get rid of warts. Having gotten 14 warts on both hands in a space of two months, I was interested. His advice: warm castor oil on gauze, applied three times a day for one-half hour. I modified this with oil on a bandage, which I changed twice a day. Within three weeks all the warts were gone.*

Wiekens reported that her friends had likewise successfully treated warts in this manner.

Other Uses   Although it is native to the tropics, castor has become a common ornamental in the southern United States and has naturalized in vacant lots and in the lower elevations of mountains. The castor has other redeeming qualities, as well. For example, it is an effective mosquito repellent when planted in the mosquito's presumed direction of flight.

Castor oil has numerous industrial uses. Perhaps the best known is the Castrol motor oil for automobiles, which once was made from castor oil.

Detrimental Properties

This is one of the most poisonous plants in the United States. Although ricin can be found throughout the plant, it is most concentrated in the seeds. When ingested, the ricin causes stomach cramps, vomiting, diarrhea, and/or convulsions. If three or more seeds are eaten at once, death can result in 24 to 48 hours (two to three seeds are generally fatal to a child; six to eight seeds are fatal to an adult).

The ricin in castor beans has reputedly been a poison of choice among some members of the Intelligence community. In one widely publicized incident, a spy, who just got off a bus in London, felt a prick on the back of his arm and noticed a man disappearing into the crowd carrying an umbrella. The pricked man died a few days later of ricin poisoning, which had apparently been administered via the tip of the umbrella.

Where Found
Native to the tropics, castor is a common ornamental in the southern United States, growing in vacant lots and in the lower elevations of mountains.

Growing Cycle
Depending on the environment, castor can be an annual, perennial, shrub, or a tree. In the eastern United States, it grows like an annual. In the Oregon area, it is a perennial. In most of southern California, it is a shrub. In San Diego, it often grows to a tree.

Lore and Signature
There is much lore surrounding the castor plant. One of its common names is Palma Cristi, meaning *palm of Christ*. Apparently, Edgar Cayce often spoke of the healing properties of the processed castor oil, and such oils are still available from Cayce's A.R.E. foundation in Virginia Beach, Virginia. It would appear that we have only scratched the surface of the many virtues of this often scorned plant.

Cattail (Typha spp.)

Cattail Family (Typhaceae)
Common Names Tule, cat o'
nine tails, bulrush, rush

Most Prominent Characteristics

Overall Shape and Size Cattails
are marsh-inhabiting perennials
with long, erect grasslike leaves
and an overall height of about
seven to eight feet.

Stalks and Stems The flower
stalks are approximately ¼ inch in
diameter, almost woody, green at

The young tender base of a cattail stalk is good raw or cooked.

first and turning tan in color as the flower spike matures.

Leaves These three- to six-feet long leaves are swordlike, soft, and pithy.

Flowers The flower is a cylindrical spike perched visibly at the top of a
long, sturdy stem. It consists of the female section of the flower spike—
the section that appears green in the spring and then matures into the
familiar brown hot dog on a stick. The male section of the flower is the
cylindrical pollen-filled tuft on the top of the female section. The mature
flower spikes have been described as resembling peeled corn-on-the-cob.

Roots Cattail forms a great underground network of rhizomes (technically, prostrate elongated stems), growing horizontally a few inches below
ground level. These rhizomes are about one inch thick, consisting of a
fibrous core and a spongy outer layer. The actual roots are ¹⁄₁₆ to ⅛ inch in
diameter, white and stringlike, found along the length of the rhizome.

Beneficial Properties

Edible Properties In the early summer, the new flowers appear as green
bloom spikes (soon to be the decorative brown cattail stalk). These tender
spikes make an excellent vegetable when still young and green, requiring
only 10 to 20 minutes of cooking. They can also be roasted, buttered, and
eaten like corn-on-the-cob.

As these early green spikes get taller, a fine yellow pollen forms at the
very top of each flower stalk. This pollen can be easily gathered without
harming the plants by shaking the heads into a bag or neckerchief. Once
sifted, the pollen can be easily blended with regular flour or can be used
alone to make delicious foods, such as yellow-colored bread, muffins, and
pancakes.

Once their spongy outer layer is removed, rhizomes can be processed
into a flour whose carbohydrate (77 percent), protein (8 percent), and fat

(2 percent) content is comparable to corn and rice. The Iroquois dried the rhizomes, pounded them, and then sifted out the fiber. The resultant flour was used for bread.

The rhizomes can also be processed by a method suggested by Euell Gibbons. Fill a large container with cold water and then crush the cores by hand in the water until the fiber is separated. The flour is allowed to settle to the bottom and then the fiber can be poured out. Repeat this two to three times until the flour is free of fiber. This flour can then be used wet or dried for later use.

Just above the rhizome where the base of a shoot connects, there is found a sizeable lump of nutritious carbohydrate material called the *heart* or the *root* (not a root, botanically). Though they can be eaten raw, the hearts are generally peeled, then cooked (or baked) and seasoned as you'd prepare Jerusalem artichokes, turnips, or potatoes. As the plant sends up its flower stalk, this starchy core becomes tougher and less palatable.

In the winter and spring, the young cattail shoots can be eaten. Pulling back the outer green leaves, grasp the white inner leaves of the young shoot and briskly pull it up. Approximately the bottom 12 inches of the shoots are eaten, since this is the most tender and palatable. The outer fibrous layers should be peeled back to get to the tender insides. This is probably the best food from the cattail, described by various people as tasting like celery or cucumber. These peeled shoots can be added raw to salads or eaten as is, or can be boiled, baked, and added to stews as a wild vegetable. These shoots are commonly referred to as Cossack asparagus, due to the Cossacks' fondness for this food. One hundred grams, or ½ cup, of this shoot contains 58 milligrams of calcium, 109 milligrams of phosphorus, 639 milligrams of potassium, and 76 milligrams of vitamin C.

The very young, round and pointed, still-white underground shoots (soon to develop into the long erect leaves of the young plant), which arise about an inch or two from the starchy core, can also be eaten either raw or cooked.

Medicinal Uses According to Mario Blackwolf, Gabrielino Native Americans in the old days would chew the starchy hearts of the cattail if they were bitten by a rattlesnake. Since this lower section of the cattail shoot is rich in sugar, it would help the rattlesnake victim deal with stress and shock.

When the fully mature brown flower spikes are broken open, all the fluffy hairs and small seeds attached to them are released, enabling the seeds to float in the wind long distances and reproduce elsewhere. This down can be pressed into wounds to stop bleeding.

Other Uses The long, erect leaves are used in making rush chairs, sandals, mats, and other items that your survival may someday depend on. To use, first dry the long cattail leaves to prevent later shrinkage. Then moisten the leaves before weaving to make them pliable. An excellent book that provides detailed instructions on this method of weaving is *Outdoor Survival Skills* by Larry Dean Olsen.

The down from the mature brown spikes can be used to stuff pillows or blankets and also makes excellent fire tinder. During World War II, schoolchildren in the United States collected mature cattail spikes as well as mature milkweed pods. The down from the cattail spikes and the milkweed pods was used as a substitute for kapok, which was used in items such as life preservers and sleeping bags. During the war, the primary source of kapok stuffing (a tree by the same name) was under Japanese control. Thus, alternatives to kapok were found with cattail and milkweed down, with traits only slightly inferior to goose down.

The stalks can be cut and used as chopsticks.

Cattails have also been planted in areas in order to purify the water. For example, in the Florida Everglades where phosphorous-rich fertilizers in the water from farms flow into the Everglades, cattails have been planted in the path of the runoff. The cattails have exceeded all expectations in sucking the phosphorous out of the farm runoff water, so cleaner water can be discharged into the Everglades.

Detrimental Properties
Some people notice a slightly unpleasant tingling sensation in the throat a few minutes after eating raw white cattail shoots.

Do not eat raw cattails found growing in water whose purity is questionable.

Where Found
The cattail is found year-round in swamp and marsh areas and along the banks of permanent bodies of water, such as streams, ponds, rivers, and irrigation ditches. Cattails grow throughout most of the world and are common in North and South America, Europe, Asia, and northern Africa.

Growing Cycle
Cattails are perennials. Found year-round, there is always some part of the plant at any given time of the year that can be used.

Lore and Signature
The dried cattail spikes epitomize the autumn season. Their ubiquitous presence as home ornamentals speaks volumes about the versatility of this plant. Perhaps we desire to be close to this friendly plant because we know it provides food, medicine, and craft material. It also bring light, when you dip the mature flower spike in wax or tallow and burn it like a torch.

Chia (Salvia columbariae)

Mint Family (Labiatae)
Common Names California chia, golden chia

a chia plant in flower

Most Prominent Characteristics

Overall Shape and Size The often inconspicuous chia plant rises to nearly two feet in ideal conditions, but usually grows about a foot tall. Each plant has usually one to four whorled seed clusters per stalk. When the seeds are ready for harvest, the dried stalks are barren of leaves with only the round, brown seed clusters remaining.

Stalks and Stems There is usually one main single stalk from six inches to two feet tall. Sometimes the stalk is branched once or twice along its length, and sometimes several stalks arise from the base. The usually leaf-less stalk is square-shaped (one of the signs of all true mints) with one to four evenly spaced seed buttons (whorls). The stalk is grayish green and is sometimes tinted a wine color.

Leaves Mostly oblong-ovate in overall outline, each leaf varies from one to several inches long. Each leaf is bipinnately divided; that is, the margin is indented into segments along a common axis, and each segment is further pinnately divided. The leaf surface is finely wrinkled and covered on both sides with tiny fine hairs. The leaves, mostly basal, grow in opposite pairs—generally two or three pairs of leaves per stalk.

Flowers The small, typical mint-family flowers are blue, two-lipped, about one-half inch long, and clustered into round whorls along the stalk(s). There are usually one to four whorls per stalk, with numerous sharply pointed purplish bracts at the base of each whorl. The plant is usually in flower from March through June, though sometimes a few random plants will be found flowering into summer.

Seeds The true golden chia has a brownish or goldish-tan seed that is almost pyramidal in shape. (The Salvia hispanica, on the other hand, commonly sold in the health food stores as chia, has a seed that resembles a tiny mottled pinto bean, usually dark gray or black but occasionally gray or nearly white.) The seeds will form a gelatinous outer layer when soaked in water. The seeds are best collected in July and August when recently matured, but before strong winds or rains have shaken them onto the ground.

Beneficial Properties

Edible Properties The southwestern Native Americans collected the seeds by bending the
stems and shaking them into a
finely woven basket. In a solid
stand of the plant, a surprisingly
large amount can be gathered in a
short time.

Today, the harvested seeds
are shaken on a fine mesh screen
in order to remove all foreign particles.

The seeds can be made into
drinks by simply soaking for a

Close-up of a chia flower.

few minutes in either hot or cold water or fruit juice and drinking as is.
Almost tasteless, the seeds, when so used, are inexplicably refreshing. The
Pomo Native Americans ground the seeds into meal and used as flour for
small cakes or loaves. Today, many people mix the chia flour half and half
with wheat flour to make bread. The seeds, like any other edible seeds,
can also be sprouted and eaten as a fresh vegetable.

For dishes, such as cereals, mush, and soups, add two tablespoons of
seeds per cup of water. As the mixture warms (chia doesn't need to be
cooked as do most cereal grains), the water will become mucilaginous.
This tapioca-like food can be eaten as it is (or sweetened to taste, with
honey) or can be added as a smoothening agent or extender to pancake
batter, biscuits, bread, ice cream, pudding, coffee, cold drinks, and more.

Inez Ainge wrote in an article, "Native Chia" (1967), that "Chia has
been proclaimed a high energy food not only because it contains a high
percentage of protein (30 percent), but because it also contains a natural
enzyme which acts as a catalyst for the protein."

A nutritional analysis done in 1964 shows 20.2 percent protein, 34.4
percent oil, and 5.6 percent ash, as well as significant amounts of iron, calcium, phosphorus, magnesium, potassium, and traces of other minerals
common to most seeds. The chia seed also contains the mineral strontium
(in its sulfate form) when the plant is growing in soils containing that
mineral. (Strontium sulfate is not to be confused with its isotope, strontium 90, which is radioactive.)

Tests by Harrison Doyle comparing golden chia, which grows wild in
the deserts and foothills in the Southwest, and the commercial mottled or
gray chia seeds from markets, report that the golden chia seed produces a
pronounced feeling of excess physical energy. Also, when any species of
chia growing in strontium-free soils were eaten (including S. columbariae),

this energizing effect was significantly diminished. Tests have indicated that the seeds that produce the greatest feeling of energy and general well-being were those harvested in the high deserts whose soils contain strontium sulfate.

There are several other plants commonly called chia, whose nutritional effects—while quite good—are somewhat inferior to golden chia. These include Salvia hispanica (the common commercial variety), S. lanceolate, S. polystachya, S. tiliaefolia, S. carduacea, Hyptis spicata, and others.

Medicinal Uses A tea from the seeds was used by Spanish missionaries for fevers, and they applied the dampened seeds as a poultice directly on gunshot and other wounds. The seeds, when eaten, are useful in gastrointestinal disorders and as an emollient. When drunk in tea or eaten, the seeds also aid bronchial and throat troubles. The seeds can be crushed between the fingers to produce an oil (generally called chia oil) for the skin. All members of the mint family, including chia, abound in volatile oils contained in resinous dots in the leaves and stems.

Other Uses A few teaspoons of seeds allowed to stand a short time in a quart of alkaline water from a bad water hole in the desert is said to sufficiently neutralize the water's toxicity so that it can be safely drunk if sipped very slowly.

Due to the mucilaginous properties, the whole, raw seed is sometimes used (instead of linseed oil) under the eyelids at night to help relieve the eyes of inflammation.

Detrimental Properties
We'd appreciate authenticated reports from readers.

Where Found
S. columbariae is native to California and is commonly found in the high-desert regions (1,500–4,000 feet elevations). There, winter rains and snow give the plants needed moisture to grow to maturity (although they are not restricted to areas where snow falls). They are found in the deserts, chaparral areas, foothills, and yellow pine belts of California, Nevada, Utah, Arizona, and New Mexico. The commercial chia (S. hispanica) is native to Mexico and South America.

Growing Cycle
These annual plants sprout in early spring, flower from March to June, die back in summer, and begin dropping their seeds in July and August (the time to do the harvesting). Seeds can be planted in gardens in the spring once there is no longer any danger of frost.

Lore and Signature
Some Native American tribes believed that it was good luck to carry the seeds in a pouch to ward off accidents.

Dr. J. T. Rothrock, botanist and surgeon of the Wheeler United States Geographical Survey of 1875, writes that the chia was cultivated as regularly as corn by the Nahua races of ancient Mexico. Of the seed, Dr. Rothrock writes, "An atole, or gruel, of this was one of the peace offerings to the first visiting sailors. One tablespoon of these seeds was sufficient to sustain for 24 hours an Indian on a forced march."

Harrison Doyle of Vista, California, author of *Golden Chia: Ancient Indian Energy Food*, writes:

As a boy in Needles, California, I played with the Mohave Indians my own age. I ate their foods, ran long distance races with them, rode their colorful Indian ponies bareback, whacked a tin can around the yellow silt flats in the ancient game of shinny. I remember some of the Indian boys telling me (I was interested in long distance running at the time) that Indian runners sometimes ran all the way in to the coast on trading expeditions with the Coast Tribes, carrying gourd shells containing water and a handful of chia seeds to sustain them.

Chickweed
(Stelleria media)
Pink Family (Caryophyllaceae)

Most Prominent Characteristics

Overall Shape and Size
Chickweed appears as bright green patches with the weak stem barely able to support the plant more than six inches (or so) off the ground. Since these delicate plants often grow in such dense patches, the entire patch may reach up to a foot in height.

sprawling chickweed, in flower, growing over a log

Stalks and Stems This annual has a succulent (and therefore weak) stem of up to a foot in length. Because of the weak stem, it's usually found growing low to the ground in a clump, or in clumped, intertwined masses. With close observation, you can see a single line of tiny, fine white hairs that runs along one side of the main stem.

Leaves
The small, oval-shaped leaves grow opposite, their margins are untoothed, and they come to a point. The lower leaves are petioled (have a stalk), whereas the upper leaves lack a petiole (join the stem directly).

Flowers The tiny flowers are white, ¼ inch diameter, and have five petals. Each petal has a deep cleft, thus giving the illusion of having ten petals. (Dr. Enari, botanist with the Los Angeles County Arboretum in Arcadia, has referred to this cleft petal as a Mickey Mouse petal because it resembled a pair of Mickey Mouse ears.) The flowers occur singly in the axils of the upper leaves.

Beneficial Properties

Edible Properties The entire visible plant is edible raw. Try to pick the taller, more mature plants so that the tender young plants can continue to grow. The best way to collect chickweed is to use a sharp knife or scissors, and trim off handfuls of the plant from the patch. Uprooting the plants is neither necessary nor desirable. A brief cold-water rinse and this succulent salad green is ready to be enjoyed. A simple oil and vinegar dressing with a bit of avocado creates a wonderful chickweed salad! The distinguishable flavor is mild and unobjectionable. Chickweed can also be lightly cooked and prepared like spinach, making it is a healthful addition to any meal.

One hundred grams (½ cup) of chickweed leaf contains 350 milligrams of vitamin C, 160 milligrams of calcium, 49 milligrams of phosphorus, 29 milligrams of iron, and 243 milligrams of potassium.

The seeds are relished by birds and poultry, and thus probably contain proteins, vitamins, and minerals that haven't yet been analyzed and recorded. The name *chickweed* apparently has its origins in the fact that chickens (and other birds) feasted on this plant first whenever it was available. Chickens will eat not only the seeds of chickweed but all of the leaves and tender stems as well.

Medicinal Uses Chickweed is one of the best bronchial decongestants. It is said to help reduce inflammation of the lungs, bronchials, bowels, and stomach. To receive these benefits, you are directed to either eat the raw or cooked herb or to drink a tea made from the dried or fresh herb. Chickweed has also been used as a salve and/or poultice to deal with skin problems, such as acne, burns, and small cuts and scratches. Apply the crushed raw herb (or chickweed tea) directly to the affected area.

Chickweed is regarded as an effective diuretic. The fresh leaves and stems can be infused for a tea. (Dried and powdered leaves can also be used.)

Other Uses We'd appreciate authenticated reports from readers.

Detrimental Properties
We'd appreciate authenticated reports from readers.

Where Found
Chickweed is a native of Europe and can now be found throughout the United States. It prefers secluded areas that are shady and moist, but will grow for a short time in full sun. In the canyons, it is quite common along little-traveled roads and close to bushes and trees where shade is provided. This plant flourishes even in the city.

Growing Cycle
Chickweed is an annual that flourishes during a warmish spring that has followed a wet winter. Generally, by midsummer, chickweed plants have matured, gone to seed, and are either dried up or too old to eat.

Chicory
(Cichoreum intybus)
Sunflower Family
(Compositae)
Common Names French
dandelion, blue dandelion,
ragged sailors, succory

chicory flowers

Most Prominent
Characteristics

Overall Shape and Size The
plant grows from one foot to six
feet tall, is highly branched, and
the main stalk is usually erect.

Stalks and Stems The rigid, branching main stalk grows as high as six feet. The stalk, which is covered with minute, stiff white hairs, exudes a milky white sap when cut. The petioles are often tinted red.

Leaves The leaves are covered with small coarse hairs. The leaves that cluster around the base are shaped like dandelion leaves: lanceolate in outline, pinnately lobed to entire, three to six inches long, with the mid-veins often reddish. The upper leaves are smaller, not pinnately lobed, and they clasp the stem. The leaves exude a milky juice when cut.

Flowers The heads of chicory's brilliant sky-blue flowers blossom from June to October. The heads are clustered in the upper axils of the plant singly or in groups of up to six. The unopened flower buds measure about ⅛ inch wide by ½ inch long; the opened flowers measure about 1 inch to 1½ inches across. Each blue petal has a ragged-looking edge, caused by the (usually) five teeth at each petal's end.

Roots Chicory has a deep, fleshy, dandelion-like taproot, which is generally thick and forked.

Beneficial Properties

Edible Properties In those European countries where it is cultivated, the roots are grown in the open during summer, then dug up when the weather begins turning cold. The roots are then stored in cellars and forced to produce leaf throughout the winter. One method of forcing produces *barbe de capucin*, the loose, blanched leaves that are considered a delicacy in France. There are other methods of forcing, each of which produces a slightly different quality of leaf (called "witloof" when the tight-clustered crown of leaves is blanched and eaten as a potherb).

The leaves are good in salad when young, or steamed. Older leaves become bitter and may need up to two boilings. One variety of chicory often finds its way into produce markets under the name of Italian dandelion.

Analysis of 100 grams of raw chicory greens shows that it contains 86 milligrams of calcium, 40 milligrams of phosphorus, 420 milligrams of potassium, 22 milligrams of vitamin C, and approximately 4,000 international units of vitamin A.

The roots can be boiled, steamed, cooked in stews, or roasted. Roasted, pulverized roots are used as a coffee substitute or extender. To use the roots in this fashion, dig up several larger roots. Clean them well, and dry them in the sun or oven. Grind the roots in your hand mill and then roast until brown. Percolate as you would coffee grounds. This is a good drink by itself or added to regular coffee.

The fresh root, collected in the spring, reportedly contains 36 percent insulin.

The plant is also grown as a fodder or herbage crop for cattle.

Note: The entire chicory tribe of the sunflower family contains no poisonous members. These are generally tender-leafed plants with milky sap. However, some may be too fibrous or too bitter for food.

Medicinal Uses According to herbalist Gene Matlock, keeping the liver decongested is a key to good health. Since habitual coffee drinking can congest the liver to the point that it hardens and almost ceases to function, it is no wonder, says Matlock, that Southerners and people in tropical Latin America (who drink a lot of coffee to overcome the lazy heat) add chicory to their coffee. Matlock says that chicory is "the herb for liver congestion," counteracting the negative effects of coffee.

Chicory is recognized as a diuretic, laxative, and hepatic by herbalists.

Other Uses Health aside, chicory root is both a practical and cost-effective (and probably health-promoting) way to extend your coffee supplies during times of shortage that may be experienced during an economic collapse, a war, a severe drought or famine, or the aftermath of a natural disaster. Dandelion, burdock, and sow thistle roots can be used similarly.

Detrimental Properties
We'd appreciate authenticated reports from readers.

Where Found
Evidence shows that chicory has been cultivated as a food plant since ancient Greek and Roman times. Considered a European native, it was introduced into the United States in the 19th century. Though it is still an important crop in the Netherlands, Belgium, France, and Germany, it is

generally treated as a weed in the United States. Most abundant in the eastern United States, it is now found over the entire United States, growing along roadsides, in fields, pastures, waste areas, gardens, vacant lots, and front yards.

Growing Cycle
Chicory is a perennial, producing new growth each year from the root. If you don't have the plant growing in your yard or homestead, you can transplant some there to have a fairly permanent patch. Then you'll be able to gather the young spring leaves and the roots when you need them, providing you leave roots for reproduction.

Cleavers
(Galium aparine)
Madder Family (Rubiaceae)

Most Prominent
Characteristics

Overall Shape and Size
Cleavers is a sprawling, weak-
stemmed annual that crawls over
other vegetation.

Stems The acutely quadrangular
stems, from two to three feet long,
are covered with backward-curv-
ing bristly hairs that enable it to
cling to other plants.

a young stalk of cleavers

Leaves The lanceolate leaves occur in whorls of six to eight along the
stem. The whorls are from 1½ to 3 inches apart; the individual leaves are
from ½ to 1 inch long.

Flowers In the upper axils grow the slender flower stalks, bearing small
(approximately ⅛ to 1/16 inch broad), white, star-shaped flowers. After the
flowers die, the tiny green fruits, which contain the seeds, develop. The ⅛-
inch diameter fruits are two lobed and bristly with short hairs.

Beneficial Properties

Edible Properties The early spring growth can be gathered, lightly
cooked, and served in its own juice (as you'd serve spinach). Even though
each individual plant is small, cleavers grows in clusters so that it's easy
to quickly gather enough for a dish.

Since cleavers is a distant relative to the coffee tree, the small seeds
can be dried and lightly roasted to make a coffee-flavored drink. The
brew made from cleavers contains no caffeine.

Medicinal Uses Gathered in late spring, cleavers becomes more and
more fibrous. At this stage, it can be dried and used for tea. The tea is said
to be excellent for reducing fevers, for kidney and bladder troubles, and
for the liver, due to its diuretic capabilities. For this same reason it is said
to be useful in weight reduction. Cleavers has also been used to treat
external skin problems, such as eczema, by applying the freshly crushed
herb as a poultice or as tea.

Other Uses Cleavers root can be used as a light red dye. A related
species (Galium verum) is claimed by some to be the plant that filled the
manger during Jesus' birth.

Detrimental Properties

We'd appreciate authenticated reports from readers.

Where Found

Cleavers is found most abundantly in moist, semishaded areas near streams and under trees in foothill valleys. It can also be found growing among oak trees on dry hillsides. Cleavers is believed to have been introduced from Europe. Today, it is found throughout North America, Europe, and Asia.

Growing Cycle

Cleavers is an annual, found most abundantly in the spring and early summer.

Currants and Gooseberries (Ribes spp.)
Saxifrage Family
(Saxifragaceae)

Note the three-lobed leaves of this fruiting currant.

Most Prominent Characteristics

Overall Shape and Size There are over 30 different species of currants and gooseberry shrubs. All bear edible fruit. All are more or less erect, having spreading branches, and are from two to five feet tall.

Stalks and Stems The gooseberries have thorns, while the currants are thornless. The long stalks are most reminiscent of blackberry vines.

Leaves
The leaves of both are alternate on the branch and palmately lobed (shaped somewhat like an outstretched hand).

Flowers The flowers vary in color from golden yellow to orange to pink to deep red. They are found either solitary on the plant, or arranged evenly along a common flower stalk. The five-lobed calyx (united sepal) is fused with the ovary, forming a tube up to an inch long. The five petals, with alternating stamens, extend from the throat of this calyx tube.

Fruit The gooseberries have oblong fruits; the currants have round fruits. The berries are generally small, although in favorable conditions they reach ½ inch in diameter. Some fruits are covered with soft spines, which must be removed before eating. Upon ripening, they turn red or bluish black. The dried and withered flower is often found remaining at the top of the fruit.

Beneficial Properties

Edible Properties While all gooseberries and currants are edible raw, some are sour or spiny, and are thus more palatable if cooked or dried. Dried, they make a good trail snack. Some Native Americans dried the berries and mixed them with meat to make pemmican. Pies, tarts, jellies, and wine are all further possibilities with the currants and gooseberries. The peeled and crushed fruit can be used directly on pancakes and muffins. By the way, most (but not all) currants sold in the markets are actually dried grapes (in other words, raisins).

Some Native Americans boiled and ate the leaves, usually with meat. The leaves also make a bland tea.

Medicinal Uses We'd appreciate authenticated reports from readers.

Other Uses When grown thickly around the borders of your property, currants and gooseberries make an ideal natural fence to keep out wandering trespassers.

Detrimental Properties
May be confused with poison oak. Be sure you're reaching into the right set of leaves!

Where Found
Considered together, gooseberries and currants have such a wide variety of habitats that they may be encountered in nearly any environment. In desert areas, look for them near water holes or along dry streams. In mountain areas, they'll be found in both shady and open areas, usually near a water supply. They are also found along the coastal mountains and canyons.

Growing Cycle
Currants and gooseberries are shrubs that can be observed throughout the year. The fruits are generally ripe from late spring to late summer.

Lore and Signature
The California golden currant has a beautiful flower of bright yellow and bright orange. Interestingly, they are often found near the decomposed granite in which gold is likely to be found.

This is also the plant of gooseberry jam fame from Dickens's *Christmas Carol*.

Dandelion (Taraxacum officinale)
Sunflower Family
(Compositae)

Most Prominent Characteristics

Overall Shape and Size
Dandelion, commonly found in lawns and fields, first appears as a ground-hugging basal rosette of leaves often reaching up to nine inches in diameter. The flowers mature into a cottony tuft of winged seeds that children love to blow into the wind.

dandelion plant in flower

Stalks and Stems Next, a single, succulent stalk emerges from the center of the rosette and rapidly grows three to nine inches. The flower stalks exude a milky juice when cut.

Leaves The word *dandelion* is derived from the French *dent de lion*, which translates to lion's tooth. This refers to the configuration of the jagged-edged leaves, which are pinnately divided into sharp lobes. The low-lying leaves often become prostrate and are thus able to hide among the blades and stems of grass. The leaves exude a milky juice when cut.

Flowers When the stalk has reached its full length, a bullet-shaped bud forms at the top, which bursts open into a globe of yellow flowers. The yellow flower heads grow singly at the tip of the vertical leafless hollow stalks. After a week to 10 days, these flowers change into a light-gray ball of fuzzy seeds. This ball, if left undisturbed, waits for a gust of wind to blow its seeds away.

Roots The brown taproot resembles a small, knotty carrot, generally from three to five inches in length.

Beneficial Properties

Edible Properties The young-to-early mature leaves are edible raw in salads or sandwiches. The older leaves become increasingly bitter and need to be cooked and prepared in much the same way one handles greens. Cooked dandelion leaves are similar to spinach.

The crown (the one-inch section between the lower leaves and the upper root section) can be eaten as a separate hot vegetable or added to mixed vegetable dishes. It should be steamed or boiled if too bitter.

The roots are commonly roasted to make a good tasting noncaffeine coffee. To do this, you first dig up the largest roots available and thoroughly wash until free of dirt. Dry them (in the sun or oven at low heat), then grind them in a grain or coffee grinder, mortar and pestle, or electric grinder. Roast in 225° F oven until brown, then percolate the same as with coffee grounds. Drink plain or try adding raw cream and/or honey. Unseasoned, it tastes something between coffee and Postum (a popular commercial cereal beverage made of barley, wheat, and molasses).

The cleaned roots can also be cooked (steamed or boiled if older and bitter) and eaten (something like parsnips).

The fresh, dew-covered flowers, carefully gathered in the early morning, are fermented to make the unique-tasting dandelion wine.

Due to its rubber content (see Other Uses), dandelion has been used as a binder for food items such as turkey stuffing, meatloaf, and walnut loaf.

One analysis of 100 grams of raw dandelion leaves yielded 14,000 international units of vitamin A (hey, folks, that's a lot!), 35 milligrams of vitamin C, 187 milligrams of calcium, 76 milligrams of sodium, and 397 milligrams of potassium.

Medicinal Uses Herbalists believe that dandelion is the perfect herb for coping with anemia. The leaves eaten fresh purge the uric acid from the blood and are said to be excellent for liver ailments. Dandelion is a mild diuretic and a mild laxative. The fresh leaves are used by herbalists for skin diseases, diabetes, pancreas and spleen problems, and fever. The root is a tonic, mild laxative, and diuretic. Dandelion roots were included in the *United States Pharmacopoeia* from 1831 to 1926.

According to a study published in 1990 in the *Berkeley Wellness Letter*, dandelion greens are a rich source of beta carotene. (Beta carotene is one of a large group of substances called carotenoids.) It used to be thought that the benefits of beta carotene were due to its conversion to vitamin A, but research suggests that beta carotene itself is the more potent protector against cancer. Numerous animal studies have suggested that beta carotene can defend against tumors and enhance the immune system. At least 70 studies on humans concluded that humans who don't eat enough fruits and vegetables rich in carotenoids have an increased risk of cancer, and lung cancer in particular. One large study, presented at the London conference by Dr. George Comstock of Johns Hopkins University, found that individuals with low levels of beta carotene in the blood had a far greater risk of developing lung cancer as well as melanoma, a lethal form of skin cancer.

Interestingly, in the published report, there was an accompanying chart listing dandelion greens as the richest source of beta carotene: one cup of the cooked greens yields 8.4 milligrams. Yet, in spite of this, not a single mention of dandelion was made in either the headline or the article. One large carrot contains 6.6 milligrams of beta carotene, and so carrots were mentioned in the headline, and the article emphasized that "Mom was right! It is good for you to eat your carrots." While we have no quarrels with eating carrots, this was a prime example of prejudice against weeds. Even though dandelion is found to be the richest source of beta carotene, it is virtually ignored in the reporting. (For the record, the other top beta carotene sources were one medium sweet potato [5.9 milligrams], ¾ cup cooked watercress [5.6 milligrams], ¾ cup cooked kale [5.3 milligrams], ½ cup cooked spinach [4.9 milligrams], ½ medium mango [2.9 milligrams].) Since some beta carotene is destroyed by cooking (the longer you cook, the more is destroyed), the beta carotene content of dandelion and other foods would be even higher when consumed raw.

In July of 1998, Vonda White wrote me the following from the California Institute for Women:

One morning in May of this year, I awoke with what I realized was a bladder infection. . . . I have long been accustomed to seeking herbal remedies when ill, so I looked into what was readily available to me. One of the most commonly found herbs growing here is dandelion—a specific remedy for such problems as mine. On my way into the dining room for breakfast, I saw some nice dandelion plants growing at the edge of the sidewalk, and I picked and ate a few tender leaves. The leaves were mildly bitter but tasted very good to me. Growing next to the dandelion was some young prickly lettuce, which I also ate. On my way out of the dining room, I picked and ate more of both. I did not notice any immediate or miraculous improvement in my condition through the day, but I continued to drink extra water. On my way to dinner that evening, I picked and ate more dandelion and prickly lettuce. The miracle was that the next morning there was no more problem.

Due to dandelion's richness in vitamins and minerals, the plant is sometimes called poor man's ginseng. It is readily available around the world, is far cheaper than ginseng, and will likely improve your health as much as ginseng—especially if you're out on fields and lawns collecting it yourself.

Other Uses During World War II, dandelion was used as a rubber source. The fresh plant contains 1 percent rubber, and the dried plant contains 16 to 17 percent rubber. Specially cultivated dandelion (such as the Russian species, T. koksaghya) can yield as high as 20 percent rubber. When, during World War II, the Germans invaded Poland (where dandelion grows best), they were amazed to see mile after mile of dandelion fields under cultivation for rubber production. Thereafter, they used the dandelions for their own purposes throughout the rest of the war. Today, some dandelion is still cultivated in Poland, as well as sections of western Asia and eastern Europe.

Because of all the foregoing usefulness issues, a Save the Dandelion organization was formed in England in 1973 to protect this versatile plant. As a result of a renewed interest in wild foods, there were fears that the plant might become extinct in England from so many people picking it.

Detrimental Properties
At your local nursery, you can inspect the broad array of persistent herbicides developed to kill dandelions. Lawns and fields thus poisoned are your greatest threat when you forage for dandelion.

Where Found
Dandelions are found throughout the world (though it appears that it is a native to Greece). It has established itself all over the United States (fortunately for the itinerant forager), and can be found on virtually any lawn, field, or similar area that has fairly consistent moisture.

Growing Cycle
Dandelion is a perennial that flowers most prolifically in the spring and early summer. The leaves of spring are the most palatable for raw or cooked dishes. The roots can be gathered year-round. When you collect roots take the largest roots and replant the younger ones for subsequent seasons.

Lore and Signature
I sent a copy of an earlier manuscript to Rebecca Wilson of San Gabriel, California, with the inscription "May all your camels reach Mecca." She sent me a card depicting a "dandelion boy," with her poem:

Dandelions,

  not

  for dreaming.

Breath to them,

  a treasure set

  a seed in motion,

  for all camels, eagles,

  even lizards and snails

    to reach

      Mecca.

Valuable book,

  is like an eagle in flight.

Within it are

  the wings to fly,

  to the open

  windows

  of knowledge.

    So,

No longer do I fear harm

  from poisonous plants, or

  death from starvation.

—Rebecca Wilson, April 17, 1982

Dandelion Celebration

When I think of dandelions, I think of Peter Gail, author of *Dandelion Celebration*. Peter has been interested in wild plants since his childhood when necessity forced his family to utilize goosefoot and other wild greens for meals. Eventually, he earned a Ph.D. in plant ecology at Rutgers University. In the 1970s, Peter Gail worked with Euell Gibbons in developing the National Wilderness Survival Training Camps for the Boy Scouts National Council in New Jersey. Gail and Gibbons developed a wild food foraging course for Rutgers, and Gail was often Euell Gibbons's back-up lecturer.

Gail's *Dandelion Celebration* is the ultimate word on dandelion nutrition and cookery—everything you'd ever want to know about dandelions in 150 pages.

Dandelion is so nutritious that it is sometimes referred to as poor man's ginseng. Gail lists its many uses, such as a cure for liver diseases, a tonic, a way to dissolve kidney stones, a skin cleanser, a high blood pressure preventive measure, help with bowel functioning, a prevention or cure for anemia, and help controling diabetes.

Still, most folks think of dandelions as food, not medicine, so Gail provides us with recipes he has collected over the entire United States. Some of the recipes are Amish, some are his own, and many are from his travels throughout the United States.

Christopher Nyerges with Euell Gibbons (left) at a Pasadena City College press conference, 1975.

Dock (Rumex crispus)

Buckwheat Family
(Polygonaceae)
Common Names curly dock,
Indian dock, yellow dock

Photo by Doug Haipt

Most Prominent Characteristics

Overall Shape and Size The
dock plant of spring appears as a
tuft of long narrow leaves with
the entire plant arising no more
than a foot off the ground. As the
flower stalk arises, and the lower
leaves die off, the plant takes on a

Christopher with curly dock stalk and the leaves

more vertical appearance, and rises up to four feet in ideal soil conditions.

Stalks and Stems Dock stalks can be up to ⅜ inch thick. When mature, they are reddish brown with darker brown striations. The mature stalk is hollow and quite rigid.

Leaves Most of this perennial plant's dark-green leaves are basal, 4 to 10 inches in length, lanceolate-shaped, with wavy, curved margins. The older leaves often have scattered red splotches. The upper leaves are smaller and less numerous.

Flowers The light-green flowers, growing in dense whorls, are only ⅛ inch broad and thus rather inconspicuous.

Fruit The mature, red-brown, papery, three-winged fruits, ¼ to 1 inch broad, are produced in abundance every late summer and autumn.

Roots The long taproot is yellow, shaped like a slender carrot.

Beneficial Properties

Edible Properties Dock leaves, best gathered in the spring, have a vinegar tartness when eaten raw. Thus, they add vigor to lettuce or wild green salads. Gather the leaves, add to hot water, and let steep or simmer until tender. Season lightly and enjoy the superb taste and texture.

One of my favorite dock recipes was the result of an experiment one Christmas weekend while camping with Leo Weiskircher and friends north of Big Sur. Into our cast iron skillet we placed equal portions of chopped dock leaves, diced tomatoes, and diced brown onions. We covered the skillet and gently sautéed until everything was tender. We added no seasoning. The blend of sour (dock) and sweet (cooked onion) and salty (tomato) resulted in quite a toothsome dish, one that I've repeated often.

A tasty green dish can be made by steaming equal parts of chicory greens and dock greens. Season the greens with butter or soy sauce and mix in liberal amounts of chopped hickory nuts. I've named this dish Hickory, Chicory, Dock.

William Biewener of Studio City, California takes the stems of the dock leaves and treats them as he'd treat rhubarb. Following a recipe for rhubarb pie, but substituting dock stems for rhubarb, he makes a delicious wild dock pie. As a long-time regular on my wild food outings, I've enjoyed many of Biewener's unique pies from wild ingredients.

Dock leaves are richer in vitamin C than oranges and richer in vitamin A than carrots. They have an abundance of easily digested plant iron. One hundred grams (about ½ cup) of the leaf contains 66 milligrams of calcium, 41 milligrams of phosphorus, 338 milligrams of potassium, 12,900 international units of vitamin A, and 119 milligrams of vitamin C.

The dock plant sends up a three- to five-foot stalk in late summer and autumn, deep brown in color. These seeds can be gathered, winnowed, ground, and used as flour (either by itself or mixed with other flours).

Medicinal Uses The fresh leaves are said to promote healing when applied to ulcers, wounds, and raw, itching skin. Another folk remedy is that if you are stung by nettles, rub on dock leaves, the saying being "Nettle in, dock out." I've experimented with this and, although the expressed juice of dock leaves does relieve the sting of nettle, the juice of aloe vera does a superior job. (See my comments in the Nettle listing.)

The dock seeds were made into tea by the Yuki Native Americans and used in cases of dysentery.

The root is said to have medicinal qualities. Dried, ground, and steeped in boiling water, it's a mildly laxative tea and is said to also be a good general tonic.

Other Uses The Latin name *Rumex* comes from "to suck", because the Romans used to suck the leaves—principally the leaf stems—to allay thirst.

Detrimental Properties

Dock contains soluble oxalates, the amount varying from location to location. Oxalates are found in toxic quantities in some plant leaves (such as rhubarb) but rarely occur in toxic amounts in dock.

Where Found

A native of Europe, dock is found throughout the United States in a variety of habitats from fields to lawns, dry, open areas, to wet, swampy areas. It establishes itself quite readily, so be certain you want it before planting it in your yard or fields. Once established (by seed or root) in your yard, you'll most likely have it there as your companion forever.

Growing Cycle
Dock is a perennial, producing new young leaves in the spring, sending up a flower stalk in early summer, with the deep-brown seeds maturing in the autumn.

Lore and Signature
This plant has also been referred to as Indian tobacco. Though some people have told us they smoke this tobacco, the dried stalks are usually used for decoration, as you might use mature cattail stalks. I have also seen it hung around the edges of houses and was told this was to keep the vampires away. Could it be that consuming dock helps protect you from blood suckers? Certainly dock's richness of vitamin A will keep you healthy.

Elder (Sambucus spp.)
Honeysuckle Family
(Caprifoliaceae)

elder flowers

Most Prominent Characteristics

Overall Shape and Size Elders can grow either as shrubs or as small trees to 10 feet tall.

Leaves The light-green compound leaves are divided into 5 to 11 leaflets. The leaves are opposite each other and have slightly serrated margins.

Flowers

The small, white flowers grow in flat-topped clusters or conical clusters of two to six inches across. The flowers are followed by small ⅛- to ¼-inch purple, black, red, or white berries, depending on the particular species.

Beneficial Properties

Edible Properties The dark purple berries, rich in vitamin A, with fair amounts of potassium and calcium, can be eaten raw, or can be mashed and blended with applesauce for a unique dessert, especially if you are using wild apples. The berries can also be used for making wines, jellies, jams, and pies. The red and white berries are not recommended for food, some having toxic qualities.

The whole flower cluster can be gathered, dipped in batter, and fried, producing a wholesome pancake. Try dipping the flower clusters in a batter of the sweet yellow cattail pollen (see Cattail) and frying it like pancakes. This is wild food at its best.

The dried flowers, removed from the cluster, can also be mixed into flour for baking pastries, breads, and more.

Medicinal Uses Tea made from the flowers induces sweating; as such, it is said to be useful for colds, fevers, and headaches associated with colds. A poultice of the leaves is used for wounds, sprains, and swellings. When I visited my grandfather's farm in Chardon, Ohio, after he died, I found only one bottle of his herbal remedy: it was dried elder flowers.

A tea of the fresh or dried leaves is used as a wash for skin infections.

In the Middle Ages, the elder was considered a holy tree, capable of restoring and keeping one's health, and as an aid to longevity.

Other Uses Elder's botanical name, *Sambucus*, comes from the sambuke, a musical instrument made of elder wood. This is because the branches

have a central pith (core) that is
soft and can be easily scooped
out; the branch is then made into
a flute.

A straight elder branch makes
an ideal stem for a calumet. The
pipe stem is carved to fit the catli-
nite (or clay, bone, wood) pipe,
and the stem is hollowed out with
a hot wire. Additionally, an entire
pipe can be fashioned from a
piece of elder stem where a second stem is growing perpendicular to the first. Both the bowl
and stem are one piece and are
hollowed out with a hot wire.

ripe Mexican elderberries

Long straight elder branches can be hollowed out and used as blowguns. Branches five feet or longer are best, but shorter ones can also be
effective. The key is to select an elder branch that is as straight as possible.
There are two methods of hollowing the blowgun. One method is to use a
hot wire and slowly hollow it out. The second is to split the elder lengthwise, scoop out the pith, and then reseal the elder branch with glue or
resins. In this second method, the entire elder branch is usually wrapped
with leather to bind it.

Detrimental Properties

The foliage and root are poisonous if eaten. It affects like a purgative. The
red and white berries are not recommended for food, some having bitter
or toxic qualities. The edible purple and black berries cause nausea for
some if eaten raw. Cooked, they are harmless.

I've seen children chewing on the pithy core of the dried elderberry
stems many times. I have often done so also, and thus conclude that the
dried stems are not harmful, at least not in small amounts. However, the
green stalks can be harmful if eaten. Wilma Roberts James, author of *Know
Your Poisonous Plants,* says that children who have made whistles and
blowguns from the dried elder stems have been poisoned. Unfortunately,
she does not list the specific incidents, nor does she tell what type of poisoning or how much the children in question actually consumed.

Where Found

Elder is found throughout the United States. It does well along rivers and
streams. There are many species of elder, and their preferred locales
include chaparral hillsides, high elevations, low canyon bottoms, open
fields, and even vacant lots.

Growing Cycle

Elder grows to a small tree. The flowers can be gathered in spring and the berries ripen around late summer.

Lore and Signature

Explore the meaning of the word *elder* as well as the respect bestowed upon the elders of all cultures. Keep that in mind when you review the many virtues of this tree.

Epazote (Chenopodium ambrosiodes and C. botrys)

Goosefoot Family (Chenopodiaceae)

Common Names Jerusalem oak, Mexican tea, wormseed, Mexican goosefoot

a young epazote plant

Most Prominent Characteristics

Overall Shape and Size Epazote has a branched stem reaching up about three feet. It is very similar to Chenopodium anthelminticum, which is not as common, although it seems that C. ambrosiodes tends to hybridize with it.

Leaves The light-green leaves are elliptical, two to five inches long, and sometimes reddish tinged or blotched. The uniquely aromatic leaves are arranged alternately. The leaf blade tapers at both ends and is slightly petioled. The undulating leaf margin is slightly or entirely toothed. The leaf surface is hairless, although it may be slightly tomentose when very young.

Flowers The inconspicuous 1⁄8-inch yellowish-green, oval-shaped flowers, dotted with glands on the underside, appear in summer in dense axillary clusters upon the branches to form terminal leafy spikes. These sessile flowers have a five-part calyx and five or fewer stamens. Numerous black seeds ripen in autumn.

Beneficial Properties

Edible Properties Epazote is very popular in Central and South American and Mexican cookery, especially in bean dishes since it prevents gas. It adds a unique flavor to beans, and as an herb, it is as cherished as cilantro by some. To use, crumble dried leaves into the pot of beans, or add some fresh leaves to your particular taste (five is usually plenty). Epazote can be eaten once cooked, but it can be toxic in large amounts (see Detrimental Properties).

It can also be made into tea to prevent or stop excessive gas.

Medicinal Uses

Epazote is one of the best antiflatulents, also aiding the digestion. It acts as a vermifuge, expelling intestinal worms (such as roundworms and hookworms) and other intestinal parasites. It is said to be less effective against tapeworms. The Natchez Native Americans used epazote to expel worms in children. It is used by the Chinese as a diaphoretic, to strengthen the eyes and the circulation, to cure coughing up blood, and for dysentery. The herb is taken either in powder form or infused into a tea.

Epazote is effective in ridding cats and dogs of worms. Simply sprinkle a small amount of the dried and powdered leaves into their food. Epazote seeds and leaves in chickens' water will also cure and prevent some diseases common to fowl.

Other Uses We'd appreciate authenticated reports from readers.

Detrimental Properties

Pure oil of chenopodium is toxic. However, epazote leaf contains only 1 percent of this oil, and such small amounts are ideal as a vermifuge or antiflatulent. The seeds contain approximately 10 percent oil of chenopodium; a teaspoon or so of the seeds added to dog and cat food works wonders as a dewormer and does not pose a threat to the animal's health in such low dosage. Eating moderate amounts of the cooked greens poses no health hazard whatsoever. However, due to the strong aroma of epazote, it is rarely cooked alone. Generally, epazote greens are mixed with other greens before cooking.

Where Found

Epazote is abundant along inland stream beds in sandy soil and common in seaside salt marshes. The plant, which is sometimes cultivated, generally prefers waste locales and areas with somewhat poor, sandy soil. It seems to prefer the semishade along the bank of a sandy river or stream but will do well in rich garden soil when cultivated. Native to Central America and Mexico, it is now well naturalized throughout parts of southern California and the southern United States. It has been found grown in the wild as far north as New England and even in big city parks, such as those in New York City, Cleveland, and Detroit.

Growing Cycle

This plant grows as an annual in colder northern climates, but acts as a perennial in the warmer southern climates. The new leaves appear in spring, the plant flowers in summer, and by fall it goes to seed and dies back. Generally, the leaves are collected from the plant in the spring before the plant flowers.

Eucalyptus
(Eucalyptus spp.)
Myrtle Family (Myrtaceae)
Common Names Gumwood, gum tree, red gum, blue gum, cider gum, white gum, yellow gum, mallee

Most Prominent Characteristics

Overall Shape and Size These evergreen trees and shrubs have become common ornamentals because they are beautiful, fast

eucalyptus leaf and pods

growing, and drought tolerant. The height of eucalypti range from 10 to 150 feet. Most have a gray-green appearance, with the overall shape varying from bushy and weeping to slender and vertical with a crowned top. In order to identify a particular variety, it is necessary to observe the bark, leaves, buds, flowers, and fruits.

Leaves The leaves are sharp pointed, toothless, simple, petioled, either pale green to bluish, or gray to light brown or tan, often with a waxy sheen. Some varieties are highly aromatic. The leaves appear opposite each other on the young plants, then become alternate on the older eucalypti.

Bark The mottled or smooth bark is either persistent or peeling. If the latter, it exposes a smooth, whitish trunk surface underneath.

Flowers The flower buds resemble acorns. The petals stick together to form a fuzzy cap, then fall off when the flower cluster opens, revealing the bright orange, yellow, or red stamens. The sepals are small or absent. The flowers are arranged in stalked umbels, panicles, corymbs, or singly.

Fruit The fruit is a woody capsule that opens at the top by three to six valves.

Beneficial Properties

Edible Properties A tea from the leaves can be infused and used as a beverage.

The mallees, Australian dwarf species of eucalyptus, were once an important staple food for the Australian Aborigines and a survival food for a number of explorers. Surface roots would be cut—usually in pieces several meters long and 2.5 centimeters in diameter. One end of these porous root sections would then be blown into and an astringent sap would bubble out the other end. The water from these roots is to the Australian desert what cactus juice is to the deserts in the southwestern

United States. Of all the mallees used this way, E. dumosa, E. gracilis, E. incrassata, E. oleosa, and E. microtheca were said to be the best water producers.

The roots of several mallee species were dried, powdered, and eaten. The best are said to be E. caesia, E. dumosa, and E. gracilis. The finely powdered seeds of one mallee, E. microtheca, have been reportedly used for food.

In Australia, the eucalyptus provides nectar and pollen to bees, who in turn provide beeswax and honey. Beehives that I've kept near a eucalyptus grove in Los Angeles have produced a honey as dark as molasses and extremely fragrant.

Medicinal Uses The young fruits can be sucked to ease the pain of sore throats. According to Alma R. Hutchens, author of *Indian Herbology of North America*, "Among the diseases in which it is employed are croup, diphtheria, bronchitis, asthma, piles, neuralgia, malarial diseases, catarrh, in subacute or chronic inflammation of the urinary organs, ulcers and sores. It has proven an effective remedy in some cases of rheumatism. For some, the mode of using it in asthma is to smoke the dried leaves."

The tea of eucalyptus leaves, well known for its efficacy in dealing with sinus congestion, also has sufficient antiseptic properties that can be used to clean wounds.

Eucalyptus oil (obtained from the leaves by distillation) is rich in the therapeutic agent cineole. Cineole is used as an active ingredient in inhalants, gargles, lozenges, and more, because it has a pleasant odor and is efficient in killing bacteria. Rutin, used medicinally for diabetes and high blood pressure, occurs in the leaves of some eucalypti.

In emergencies, the crushed, fresh leaves of any of the eucalypti can be placed directly on wounds to help reduce swelling and prevent infections.

We have taken the caps off some of the smaller capsules and used the powdered insides (which consisted mostly of stamens) as a first aid remedy for cuts. In all cases, this resulted in rapid healing and very little scarring. We suggest that the smaller, unopened capsules be included in first aid kits.

Other Uses The variously scented eucalyptus leaves (peppermint, lemon, and medicinal) tend to repel insects. A necklace of young fruits is used as a safe flea repellent for cats and dogs.

Medicine and industry are the two main consumers of eucalyptus oils, with a small percentage being used by the perfume industry. Eucalyptus is used in soaps, antiseptics, and deodorants. The oils, useful solvents for varnish resins, grease, and rubber, can be safely used for cleaning greasy hands. Eucalyptus oil is a source of piperitone, from which menthol is manufactured. The rutin that occurs in some of the

eucalyptus leaves can be boiled
out and used as a yellow dye.
   Whole books have been written on the many uses of this valuable plant. We've only scratched
the surface here. For further information, we suggest you check
with your local public library,
bookstore, or search the Web.

Detrimental Properties

Perhaps the biggest hazard with
eucalyptus is the fact that older
branches readily break off in the
wind or when someone is climbing

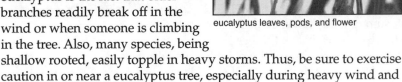
eucalyptus leaves, pods, and flower

in the tree. Also, many species, being
shallow rooted, easily topple in heavy storms. Thus, be sure to exercise
caution in or near a eucalyptus tree, especially during heavy wind and
rainstorms.
   It is also more difficult to garden under the areas where eucalypti are
growing. Your garden plants will produce smaller fruit or tubers, and the
plants will require more fertilizer. This is apparently the result of the dis-
persion of the various eucalyptus oils into the soil.

Where Found

Eucalyptus is native to Australia. There are about 90 varieties which have
naturalized in California. Eucalyptus is also found in warmer climates as
an ornamental.

Growing Cycle

These plants grow as shrubs or trees. The flowers and new leaf growth
appears in the spring. The woody capsules follow the flowers and mature
by midsummer.
   For their medicinal virtues, the leaves are best collected in the spring
of the year.

Fennel (Foeniculum vulgare)

Parsley Family (Umbelliferae)
Common Names Wild licorice,
wild anise, finocchio

a ferny fennel shoot

Most Prominent Characteristics

Overall Shape and Size In winter and early spring, the plants begin to appear. They first establish a ferny, bushy, two- to three-foot broad base. By spring and early summer, the flower stalks rise to a height of six feet (higher in ideal conditions). The entire plant has a slightly bluish-green cast, due to a thin waxy coating on the stalks and leaves. All parts of the plant have a licorice taste and odor.

Stalks and Stems The stalks and stems are coarsely, striately grooved.

Leaves The leaf ends are dissected into many fernlike leaflets. Each leaf stalk adheres to the stem from which it grows with an easily distinguishable base that resembles the flared base of a single celery stalk.

Flowers The yellow flowers are large compound umbels up to six inches in diameter.

Seeds The ⅛-inch seeds are oblong with prominent ribs. The mature seeds sometimes persist on the plant for a few months after the plant has died and dried.

Roots Fennel root is large and fat; it continues growing larger as the years go by. It begins as a taproot.

Beneficial Properties

Edible Properties Due to its succulence, fennel is very refreshing to eat when you're thirsty. In spring, the entire young tender base of the newly emerging flower stalks (the section between the root and the leafy ferny tops) can be eaten. Eat this most delicious part as you would celery. Towards summer, as the plant's flower stalk develops, individual leaves can be pulled off and their enlarged base eaten like celery; or the leaves can be cooked.

The seeds can be steeped to make a licorice-flavored tea. The seeds are used commercially both in making candy and in French and Italian cooking. They are also used to flavor medicine.

Fennel seeds have been used to flavor salads and other dishes. In Indian restaurants, one is served an after-dinner fennel tray as a breath freshener.

One hundred grams of raw fennel leaf has been found to contain 100 milligrams of calcium, 51 milligrams of phosphorus, 397 milligrams of potassium, 31 milligrams of vitamin C, and 3,500 international units of vitamin A.

Medicinal Uses Eating fennel is said to relieve gas. The best way found to use fennel as a gas preventive is to eat the raw young stalks or the fresh foliage. Fresh or dried fennel in dishes, such as soups or stews, is equally effective as an antiflatulent. Fennel also has a diuretic effect. Infused into tea, it is used for gas, upset stomach, and cramps.

Fennel seeds in milk is said to combat giddiness and nausea.

Other Uses Sprinkling fresh or dried fennel leaf parts in dogs' sleeping areas is reputed to repel fleas. The old flower stalks make attractive dried floral arrangements. Oil of fennel is used in soaps and perfumes.

The pithiness of the dried flower stalk can be useful for tinder when starting a fire.

Detrimental Properties

Warning! Be *sure* you've correctly identified this plant! Poison hemlock, an *extremely* poisonous member of the parsley family that often grows along with fennel, is deceptively similar—especially to the amateur naturalist. Poison hemlock, however, has no licorice odor and has characteristic purple marks or blotches along the stem that fennel lacks. Furthermore, poison hemlock's leaves closely resemble parsley, whereas fennel's leaves are finely divided into needlelike segments.

Where Found

Fennel is a European native. It is extremely common along the United States Pacific Coast, in coastal streams, vacant lots, and extending to the San Gabriel Mountains to the north.

Growing Cycle

This plant is a perennial, appearing bushy and ferny every early spring, with flower stalks rising by summer and maturing in late summer and autumn.

Lore and Signature

Prometheus was said to have brought fire to earth in a dried fennel stalk. Also, the fronds of fennel are said to ward off evil spirits and witches.

Filaree (Erodium circutarium and moschatum)

Geranium Family
(Geraniaceae)
Common Names Heron's bill,
scissors plant, alfilarea

The common filaree can be found just about every-where.

Most Prominent Characteristics

Overall Shape and Size The
low plant first manifests as a
rosette of ferny leaves, then sends
up a flower stalk of up to 1½ feet.

Stalks and Stems The erect
flower stalks are stout and fleshy and vary from ⅟₁₆ to ⅜ inch in diameter.
The same is true of the leaf petioles, which, in ideal conditions, can be
found up to 1½ feet long.

Leaves The leaves are pinnately compound and oppositely arranged.
Each leaflet is ovate, petiolate, with a serrated margin, sparsely incised,
and from ¾ inch to 1½ inches long. The leaves are covered with short,
coarse, stiff hairs.

Flowers Each flower stalk bears ¼- inch pink to rosy purple flowers. Each
flower has 5 petals and 10 stamens (5 of which lack anthers and are therefore infertile).

Fruit The awl-shaped fruits measure about one inch long along their longitudinal axis. The plant's Spanish name, *Alfilarea*, refers to the fruit's pinlike
appearance. The fruit consists of five carpels, each of which separates from
the central axis when mature and, beginning at the apex of the fruit, coils
up into five spiral-shaped carpels, still attached to a common base.

Beneficial Properties

Edible Properties The mild-flavored stems can be eaten raw. The green
leaves, though slightly fibrous, can be eaten raw in salads, the small
coarse hairs requiring some extra mastication to ensure digestion. They
can also be cooked like spinach, and provide spinachlike flavor.

E. moschatum is an important winter and spring forage crop for livestock in the northeastern United States and parts of Canada.

Medicinal Uses We'd appreciate authenticated reports from readers.

Other Uses The ripe fruits can provide a source of amusement for people who may have been forced by circumstances to return to life's simple

pleasures. It can be fascinating to watch the carpels unfold into coils, and can be diversionary to attach two of the fruits together by piercing the body of one with the sharp point of another (the resulting object closely resembling a miniature pair of scissors, thus the common name scissors plant).

Detrimental Properties
We would appreciate authenticated reports from readers.

Where Found
Filaree prefers disturbed areas such as soil that has been recently cleared. It is also found in fields and lawns. The plant is native to the Mediterranean region.

Growing Cycle
This annual's leaves are best gathered in late winter and early spring for food.

Glasswort
(Salicornia spp.)
Goosefoot Family
(Chenopodiaceae)
Common Names Samphire,
pickleweed, saltwort

glasswort

Most Prominent
Characteristics

Overall Shape and Size These
low-growing plants are either
perennials or annuals with their
erect or decumbent stems rising
up to one foot tall out of the sand
(which they nearly always inhabit).

Stalks and Stems Glasswort is characterized by its succulent and cylindrical stems which are oppositely arranged. The slender, greenish stems
are approximately ⅛ to ¼ inch thick. This branched plant with its many
jointed segments appears leafless. The entire plant turns red in the
autumn, beginning from the base.

Leaves The degenerate leaves appear as opposite inconspicuous scales
at each node.

Flowers The flowers, borne on cylindrical spikes, are less conspicuous
than the leaves, since the flowers are hidden under the scaly leaves. The
flowers appear in opposite groups of three to seven.

Beneficial Properties

Edible Properties Every observant explorer of the Pacific Coast salt
marshes has noticed glasswort, especially in the fall when it covers the salt
marshes in a beautiful carpet of scarlet and bronze. Others have possibly
nibbled on some of its raw branches while walking along the beach. Glasswort is at its best eaten raw, eating only the upper and more tender parts of
the plant. Glasswort can be used alone as the main salad ingredient, mixed
with other salad greens (wild or domestic), or even as a garnish with any
seafood dish (same as restaurants use watercress and parsley springs).
Mixed with stews and soups, glasswort provides all the salt needed.
    Glasswort can also be cooked or steamed, seasoned, and served as a
hot vegetable. This is good, but cooked glasswort loses much of its
appeal. Use only the tender upper tips of the plant.

Tender glasswort stems can also be pickled. One method involves first washing the freshly gathered plants and packing them into jars. A pickling mix is then made by combining one cup of vinegar, ¼ cup of honey, a few tablespoons of pickling spices (such as dill or garlic), and a sliced onion and boiling for 10 minutes. This mix is then poured boiling hot over the glasswort until the jars are level full. The full jars are then sealed airtight and stored for two to three weeks before serving. Warning: Since there are many more elements to a successful—and safe—pickling and canning operation, I strongly suggest that anyone caring to pursue this further first glean additional facts from a good cookbook (such as *Stocking Up* by Rodale Press).

In the desert marshes of Nevada and Utah, the Native Americans ground glasswort seeds into flour.

According to Bradford Angier, snow and Canada geese eat the fleshy glasswort branches. In the autumn, the reddening glasswort stem tips are eaten by ducks, especially pintails, who are mainly interested in the seeds.

Medicinal Uses We'd appreciate authenticated reports from readers.

Other Uses Glasswort ashes, called barilla, have a high soda content and are used in the manufacture of soap and glass.

Detrimental Properties
We would appreciate authenticated reports from readers.

Where Found
Most glasswort grows in coastal salt marshes (from Canada to Mexico and all along the Atlantic coast). Some glasswort is also found in the southern California alkaline marshes of the deserts. The plant is also found in Europe and Asia.

Growing Cycle
In the fall, glasswort matures to a beautiful shade of red, at which time the core of each stem becomes extremely fibrous, making the plant inedible. One could, however, pick the stems and chew off the outer tender section of each stem, and then discard the fibrous core. Due to this fibrousness, glasswort is not used in salads, as a cooked vegetable, or pickled at this stage of its growing cycle. Glasswort is best gathered in the spring when the new growth is abundant. However, even in the fall and winter, tender green glasswort may be available in small amounts.

Grass (All species)
Grass Family (Gramineae)

Most Prominent Characteristics

Overall Shape and Size There are numerous varieties of grasses. Some are ground-hugging, lateral-spreading, carpetlike plants (such as crabgrass, St. Augustine, rye, and bluegrass). Then there are the tall, erect, agriculturally important grasses such as corn, wheat, rice, sorghum, and sugar cane. And finally there are the forest grasses—those unmistakably towering plants called bamboos.

Wild oats is a type of grass.

Stalks and Stems These are usually round in cross section and are hollow except at the nodes where the leaves are attached. The nodes—easily seen and felt—create a visible bulge. Hollow stems such as these are commonly referred to as culms. The stems can be solid (such as in corn or sorghum), woody (as in bamboo), or succulent (as in most lawn and grain grasses).

Leaves The parallel veined leaves consist of two basic parts: the sheath, which envelops the stem, and the blade, which projects forth in a linear shape. There is also a hairlike membranous projection called a ligule inside of the grass sheath (where it meets the blade).

Flowers The flowers—usually, but not always, quite small—nearly all contain a functional pistil and stamens. They are, however, without distinct petals or sepals. Flowers are arranged in spikelets from which grow either one or many flowers. Spikelets consist of a straight axis (rachilla), two empty scales (or bracts) at the bottom, and then two more bracts in which grows the flower. Grass flowers are usually composed of three stamens, each bearing delicate filaments and two-celled anthers, one pistil (which has two styles), and feathery projecting stigmas.

Fruit The fruit, or grain, is technically referred to as a caryopsis. These grains are composed of the familiar exterior hard, starchy substance (endosperm) that surrounds an embryo (commonly called the germ). The germ is a concentrated source of vitamins and protein, the endosperm a storehouse of minerals and carbohydrates. Grain's extremely low moisture content makes it easy to store and transport, which is why it has become a major food source.

Roots Many of the grasses spread by means of rhizomes (horizontal stems). Rhizomes can send out their roots and shoots either above or below ground. The roots tend to be extremely tough and fibrous, and usually grow in dense, extensively branched clusters or clumps.

In one well-publicized study, the root cluster of a single four-month-old rye plant was spread out and each root strand measured; the total combined length was 387 miles!

Beneficial Properties

Edible Properties Of the 15 crops that are traditionally considered to stand between man and starvation, 10 are grasses. These included the grains of wheat, rice, corn, rye, oats, barley, millet, and sorghum.

The grains of every grass plant—even the wild weeds that everyone is so bent on getting rid of—can be eaten. Harvesting may be more difficult with the uncultivated species, but for the food value returned, harvesting is not a serious problem. Grass seeds can be roasted, ground into meal for bread and cakes, soaked in water and boiled into mush.

Since one is likely to encounter grass almost anywhere in the world, this is probably the most valuable plant family to become familiar with.

The very young, newly emerging grass shoots, under six inches, can be eaten raw in salads or cooked. Generally, these have little flavor, with the exception of some bamboos, which are quite bitter. Mature grass leaves become so fibrous that they're just too tough for the human digestive system; however, they can provide lifesaving nutrition to anyone willing to chew and chew and chew and chew them.

Acres USA, the journal of organic farming, published two features on grass in their December 1979 and January 1980 issues. The articles revealed that the very young grass leaves are the ideal supplement to the grain of the same plant. The grasses must be used at or before the jointed stage. (Unjointed grass has no stem; what appears to be a stem is several leaves rolled together.) Once the jointed stage is reached, the protein and vitamin content drops quickly since the growing plant uses up much of it. Grass picked at or before the jointing stage typically has approximately 40 percent protein, compared with approximately 4 percent protein at the mature stage.

Most cereal grasses joint about three weeks after being planted. Grass picked at this stage can be eaten as is in survival situations, or can be dried and powdered and added to other staples. A grass culm will grow up again and again if it is cut before the first joint forms.

Here is a list of the vitamin content of 100 grams of dehydrated cereal grasses cut when the first joint forms: carotene, 30–70 milligrams; vitamin C, 300–700 milligrams; riboflavin, 2,000–2,800 milligrams; thiamin, 300–500 international units; vitamin K, 30,000–80,000 standard units; nicotinic acid, 7.5–15 milligrams; vitamin E, 20–44 milligrams.

Medicinal Uses Although there are scattered references to Native American medicinal uses of grasses, grasses are generally not considered important medicinal plants except in the sense that all edible plants can be said to be medicine for the body. For example, young grass sprouts (and the juice from these sprouts, such as wheat grass juice) are *rich* in vitamins.

If readers know of any specific medicinal properties of any of the grasses, or of grasses generally, we'd appreciate hearing from you.

Other Uses Of all the grasses, the bamboo has the broadest range of uses. Bamboos have supplied—and still do supply—untold numbers of cultures with virtually every needed item: house and temple construction; water-piping; ladders, stairs, and scaffolding; home and outdoor furniture; knifes, swords, and spears; tools; kitchen utensils; bowls and cups; shingles and siding; motor vehicles and airplanes; and more.

Less woody grasses can be twined into cord or rope.

A good whistle can be made with any blade of grass: When you hold your hands and fingers together, notice the narrow elliptical opening at the base of where the thumbs meet. Place a blade of grass in this opening so that it is held tight between the top joints of the thumb meeting place and where the thumbs meet again at their bases. The edge of the grass must face you as you look at it. Held thus, the grass serves as a reed, and can be loosened or tightened by small movements of your thumbs. By blowing through the aforementioned elliptical opening (across which the grass blade is stretched), you can produce anything from a soft buzzing to a loud shrieking whistle, similar to a peacock call. With practice, many sounds can be produced. These noises can be useful for beckoning help, for attempting to attract animals for food, or for scaring away unwanted company.

Detrimental Properties

Although 99 percent of grass seed is entirely safe to eat, the seeds of Darnel (Lolium temulentum) and some sorghums are said to be toxic. Cyanide, the usual cause of their toxicity, can be eliminated by cooking or thoroughly drying the grain. Since only a few grasses exhibit this toxicity, and since most grains are cooked or dried before consumption, there is virtually no chance of poisoning if one is cautious. Grazing cattle have sometimes been poisoned by consuming these few grasses, but this is rare.

Never eat grains that have a mold or funguslike growth on them. Lysergic [lys(o) + erg(ot) + ic] acid, a crystalline alkaloid ($C_{16} H_{16} N_2 O_2$), was originally discovered in fungus ergot, a rye grain parasite. From lysergic acid, the powerful hallucinogen LSD-25 (lysergic acid diethylamide ($C_{20} H_{25} N_3 O$), was developed. In the Middle Ages, whole towns in Europe suffered intoxication, insanity, and even death when they ate ergot-infected rye. There has also been speculation that many of the so-called witches burned at Salem and at other witch trials could, in fact, have been suffering from the effects of infected grains. (We'll never know for sure. Remember that in those times, to simply be accused of being a witch virtually assured your death.)

If you plan to taste-test the young grass leaves of a cultivated lawn, first ascertain that the lawn has not been sprayed within the present growing season with chemical herbicides or chemical fertilizers.

Where Found
Grasses are found growing upon most of the land on Earth; grass covers approximately half of the lower 48 United States. The number of species in the grass family is exceeded only by the orchid family and the sunflower family.

Growing Cycle
Some grasses are perennials, some annuals. Those annual grasses that reproduce by seed generally follow the seasons (in other words, sprout in spring, go to seed by late summer or fall).

Horehound
(Marrubium vulgare)
Mint Family (Labiatae)

Horehound is a bitter mint.

Most Prominent Characteristics

Overall Shape and Size
Horehound is a perennial herb that seldom rises more than two feet. The square stem, whorled flower clusters, and opposite leaves are characteristic features of the mint family.

Stems The squarish stems and the leaves are conspicuously covered with a fine, downy white hair.

Leaves The oval, toothed, opposite leaves have the appearance of wrinkled skin.

Flowers The flower clusters are in whorls along the square stem at even intervals.

Beneficial Properties

Edible Properties We'd appreciate authenticated reports from readers.

Medicinal Uses Though it's a member of the mint family, if you chew a raw horehound leaf while hiking, you probably won't notice any strong minty flavor. Rather, it will be uniquely bitter.

The dried or fresh leaves of horehound can be made into tea. As a hot tea, horehound has been commonly used as a tonic, and for chronic sore throat, coughs, colds, and breathing problems associated with asthma. The tea has a strong bitter mint flavor, improved greatly by adding honey. Horehound leaves should be gathered in the spring when the plant is young and the leaves are large.

This plant provides the raw ingredients for horehound candy, which has long been sold in drugstores and markets as a mild cough drop. Here is a recipe for those of you who'd like to try to make the candy yourself. Cook (don't boil) one cup of the fresh herb (or ¼ cup of the dried herb) with two cups of water for about 15 minutes. Strain. To each cup of liquid, add one cup of honey. Cook until the mixture thickens. Keep at a low heat or it will run over. Pour onto a cookie sheet and let it cool. Break (or scoop) off pieces as you need or want it. It is best to refrigerate it, since it tends to spread. This candy is pleasant as a snack or energy food on the trail, as well as being useful for sore throats.

Other Uses The dried seed
stalks are attractive in dried floral
arrangements, alone or mixed
with other wild vegetation.

The seed whorls can also be
gathered and scattered in your
yard at the end of winter when
the ground is damp. Chances are
that some horehound will come
up. Horehound plants need little
care in the garden, for in the wild
they do well in dry regions in
even the poorest soils.

Detrimental Properties
We'd appreciate authenticated
reports from readers.

a horehound flower stalk

Where Found
Although horehound is a European native, it is naturalized in much of the
southwestern United States and is now very common in the foothill
regions. It grows by the roadside, in very open areas, and in disturbed
areas (such as plowed or disced land).

Growing Cycle
Horehound is a perennial herb whose leaves are best gathered during the
spring before the flowers appear.

Horsetail
(Equisetum spp.)
Horsetail Family
(Equisetaceae)
Common Names Scouring
rush, mare's tail, baby bamboo,
equisetum

fertile horsetail stalks with the spore-bearing tips

Most Prominent
Characteristics

Overall Shape and Size This is a
perennial rushlike plant, which
sometimes resembles a narrow
bamboo. Many people consider
the horsetails—common in the
roadside ditches—very similar in appearance to certain ferns.

Stalks The shoots can be easily pulled apart at the nodes. Each individual shoot has vertical grooves or ridges along its length and is covered with gritty silica. The internodes are hollow. Chlorophyll is produced in all of the stem.

Leaves The bristly black, needlelike leaves are small sheaths that appear at the nodes of the shoots. There is no chlorophyll in the leaves.

Reproduction Since horsetails have no flowers, they reproduce by spreading underground rhizomes and by airborne spores. The fertile stalks terminate in a conelike spike, which bears the spores.

Beneficial Properties

Edible Properties Although horsetails are not an important food source, the very young, newly emerging shoots (about one inch tall) can, if as large as your little finger, be eaten if first carefully peeled of their thin outer layer of gritty skin.

Medicinal Uses Best gathered in spring, horsetail is highly regarded by herbalists for its medicinal value. The shoots, used fresh or dried, are ground and cooked in water to make a tea. This tea is then used for cases of nervous breakdown, for insomnia, or for purifying the blood. To treat any wounds, cuts, sores, swelling, or rashes, one is told to wash the area with horsetail tea and then apply compresses. The tea is also useful for bad breath, stuffed-up nasal passages, and cases of extreme tension.

Other Uses The dried or fresh shoots can also be used for cleaning pots and pans due to their gritty silica coverings. The same quality makes the plant ideal for use as a fingernail file, for polishing hardwood, ivory, or

brass (to which it imparts a natural sheen), and even (in emergencies) chewed as a dentifrice
(although this can be abrasive to
the teeth).

Detrimental Properties
Horsetail causes mild poisoning if
grazed in large quantities by horses, cattle, and sheep, although it
doesn't kill. Symptoms include
weakness, nervousness, staggering, and unsteady gait.

Where Found

nonfertile horsetail which appears ferny

Horsetails are commonly found
along streams in sandy, wet soil, in swamps, or in roadside ditches.

Growing Cycle
Horsetails are perennials, and although they can be gathered year-round
for their practical uses, they are best gathered in the spring for their medicinal uses.

POISON

Jimsonweed (Datura meteloides and D. stramonium)

Nightshade Family
(Solanaceae)

Common Names Jamestown weed, toloache, sacred datura, stinkweed

Jimsonweed is also called thornapple.

Most Prominent Characteristics

Overall Shape and Size Jimsonweed is a branching, shrublike plant, reaching vertically two to three feet.

Leaves The large (3 to 10 inches long) petioled leaves have a fuzzy, grayish appearance. They are ovate with a coarsely toothed, recessed margin. The rank odor of the fresh leaves is unmistakably similar to rancid peanut butter, thus its other common name: stinkweed.

Flowers The large white trumpet flowers, up to 10 inches in length, resemble morning glories; they are often tinged with purple. The flowers are sometimes called Datura lilies. The calyx is five toothed.

Seeds The spiny seed capsules are spherical, full of seeds, approximately one inch in diameter and bursting at maturity.

Roots The rather large forking taproot is the size of a slender carrot and grows to a depth of approximately two feet.

Beneficial Properties

Edible Properties Poisonous. The name *Jimsonweed* is a corruption of the word *Jamestown*, after Jamestown, Virginia. It was there, in 1676, that soldiers confused D. stramonium for a potherb (they probably thought it was a chenopodium or an atriplex) and ate it, afterwards experiencing visions and hallucinations. The plant was then referred to as Jamestown weed and has steadily evolved to its present form.

Medicinal Uses Although the plant is classified as poisonous, it does have claimed medicinal value. The dried leaves, sometimes mixed with dried mullein leaves, are smoked in cigarettes or in pipes to give some relief to asthma sufferers.

Used externally, the crushed root and leaves were regarded by some Native Americans as an effective rattlesnake-bite cure when applied to the bite. The plant has a history of being used as a pain reliever (the crushed leaves and stems may be packed against the gums for toothache, being careful not to swallow the saliva or any plant parts).

Other Uses We'd appreciate authenticated reports from readers.

jimsonweed in flower

Detrimental Properties

Poisonous! This is one of the plants witches are said to have made into an ointment, which they rubbed all over their bodies in order to fly. Lest you be tempted to casually experiment with this mind-altering plant containing solanaceous alkaloids, be warned that its effects when taken internally include dry mouth, thirst, nausea, vomiting, incoherence, delirium, convulsions, coma, and sometimes death (though death is rare). The seeds are the most potent.

Where Found

D. meteloides is found throughout the dry, sandy valleys of the Southwest, often along roadsides. D. stramonium is found throughout the eastern United States, frequently in fields and along roadsides.

Growing Cycle

The plant has a rather large forking taproot, about the size of a slender carrot and reaching about two feet into the ground. The persistent root produces new foliage each spring; thus it is a perennial. During the winter, you'll see the dried stalks with the seed capsules still clinging.

Lore and Signature

The most widespread use of the plant has been as a drink made from the roots and seeds, used as a ceremony for Native American boys' puberty rites. Native American shamans are also said to have used this plant to induce a state of mind where they could see future events and learn some of nature's secrets. The Native American ceremonial uses of this plant are described in detail in *The Teachings of Don Juan* by Carlos Castaneda.

There is a saying: "The stems and leaves are used for medicine, the roots and seeds for divination, but the flowers will drive you mad."

The root often has the appearance of a human body, somewhat akin to the appearance of a ginseng root, though the jimson root is much larger.

Lamb's Quarter
(Chenopodium album)
Goosefoot Family
(Chenopodiaceae)
Common Names Belgian
spinach, white goosefoot, pigweed, middens miles, Seh eh teh
(northern Cheyenne)

the young tender top of lamb's quarter

Most Prominent
Characteristics

Overall Shape and Size Lamb's
quarter is an annual with an erect
stem that normally reaches one
foot to three feet high, reaching
above five feet in ideal conditions.

Stems Characteristic vertical red markings are often observed on the plant's mature main stem.

Leaves The alternate roughly toothed leaves are either ovoid or some-what triangular in shape about two to four inches long. The whole plant (and the leaf undersides in particular) is covered with a white meal-like powder, which gives the plant a sparkly appearance and causes raindrops to bead up on the leaves.

Flowers The tiny, light-green, inconspicuous flowers are clustered at the top of the plant in spikes. As the flowers mature, numerous small black seeds develop.

Beneficial Properties

Edible Properties The leaves and tender tips can be briefly steamed or cooked with onions or garlic and lightly seasoned with powdered herbs for a delightful, hearty dish. They are equally tasty (and far more nutri-tious) when added raw to salads. This plant is one of the finest tasting wild edibles, the flavor being similar to (but better than) spinach. The plant is, in fact, related to our common spinach and beets.

The seed clusters of late summer can be ground, winnowed, and added to pancakes and breads, or used alone, replacing flour in baked products. It gives the finished product a unique hearty flavor. I have used lamb's quarter seeds instead of wheat flour in my acorn bread recipe (see Oak Tree for recipe).

According to the United States Department of Agriculture (USDA), 100 grams of lamb's quarter leaf contains 4.2 grams of protein, 309 mil-ligrams of calcium, 72 milligrams of phosphorus, 11,600 international units of vitamin A, and 80 milligrams of vitamin C. Another analysis (Duke and Atchley) shows 684 milligrams of potassium per 100 grams.

Analysis of 100 grams (½ cup) of lamb's quarter seed shows 1,036 milligrams of calcium, 340 milligrams of phosphorus, 64 milligrams of iron, and 1,687 milligrams of potassium.

Medicinal Uses We'd appreciate authenticated reports from readers.

Other Uses A related species, C. californicum, has been used as a soap. The entire plant is used while still young (before the flowering and seeding stage). The best part to use for soap is the grated root. The plant's tender portions or grated root are mixed with water and then agitated between the hands, resulting in a frothy soap. Though this can be done with lamb's quarter, an inferior soap results.

Detrimental Properties

We'd appreciate authenticated reports from readers.

Where Found

This is such a common city plant that it is widely regarded as a weed. It can be found in most vacant lots, parks, and lower parts of mountains and hills, and in virtually everyone's garden. The plant is a native of Europe and has now spread all over the United States. No homeless person should go hungry where lamb's quarter grows.

Growing Cycle

This is an annual plant. Though it is best gathered from midwinter to summer when the leaves are young and large, the smaller leaves that appear as the plant goes to seed can also be used.

Mallow (Malva parviflora)

Mallow Family (Malvaceae)

Common Names M. neglecta (formerly), malva, cheeseweed

Most Prominent Characteristics

Overall Shape and Size Mallow is one of the most common vacant lot weeds. This spreading and highly branched annual reaches to about three feet tall and is seen as mounds of green in the lots.

the mallow plant

Leaves Each petiole is usually three times as long as the leaf blade. The leaf is roundish in outline, palmately divided into 7 to 11 shallow lobes, and has a margin of small teeth. Where the petiole meets the base of the leaf blade, you will notice a red spot on the upper surface of the leaf. The leaves are alternate and almost hairless.

Flowers The flowers are arranged in close axillary clusters along the branches. There are bracts at the base of each of these rose-colored flowers, and each petal is notched at its apex. The floral parts are five sepals, five petals about ⅛ inch long, numerous stamens, and one pistil.

Fruit Circular flat fruits develop from the flowers. These ¼-inch green fruits split when ripe into up to a dozen nutlets, resembling packaged cheese, thus its common name: cheeseweed.

Roots The taproots are long, thin, and fibrous.

Beneficial Properties

Edible Properties There are no poisonous malvas. Mallow leaves are edible raw in salads, and they impart a slightly mucilaginous texture. The leaves are commonly cooked and eaten like spinach; they can also be added to soup. The leaves can be dried and infused into tea, and although bland, are a good source of vitamins and minerals. According to the USDA, 100 grams (½ cup) of the mallow leaf contains 249 milligrams of calcium, 69 milligrams of phosphorus, 2,190 international units of vitamin A, and 35 milligrams of vitamin C. An analysis of the same volume of mallow leaf by Duke and Atchley showed 90 milligrams of calcium, 42 milligrams of phosphorus, 410 milligrams of potassium, and 24 milligrams of vitamin C. This second analysis also revealed 3,315 micrograms of beta carotene.

The raw round fruits can be eaten as is, having a nutty flavor. The mature fruits can be gathered, dried, and then the seeds separated from the chaff and other debris by winnowing the plant through a soft breeze. Then wash the seeds, dry them, and grind them for flour. The seeds can also be simmered in water until they swell up. Then they are lightly cooked and eaten like rice.

Mature mallow plants can be gathered in abundance in some areas and the seeds easily harvested.

Medicinal Uses Herbalists use this mucilaginous herb as a demulcent and emollient. An infusion of its leaves is used for coughs. In Mexico, the raw leaves are chewed to alleviate minor sore throats. The leaves were used externally by Native Americans as a poultice on sores and swellings.

Interestingly, this plant is related to the marsh mallow (Althea officinalis), the root of which was boiled to yield a slimy juice. This was whipped into a froth and made into a medicine for sore throats, bronchial troubles, and coughs. Today, marshmallows have no marsh-mallow root extract, but are made of eggs, sugar, and other ingredients and sold as candy. Common mallow root (Malva parviflora) will not yield as thick and slimy a juice when boiled, but the green fruits (and the roots) can be boiled and the water beaten for an inferior substitute.

Other Uses Chewing the fruits is believed to keep the mouth moist when water is scarce.

Detrimental Properties
Abnormally large (and thus unlikely) amounts of mallow eaten at one time may cause digestive problems.

Where Found
Mallow has naturalized here from Europe. It is almost always found around civilization and tends to be absent from wilderness areas. Look for this plant in vacant lots and waste areas.

Manzanita
(Arctostaphylos spp.)
Heath Family (Ericaceae)

ripe manzanita berries

Most Prominent Characteristics

Overall Shape and Size Most varieties appear as shrubs or small trees with crooked branches. At least one species is a vining plant.

Stalks and Stems Perhaps the most characteristic feature of the manzanita is the striking maroon-colored bark that appears smooth and polished.

Leaves All manzanita leaves are leathery and tough. The leaves vary in outline from round to oblong or elliptic. The margins of the leaves are entire (in rare cases there are serrations).

Flowers In the spring, you can observe the small tubular or urn-shaped white or pink flowers on the manzanita bushes. The flower parts are usually in fives.

Fruits The small fruits externally resemble apples. The fruits that develop in the summer and into the fall are first green, with a smooth surface. As they mature in late summer, they turn a dark red or maroon color and the flesh becomes mealy or powdery. The hard inner seed is usually composed of two or three nutlets, and sometimes there is just one single seed.

Beneficial Properties

Edible Properties The most valuable resource from all manzanita species are the small berries, which externally resemble apples. *Manzanita*, in fact, means "little apple" in Spanish.

If you pick a green fruit and suck on it, you'll discover an interesting trail nibble. Chances are you'll spit out your first taste. It's sour. But, there's also sugar in there, and if you try it again, and again, the flavor will grow on you. Some pretty good jam and jelly is made from the green fruit.

However, in the past, it was mostly the ripe fruit that was used, the fruit that has matured to a dark red or maroon color, almost like the bark. The ripe fruit may be sticky, and there is typically a thinnish shell covering a hard seed. Collect all you can when the fruit is in season. If you are collecting the sticky variety of fruit (such as A. glauca), be sure to clean off as much of the stems and leaves as possible while collecting; otherwise, you'll have a difficult task later.

Among the Cahuilla Native Americans of southern California, manzanita was regarded as a primary food source since it could be collected in volume and stored. Though the use of manzanita seems to be nearly a lost art today, it was once considered an important food additive. Typically, manzanita was used as an aspic, a thickener, or a sweetener to other foods. It also makes a pleasant beverage.

Let's review the way to process manzanita for each of these foods.

Collect the ripe fruit, and pick out any foreign matter, such as leaves or stems, bugs, and so forth.

Wash it all, and let it dry in a colander. I typically put all the berries in a cookie pan and let them then dry in the sun or in the oven at pilot-light temperature.

Next, I put some of the berries in my old fashioned Mexican metate, a stone grinder. I grind away at the entire seeds for awhile until I have removed the covering from each fruit and have ground up most of the covering. The actual seed will get ground down a bit, but it is harder and takes more work to reduce to a powder.

Then I put the ground material into a sieve and shake out the fine powder. This fine powder is then added in varying amounts to bread or pastry products. I like to add it to my acorn pancakes (see Oak Tree for recipe), and it both sweetens the dough and gives it a smoothness that's a bit hard to describe. Well, it's good. In fact, you can save this fine powder and add it to a lot of dishes. Experiment. Use it wherever you might have used aspic or a thickener, such as in gravy, jellies, or sauces.

According to Linda Sheer, who grew up in rural Kentucky living many of the old ways of storing and processing foods, the manzanita powder can also be added to meat, in much the way that wild berries were added to meat to produce the original pemmican. Again, you'd need to experiment to get the right flavor, but you'd be adding powdered manzanita to a dry meat that has been ground. The manzanita acts as a preservative and flavoring.

Put into a pan the coarse meal that was left in the sieve and cover with water. Simmer for about 10 minutes. Taste just a bit of that water. You'll find it is terribly sour, but still, there's that sweet aftertaste. Strain out the coarse meal, and then add an equal amount of water to your sour manzanita water. Also add about a tablespoon of honey for each quart of liquid. You could also add deseeded cactus pulp. Now taste it to see how tolerable it is. Don't get too concerned about the exact measurements of water or honey; just make it so it tastes good to you. To me, it is just right when the flavor is somewhat like a weak lemonade. It is subtle in flavor, yet uniquely refreshing.

This drink also helps your body to hydrate, and thus, it is good to drink during heat waves or if you're in the desert. You could also just add a few of the dried fruits into your canteen and take advantage of these hydrating qualities that way.

Another use of this sour liquid is as a vinegar for a wilderness salad dressing. It makes a surprisingly good substitute, especially when you consider all that goes into making regular vinegar. This undiluted manzanita liquid can also be frozen for later use.

The coarse meal is typically discarded after one boiling. However, if it's a bad year, you could actually get several boilings out of the meal before you need to discard it. Between boilings, you could put the meal into a cooking or pie pan, thin, and allow it to dry out. You do this so you can keep it for later without it going moldy.

Medicinal Uses The leaves of various manzanita species are also used medicinally. According to Michael Moore, author of *Medicinal Plants of the Mountain West*, the leaves of all species contain arbutin, a glycoside that is broken down to hydroquinone in the urine, which is the reason that manzanita leaf tea has disinfectant qualities. Moore suggests this tea in cases of mild urinary tract infections, chronic kidney inflammations, and water retention. The tea from the leaves also acts as a mild vasoconstrictor for the uterus and therefore can be helpful during painful and heavy menstruation. However, he does not advise its use during pregnancy.

Incidentally, I regard Michael Moore's books as the best available sources on the medicinal properties of wild plants. He has written several books for various geographical areas.

Other Uses I first became aware of the usefulness of manzanita when I learned about the desert species, a vining, crawling plant known as kinnikinnick (Arctostaphylos uva-ursi). The leaves of this manzanita species have long been used as a tobacco substitute or added to tobacco mixes. To me, there isn't a lot of flavor, though I have heard that the leaves need to be slightly fermented to truly bring out the flavor and aroma of this smoke. It does smoke well, and so I enjoy adding it to my nonnicotine smoking mixes.

The beautiful wood of this plant makes it a favorite for crafts projects. It is often used for such items as lamp stands, candleholders, and tobacco pipes.

Hunters in the old days and even today would often take special note of the manzanita patches. This is because the fruit provides food for a wide variety of game including all small game and birds, of course, but also larger animals. In the Angeles National Forest, which constitutes the northern third of Los Angeles County, I have often observed large bear droppings in late summer and fall. Their primary diet had been either manzanita berries or the two varieties of native wild cherries.

Detrimental Properties

We'd appreciate authenticated reports from readers. I was once told that one of the detrimental effects of collecting manzanita berries is that a bear might chase you out of its patches. That's pretty unlikely, isn't it?!

Where Found

Several species of manzanita (Arctostaphylos spp.) are found throughout the West and Southwest, even though it is commonly associated with southern California coastal mountains. (There are believed to be at least 43 species of manzanita in California alone.) But you'll find manzanitas in areas such as the deserts of California, Nevada, Arizona, New Mexico, parts of Utah, southwestern Colorado, and into Mexico. The range of the uva-ursi plant, perhaps more commonly known as kinnikinnick, is found up the Pacific Coast to Alaska. In fact, the manzanitas have a fairly large range.

Growing Cycle

Manzanitas are perennials. The flowers typically appear through the spring and early summer, depending on how long the winter lasted. The fruits appear in summer and are usually available for picking in August and September.

Lore and Signature

I am vaguely aware of some folklore associating bears with the manzanita plants. We know that bears like the berries, and one species of manzanita is even known as bearberry. Though I may be on thin ice here, the Latin name's root of *arktos* suggests a connection between King Arthur and the Big Dipper, at least as far as mythology and lore are concerned. This is just food for thought, so let me know if you discover more.

Keep in mind that the pursuit of the lore can often reveal more about the plant than the hard facts only.

Milkweed (Asclepias syriaca and A. california)

Milkweed Family
(Asclepiadaceae)
Common Names Common milkweed, silkweed

a young milkweed shoot

Most Prominent Characteristics

Overall Shape and Size This plant grows erect, from two to five feet tall, is stout and whitish-green in color. It is usually found in patches.

Stalks and Stems Thick milky-white sap, called "latex," oozes out when the stalk is broken or cut. The stalk is fibrous and usually erect.

Leaves The ovate-to-oblong leaves are opposite or whorled, not toothed at the margins, and tapered at both ends. There are obvious central veins or ribs. The same type of milky latex oozes out when the leaves are cut or broken. The leaves measure from two to five inches long, and their surface is softly tomentose.

Flowers The white, pink, or rose/purplish flowers are about ½ inch in diameter, arranged in umbels. Each flower consists of a five-petaled corolla; each petal has an erect cowl and inwardly hooked horn. There are five sepals, five stamens, and two pistils with a superior ovary.

Fruit The blossoms develop into rough green pods (fruits), about three inches long. When the pods mature, they split along one seam, revealing the neatly packed seeds. To each seed is attached a number of downlike silky fibers. The outside of this fruit is densely wooly.

Seeds Attached to each flat, brown seed are long, silky fibers. These fibers enable the seeds to become airborne and thus to scatter sometimes great distances.

Roots The roots are thick and penetrate rather deep.

Beneficial Properties

Edible Properties The tender young sprouts, below six inches tall, can be eaten. When the plant is older, the leaves and flower clusters are also used for food. The immature seed pods, before they've developed the silky fibers inside (cut one open and inspect), are great in soup or with meat. All parts of the milkweed must be boiled in water (usually at least twice with a rinsing between boilings) before they are rendered palatable. Due to the bitterness of the raw plant, human poisoning by the raw plant is rare.

Medicinal Uses The white sap was reportedly used by Native Americans to cure warts by surface application for several consecutive days. (See our comments on warts in the Poison Oak listing.)

The roots of one species of milkweed—A. tuberosa, which is one of the species that doesn't have milky sap—was listed in the *United States Pharmacopoeia* until 1936 for lung problems. Certain Native American tribes made tea from the leaf to control coughing, and others chewed the roots of A. tuberosa for respiratory problems.

The white sap was used for treating horses' saddle sores.

Other Uses The latex of this plant was experimented with for rubber production during World War II. The silky downlike filaments (technically floss or vegetable silk) attached to the seeds were used by the Department of Agriculture as a kapok replacement in life jackets and belts and life preservers because the down will still float while supporting 30 times its own weight. It is also used as upholstery padding, insulation material, and for stuffing pillows.

A fiber can be obtained from the stalks that can be used to weave such items as rope, sandals, and fishing line. The fiber has been used in limited amounts for paper making and weaving into muslins. To obtain the fiber, first peel the stalks and then roll the stalks to release the fiber. Cahuilla Native Americans used these fibers for snares, nets, slings, and more.

The sap was used by some Native Americans as a type of chewing gum. The sap was obtained from the stalks and stems and heated until it solidified, or just allowed to stand until it hardened.

Detrimental Properties
Milkweeds should never be eaten uncooked, due to the resins in the leaves and stems. Ingestion of raw milkweed will cause severe stomach and intestinal upsets. Symptoms, which occur within a few hours after eating, include staggering, difficult breathing, excessive perspiration, enlarged pupils, weakness, muscle spasms, and high temperatures. A. speciosa has resulted in livestock poisoning, but animals tend to avoid it. Most milkweed species are generally regarded as toxic to cattle. There are several species of milkweed across the country, and A. syriaca (common in the East) and A. california (common in the West) are the ones most commonly eaten. Nationwide, there are about 60 species, 25 of these occurring in the West.

Where Found
The plant resides in dry fields, hillsides, roadsides, woods, yards, pastures, marshes, deserts, along chaparral trails, and waste places. In other

words, it is one of the plants you can find in virtually any environment. It is thus most worthwhile to be able to identify milkweed (there's possibly one in your—or your neighbor's—yard right now).

Growing Cycle

Milkweed flowers from May to July, fruiting in the summer and fall. The plant is a perennial.

Lore and Signature

The botanical name comes from the Grecian God of Medicine— Aesculapius. Hopi Native Americans believe that one species, A. subverticillata, increased the milk flow in mothers.

Miner's Lettuce
(Montia perfoliata)
Purslane Family
(Portulacaceae)

Most Prominent Characteristics

Overall Shape and Size This annual plant grows to its maximum 12-inch size only in ideal conditions, which are warm to cool to warm temperatures, shade, and regular moisture.

Notice the characteristic flower stalk growing through the round leaves in this young miner's lettuce patch.

Stalks and Stems Each plant is composed of one to two dozen erect or diffuse 3- to 12-inch succulent stems.

Leaves The unmistakable feature is the leaf. It is cup shaped or saucer shaped, and directly through its middle pushes the flower stalk. The basal leaves are either quadrangular, triangular, ovate, or lanceolate (three to four times longer than broad, widest below the middle, and tapering to the apex and base). When young, the leaves appear to be somewhat water spotted.

Flowers The small, white-to-pink ¼-inch broad flowers (two sepals, five petals, five stamens, and a three-styled pistil), growing together in close clusters are borne along the stem in racemes (growing outward along the stalk from the stems of nearly equal length).

Beneficial Properties

Edible Properties The whole plant can be used in salads. The chopped leaves, lightly seasoned with apple cider vinegar (or lemon juice), and a high quality cold-pressed oil (such as Olio Sasso) make an excellent salad. The succulent leaves not only taste good but are also rich in vitamin C and iron. The name, miner's lettuce, refers to the California '49ers, who, while mining along California's remote rivers and streams, ate this plant to prevent vitamin deficiency.

Miner's lettuce can be lightly cooked and eaten like spinach. Tuna or hard-boiled eggs eaten with miner's lettuce provide the protein that's missing in the plant, and small quantities of seasoning enhance its unique mild flavor. Or, if you're particularly industrious, you could try the trick used by some of the Native Americans, who laid miner's lettuce around red ant holes. The formic acid that came from the ants as they walked over the leaves was said to impart a vinegar flavor to the greens.

Medicinal Uses This plant was regarded as a medicine only to the extent that, due to its vitamin C content, it was useful in preventing scurvy.

Other Uses We'd appreciate authenticated reports from readers.

Detrimental Properties
We'd appreciate authenticated reports from readers.

Where Found
Miner's lettuce is often found in great abundance in naturally shady places, such as along moist canyon walls, but is generally found in any damp, shady area. Miner's lettuce is common along the Pacific Coast.

Growing Cycle
Miner's lettuce is an annual. It begins its growth in midwinter, sending up its flower stalk by early spring, and is usually dried and shriveled by summer.

Mugwort (Artemisia douglasiana)

Sunflower Family
(Compositae)

Common Names A. vulgaris (formerly), sagebrush, purple sage

a patch of mugwort

Most Prominent Characteristics

Overall Shape and Size The erect stalk normally reaches two to three feet (much higher in optimum conditions).

Stalks and Stems Mugwort stalks vary from $\frac{1}{16}$ inch to $\frac{1}{8}$ inch in diameter. They are predominantly light green, with reddish-brown striations along the stem's length.

Leaves The very aromatic leaves are ovate to elliptic and are often divided into three to five pinnate segments. The leaves near the top of the stalks become narrower, linear to lanceolate in shape, and are generally entire (not toothed). On the topside, the leaves are dark green and almost glabrous (hairless). On the underside, the leaves are covered with short, soft, white, wooly hairs, which is one of mugwort's dominant characteristics.

Flowers Very small flowers are clustered together (between 20 and 30) to make up $\frac{1}{8}$-inch high heads. These heads are tightly clustered along a spike or rodlike stalks, which in turn are alternately arranged along the main stalk. The flowers are followed by the seeds. The year-old dried seed stalks are usually found alongside the new young plants.

Beneficial Properties

Edible Properties Some people sprinkle the fresh leaves (cut into small pieces) in salad or cook them as a potherb; but the flavor is vinegary and bitter, and thus unappealing to many for use as food. Mugwort seeds can be ground into meal to make bread products; however, as a food plant, mugwort is insignificant.

Medicinal Uses Mugwort tea is said to increase the appetite, to aid in digestion, and to relieve stomach pains and fevers. An infusion from the dried leaves is applied externally to swellings. Bruises are reputed to heal more quickly if bathed with a mugwort infusion. As a bath additive, mugwort revitalizes tired legs and feet.

With some people, it is customary to rub the fresh mugwort leaves over exposed portions of their bodies before entering poison oak areas in order to prevent the rash. In fact, some Native Americans used the fresh leaves externally as a cure for poison oak and wounds.

Other Uses Mugwort gets its name from the English practice of adding a leaf of mugwort to mugs of beer to improve the flavor. (*Wort* is an Old English word meaning "herb.") This is still practiced in London pubs.

Some people have slept on pillows of dried mugwort leaves in order to induce wild, vivid dreams and visions of the future. Folklore from various parts of the world states that a leaf of mugwort in the shoe will enable you to walk all day without leg fatigue. Nathaniel Schleimer of Pasadena, a student of a therapeutic technique called acupressure, pointed out to me that there may be some factual basis for this folklore. Schleimer told me that there is an acupuncture point on the bottom of the foot that is said to regulate fatigue. The mugwort leaves, which have naturally dried on the plant, are collected and used in acupressure. When rolled into small balls or into a cigar-shaped cylinder, these dried leaves are called *moxa*. A Chinese species is said to be the best, but all species can be used in the following fashion, described by J. C. Cerney in his book *Acupressure—Acupuncture Without Needles*:

> On the outside of the lower leg, below the level of the knee, is the head of the fibula. Just below and slightly in front of the head of the fibula is what the Japanese refer to as sanri or S-36. This is an important vitality stimulating zone. It's a point where weary Oriental foot travelers applied a burning ball of moxa and with energy restored, traveled on.

One of the most effective wilderness punks is made by gathering mugwort leaves that have dried and browned on the stalk. Slide your hand along the lower stalk to gather the dried leaves and then roll them into a cigar. By lighting the end of this cigar and then wrapping the entire cigar in larger fresh mugwort leaves, you can effectively carry fire over long distances. This was the technique practiced by southwestern Native American tribes for transporting fire from camp to camp. It can still come to the aid of today's campers when matches are scarce.

The pleasant aroma of the burning leaves, used as incense, helps bring the aroma of the mountains to the home.

Dried mugwort, mixed with other herbs, can also be smoked as a nonnicotine tobacco.

Detrimental Properties
We'd appreciate authenticated reports from readers.

Where Found
Mugwort is very common along the shady banks of canyon bottoms and along riverbanks in foothill and coastal regions. You almost always find it

near streams. It can frequently be found near poison oak as well, for which the mugwort acts as a prophylactic.

Growing Cycle

Mugwort is a perennial. Its first new growth appears in late winter or early spring; it flowers in summer and goes to seed by fall. The dead stalks are usually visible throughout the winter.

Everyone would profit by becoming familiar with this valuable and versatile herb.

Lore and Signature

Some people believed that young mugwort leaves, which somewhat resemble a hand held out with fingers spread, were effective in warding off witches, Satan, and evil spirits. Mugwort was hung over doorways, windows, chimneys, and other openings on Halloween in the belief that it protected against the evil effects of witchcraft and the entrance of witches. Pregnant women and newly born babies were considered particularly vulnerable on Halloween. For this reason, pregnant women would wear dried mugwort around their necks in a small bag, and mugwort would be laid in or around young babies' cradles.

Mugwort's folklore and various nonfood uses make it an interesting plant to know. Although this is the plant that Zane Grey referred to in his *Riders of the Purple Sage*, mugwort is not a true sage. Rather, it is closely related to the common wormwood (Artemisia absinthium).

Mustard
(Brassica spp.)

Mustard Family (Cruciferae)

mustard leaf plant

Most Prominent Characteristics

Overall Shape and Size

Mustard is a slightly spreading, but more or less erect, annual usually one foot to two feet tall, but reaching to five feet in ideal conditions.

Leaves The lower leaves are generally lyrately pinnate (the end section of the leaf is large and rounded, and the lower part of the leaf is divided into smaller, more pointed sections), and the leaves on the upper part of the plant are more or less entire (margins not toothed or indented). The leaves are either glabrous (not hairy) or covered with hairs.

Flowers The relatively showy yellow flowers grow in racemes (growing outward along the stalk on stems of nearly equal length) and are followed by pods. The yellow flowers, approximately ½ inch across, have four petals (arranged in a crosslike formation) and include four sepals, six stamens (two short, four tall), and one pistil.

Beneficial Properties

Edible Properties The mustard greens are most palatable after the rains of late winter and early spring. These young spring leaves, sometimes quite large, can be added fresh to salads and sandwiches to add an oniony zing. And you'll be adding more than flavor, for these leaves are a rich source of vitamins A, B1, and B2. According to the USDA, 100 grams of the leaf (about ½ cup) contains 183 milligrams of calcium, 50 milligrams of phosphorus, 377 milligrams of potassium, 7,000 international units of vitamin A, and 97 milligrams of vitamin C.

The leaves are also commonly cooked like spinach, which renders even the older late-spring to early-summer leaves quite palatable. Leaves gathered later in the year, though certainly edible, tend to be tougher and more bitter. To prepare greens, wash them and either chop or leave them whole. Cook in hot (not boiling) water until tender, adding onion, garlic, and/or sea salt and kelp for flavor.

There are various ways of using the seed to produce common brown table mustard seasoning. One method involves baking whole wheat flour on a cookie sheet until it browns, then mixing equal amounts of the flour and ground mustard seed. This mixture can then be stored dry and used as is or moistened with equal parts of water or vinegar to taste. You can also grind just the mustard seeds (adding no wheat flour), and the resulting powder will be a faded yellow, tan, or brown, depending on the type of mustard seed used. The bright yellow color of commercial mustard comes from coloring agents, which we recommend be avoided as much as possible. Some mustard manufacturers who prefer the bright yellow color have switched to natural yellow dyes. Nevertheless, you should read the labels before making a purchase.

Mustard flowers and unopened flower buds can be added to salads and soups or used as a garnish. When you observe the unopened flower buds of mustard, its relationship to broccoli will be somewhat obvious. (What we call broccoli is a tight cluster of unopened flower buds of a cultivated member of the mustard family.)

The tender stalks and stems of mustard plants can be added to salads and stews or nibbled on along the trail. Several inch-long segments of the tender stems can be cooked and served like green beans. These stem segments are still good to use this way when they readily snap between the fingers; those that just bend but don't break have already gotten too old and fibrous.

There are no poisonous members of the mustard family. All of the Brassica species and many other species of different genera of the mustard family are commonly used for food. Several others in the mustard family are discussed in this book, but not all. Members of the mustard family are identified by their floral characteristics (see Flowers section). Most all have a pungent taste. Any member of this family that is palatable and nonwoody can be safely eaten.

A related plant is wild radish (Raphanus sativus). The size and shape of its flowers are nearly identical to mustard, except that they are purple and fade to white. The leaves of wild radish resemble mustard (although their surfaces tend to be a glossier green and lack the fuzzy surface of hairs), and they can be used in exactly the same way. A pleasant bonus is that wild radish leaves are generally milder than mustard greens. Furthermore, the young green seedpods of the wild radish are crisp and spicy (like common radish roots) and add a chili-like flavor to soup or salad. Even chewed fresh off the stalk, they're considered delectable by people who enjoy the flavor and bite of radishes or chilies. The roots of wild radish plants smell just like cultivated radish roots but are usually too fibrous to eat. When you find the wild radish in a very wet environment, the entire root (or at least the tender outer layer) is sometimes tender enough to eat. All cultivated radishes are believed to have originated from this plant, which is still found in a wild state.

Medicinal Uses When the yellow flowers fade and drop, they're followed by small pods, ½ to 1 inch long. Each pod contains seeds. The seeds of some species can be removed easily after the pod has dried on the plant. These seeds are then ground very fine to make a plaster for chest colds, muscles, and aching backs. The plaster is made by grinding one part mustard seed to four parts whole wheat flour into a paste with warm water. Make it thick enough so it will spread over a piece of cloth that will cover the irritated area. The heat generated from the plaster can sometimes be sufficient to blister sensitive skin. Blistering can be prevented by mixing the mustard and flour with egg whites instead of water.

close-up of mustard flowers

In 1984, the American Cancer Society cited seven ways to prevent cancer. They included on their list:

Include cruciferous [mustard family] vegetables in your diet. Certain vegetables in this family—cabbage, broccoli, brussel sprouts, kohlrabi, and cauliflower—may help prevent certain cancers from developing.

Three other recommendations on their list would certainly apply to those who eat wild foods:

Cut down on total fat intake.

Eat more high-fiber foods.

Include foods rich in vitamins A and C in your daily diet.

They also recommended avoiding obesity. Gardening and collecting wild foods can certainly help in this regard.

The last two commonsense recommendations on this list include:

Eat moderately of salt-cured, smoked, and nitrite-cured foods.

Keep alcohol consumption moderate, if you drink.

Detrimental Properties
Burning sensations on the skin can result when applying a mustard plaster, as described in the Medicinal Uses section above.

Where Found
Mustard is a European native that has naturalized in the United States. It can be found in vacant lots, dry arroyos, and hillsides, as well as in green open areas and well-cultivated urban properties.

Growing Cycle
Mustard is an annual whose leaves are best gathered in early spring.

Nasturtium (Tropaeolum majus and related species)

Tropaeolum Family
(Tropaeolaceae)

Common Names Indian cress, creeping canary

nasturtium plants in flower

Most Prominent Characteristics

Overall Shape and Size
Nasturtium is like ivy in that it grows sprawling across a hillside, filling a garden border, or climbing and covering fences. The colorful red, orange, or yellow flowers make this plant very conspicuous in the spring.

Stalks and Stems The round light-green stalks and leaf stems are sometimes tinged with spots of red. The stalks seldom become thicker than ¼ inch in diameter. A single main stalk can reach up to six feet in length; single leaf stems are generally from six to eight inches long. In the climbing variety, the stems often act as tendrils.

Leaves The irregularly round-shaped leaves average about 2 to 5 inches in diameter. The leaf color is light green to bright green. The succulent leaf stem is attached to the underside of the leaf, either in the center or slightly off. The leaves are alternately arranged on the stalk.

Flowers Nasturtium flowers are not radially symmetrical. The five colorful petals are distinct (not united to each other at all). Three of the petals have side projections, or guide hairs, at the base, which guide insects to the nectar. To reach this nectar, insects are brought into contact with the stamens and pistil, which is nasturtium's way of achieving pollination. The base of the top two petals is prolonged to form a long spur, which is a hollow, nectar-filled extension of the flower. The red, yellow, or orange flowers are shaped somewhat like a horn—with the spur at one end, opening into a bell shape at the other.

Seeds The seeds ripen to an approximately ½-inch two-celled wrinkled globe that bears an uncanny resemblance to the human brain.

Beneficial Properties

Edible Properties When Mrs. L. Patten of Pasadena, California, introduced me to the nasturtium plant in the early 1970s, I began by chewing on a long, succulent stem. I enjoyed the initial sweetness; but as I chewed, the sweetness gave way to a hot pepperiness—like a hot radish or horse-radish—which quickly increased in intensity. The ultimate effect was similar to the aftereffects of horseradish: open sinuses and watery eyes. "Wow," I said, blinking away the tears, "that's good!"

Although every part of the plant above ground can be eaten raw or cooked, the leaves are most commonly eaten. The leaves can simply be picked and eaten raw; they can be added to any type of salad—potato, cucumber, lettuce, and so forth. They can be chopped finely and added to soups, omelettes, and potato dishes; they can be cooked and eaten like spinach; they can be used for stuffed grape-leaf-type recipes (i.e., folded around cooked rice and/or minced meat, then tied or pinned shut and steamed until tender).

Spicy Cheese Spread with Nasturtiums

Here's a simple recipe for making a spicy cheese spread using nasturtium leaves. This should be eaten immediately—or shortly after it's made since nasturtium leaves tend to become slightly bitter if allowed to stand after being mixed with the other ingredients, and the radishes lose texture.

1 bunch small radishes
1 tablespoon nasturtium leaves, finely chopped
1 teaspoon lemon juice
8 ounces cream cheese

Wash and remove the tops of radishes. Coarsely grate the radishes, leaving a few thinly sliced for garnish. Quickly blend the grated radishes, nasturtium leaves, lemon juice, and cream cheese. Spread immediately onto thinly sliced rye or pumpernickel bread, or onto rye crackers. If you want more bite, garnish with a whole nasturtium leaf or radish slices. This recipe makes about one cup of spread.

The stems (preferably the long succulent ones) are a bit hotter and juicier than the leaves. They are best eaten raw, such as in salads.

The flowers can also be added to all salads. Their flavor is mildly hot and mildly sweet. The young green seedpods can be eaten in salads or pickled and used as a caper substitute.

Medicinal Uses The plant is a rich source of vitamin C.

Other Uses Snails, strongly attracted to nasturtiums, can often be found attached to the undersides of the leaves. Most of the conspicuous garden snails are an edible (and very nutritious) escargot (Helix aspersa); by planting nasturtiums, you'll be assured of a steady supply of this quality protein.

Detrimental Properties
If one who is unaccustomed to eating nasturtium takes too large a bite (especially the stems), an almost certain result will be opened sinuses, a runny nose, and watery eyes. This is because nasturtium has approximately the same hotness as fresh green onions. As with onion eating, these physiological effects are temporary. In fact, labeling them "detrimental" may be considered false advertising by some, since these effects are considered desirable by people who like hot foods.

Where Found
Nasturtium can be grown in most soils. It prefers poor soil, in which it usually produces an abundance of flowers (in richer soils, it produces more leaves). It has also naturalized in the sandy soil of some beach areas. This Peruvian native was first introduced to Europe in 1686.

Growing Cycle
Nasturtium begins to grow in late winter and early spring. By mid to late spring, the plant lays out a carpet of colorful flowers, forming a beautiful ground cover. The plant is relatively short-lived, for by the time the heat of midsummer comes, the entire plant will be dried up. Once established, however, nasturtium will reseed itself year after year.

Lore and Signature
In the late 1700s, the famous Swedish botanist Carolus Linnaeus, noting that nasturtium was often grown on poles, likened the plant's brilliant flowers to the tropaeum (the gold-colored, blood-stained helmets of the defeated warriors that were hung on poles of the Roman legionnaires). Hence, he called the plant Tropaeolum.

Nettle (Urtica dioeca)

Nettle Family (Urticaceae)

Common Names Stinging nettle

a stalk of nettle

Overall Shape and Size The stalks—which are usually unbranched—generally reach up to five feet, sometimes higher.

Stalks and Stems The main stalk, usually unbranched, is fibrous and covered with hairlike bristles.

Leaves The tips of the oblong leaves taper to a point. The leaves grow opposite each other on the stems. The margin is sharp toothed, and the upper leaf surface is covered with hairlike bristles. The petioles are from ⅜ inch to 2 inches in length.

Flowers The inconspicuous petal-less clusters of tiny green flowers arise from the leaf axils. Small, dry, one-seeded fruits are also present. The plant is monoecious, which means there are separate pistillate (female) and staminate (male) flowers on the same plant.

Fruit The dry, one-seeded fruits are only ¹⁄₁₆ inch long. Each fruit is elliptic, somewhat acute at the apex. The fruits are produced in dense clusters, which arise from the leaf axils.

Beneficial Properties

Edible Properties Nettle is rich in vitamins A (4,900 international units per 100 grams) and C (790 milligrams per 100 grams) and is a rich source of protein. Ideally, only the first nettle greens of spring will be eaten (before the stalks get tough), and even they should be carefully gathered with a knife (or sharp scissors) and gloves. The older the plants become, the less palatable they are. Only the tenderest nettle tops should be gathered. Once they've been cooked (steamed or boiled), their stinging properties are gone. They are delicious served with just butter.

The dried nettle plant is excellent food for goats, chickens, horses, and livestock. Dried nettle can be used as a winter food supply for chickens. Chickens fed nettle are said to lay more eggs.

There is an edible portion of the main stalk that is slightly underground but above the root stalk. It's usually pinkish. This tender pink section can be cooked with the leaves and tops. The yield from this part of the plant will be small. Also, picking this part will hurt the plant—even kill it. For these reasons, you should only collect this tender pink section

of the lower stem in genuine survival situations, from dense patches of
nettles, or after the main stalks have already been cut down (either for use
in weaving or as part of a weed clearing effort).

Krapivnie Shchi (Russian young nettle soup)

1½ pounds young nettles, blanched
1 pound sorrel
6 cups veal, chicken, or vegetable stock, or more to taste
3 sausages, fried or boiled
Sour cream to taste

Add nettles and sorrel to the stock. Simmer very gently for 1½
hours. Cut the sausages into inch-sized pieces and add to the soup
half an hour before serving. Sour cream can be stirred into the
soup a few minutes before serving or can be served separately
(from *The Green Beret Gourmet* by James Guttenberg, Guttenberg
Press, Box 973, Rockledge, FL 32955).

Medicinal Uses A tea made from the infused leaves has been used for
such things as cleansing the stomach, purifying the blood, dissolving
mucus in the chest and lungs, and for alleviating bronchial problems in
general. The tea is also used to stop diarrhea. A poultice of the steeped
green leaves will relieve pain and stop bleeding of minor wounds when
applied externally.

For more on cholesterol, see Purslane.

Other Uses Since nettles contain approximately 7 percent nitrogen
(based on dry weight), it's an excellent plant to use as a mulch or fertilizer
for your garden. Knowledgeable farmers have long taken the presence of
nettles to be an indicator of rich soil.

British poet Thomas Campbell wrote, "In Scotland, I have eaten nettle,
I have slept in nettle sheets, and I have dined off a nettle tablecloth."

The nettle stalks contain a strong, silky fiber that is in some ways similar to hemp. To obtain the fiber, dried stalks are pounded to remove the
vegetable matter, then washed in water so that only the fiber remains.
Either commercially or in survival situations, this fiber can be used to
make thread, fishing line, yarn, snares, nets, cloth, sandals, blankets,
woven socks, and more. The German army once utilized nettle fiber to
make some of its uniforms.

I have followed these instructions on numerous occasions and have
tested the resulting fiber. The fiber is easiest to weave when wet. I have
hastily woven small crude cords from this fiber in minutes and found
them strong enough to lift up to 25 pounds. I'm certain that a thick nettle
rope, carefully woven, could be functional for climbing mountains, crossing a stream, lashing a splint to a broken limb, or for other emergency and
nonemergency uses.

The Power of Nettle

In 1974, 45-year-old Herb Krueger of Greenbush, Wisconsin, suffered a heart attack. His doctor recommended (and scheduled) a quadruple bypass operation. Krueger had second thoughts and asked the doctor to postpone the surgery for awhile. The doctor agreed on the condition that Krueger take some special drugs and avoid working for two years. Krueger agreed, took the drugs, but again had second thoughts. "I knew that the medication was wrong because my body felt it and was rejecting it," stated Krueger.

Krueger went back to the doctor and demanded some answers. "The doctor admitted that 'life is an experimentation.'" So I said, then I'm going to experiment too. And in the last 15 years [as of 12/89], I have not spent a dime in the doctor's office. I cured myself. In the two years that I could not work I studied in earnest. I believe that many of the bypass surgeries that are being performed are unnecessary."

Krueger learned that he had to drastically cut back his intake of choles- terol. He became an earnest herb and vegetable gardener and discovered a novel way to reduce his cholesterol. "I think the main thing that cured my vascular system was stinging nettle. The nettles have formic acid—a sub- stance that I believe dissolves cholesterol in the vascular system. Nettle is the only plant known to the botanical world that contains formic acid." Krueger drinks three cups of his homegrown nettle tea every day, and he never had the heart surgery.

"My advice to any person who has any curiosity whatsoever about human existence is to get as close to nature as you possibly can. If you elimi- nate the so-called processing of foods, you are getting much of the nourish- ment that our Creator has put into them as you can," states Krueger.

Roman soldiers employed the nettles for another survival use. They rubbed the fresh plant over the entire surface of their bodies when they were in the bitter winter cold. Although this was painful, it brought blood to the surface and was actually warming. I have tried this with just my arms and found it to be definitely warming. I could feel heat generating within my arms after vigorously rubbing the leaves onto my skin. However, I don't recommend this as a way to keep warm if there are other viable options because the body loses heat more rapidly once heat is brought to the skin's surface. If you do resort to this method in an emer- gency, remember that it will be counterproductive over long periods of time if you don't take additional actions (such as building a fire, eating, or exercising) to protect your body from the elements.

In *Acres U.S.A.* in the December 1989 issue, a Belgian research team found a potent natural fungicide in the form of a protein in the rhizomes of stinging nettle. The protein molecule, called Urtica dioica agglutinin (UDA), strongly inhibits the growth of several pathogenic and saprophytic fungi. The UDA attacks the fungi by interfering with cell wall manufacture at the growing tips of fungal hyphae. Specifically, the UDA inhibits chitin production, and chitin is a major constituent of most fungal cell walls. The researchers believe that the gene that controls UDA production in nettle can be inserted into crop plants by genetic engineering techniques in order to make the crops immune to fungal attack.

Detrimental Properties

When you brush against the plant, the tips of numerous small hollow needles break off, forcing an organic irritant containing formic acid onto the skin. This causes an immediate burning sensation, subsequent stinging sensation, and rash-like welts. Within two to four hours (depending on the degree of contact), all effects are gone.

For this reason, you'll need to be most careful when you gather this plant. Wear gloves or some other protective device, such as mullein leaves or paper bags.

A children's jingle states: "Nettle in, dock out; dock rubs the nettle out." This refers to the effectiveness of rubbing dock leaves (Rumex crispus) over nettle rash to relieve the stinging. I once decided to test this; at the same time I compared the effectiveness of dock to that of aloe vera juice.

I vigorously rubbed a fresh nettle plant over my right and left arms. An immediate burning was followed by intense stinging, soon followed by hundreds of tiny red dots that appeared over both arms. Within five minutes, both arms were covered with swelling welts that resembled skin that has healed over after serious burns. I rubbed fresh dock leaf—crushed to express the juice—over my right arm and fresh aloe vera juice over my left arm. In both cases, I experienced an immediate relief to the burning, but the welted appearance remained.

I monitored both arms at one-hour intervals. After two hours, the aloe-treated arm felt considerably better than the dock-treated arm, but the dock-treated arm looked better. After eight hours, although both arms looked almost normal, small pinhead-size red dots could be detected over each arm. While the dock-treated arm still had sensations of mildly irritating stings, the aloe-treated arm experienced absolutely no residual discomfort or irritation. Therefore, I recommend the use of aloe over dock leaves for treating nettle. Of course, if you get nettled in the wilderness and you have no aloe with you, by all means use what is available, be it dock or any other green leafy (or juicy) plant.

I should point out that my experiment caused a more intense contact with nettle than one would normally experience by just brushing against the plant. Untreated, a normal nettle sting should last no more than two hours.

Where Found

Nettles are found near streams, in moist soil, in rich soil, and often near raspberries and blackberry vines. This European native is common throughout most of the United States.

Growing Cycle

These perennials are best gathered for food in the springtime when the new growths are just beginning to sprout. The plant becomes steadily less palatable as it matures and goes to seed and is all but inedible once it has begun to die back.

Lore and Signature

In 1976, Dr. Leonid Enari told me the following story about nettle:

An Oregon Native American tribe has especial respect for spiders because a spider is believed to have saved the tribe from starvation during a hard winter many moons ago. During that winter, the Columbian River was full of salmon, but the people couldn't catch any. A spider saw the misery and decided to assist. He transformed into a man, married a Native American girl, and taught her how to extract fiber from the nettle and how to make nets from the nettle fiber. Who else but a spider would know how to weave such nets? The girl then taught the others how to make these nets, with which they caught salmon; and there was plenty to eat.

Oak Tree
(Quercus spp.)
Beech or Oak Family
(Fagaceae)

Before leaching, this acorn must be peeled.

Most Prominent Characteristics

Overall Shape and Size Quercus is a large genus of more than 200 species including deciduous and evergreen trees and shrubs.

Leaves Among the many varieties, the leaves, which are always arranged alternately, vary in shape from small, hard, oval and toothed to large, flexible, and almost like a maple leaf.

Flowers Oaks are monoecious; that is, they have separate male and female flowers on the same plant. The inconspicuous female flowers are small and greenish brown. They look like small acorns and appear solitary or in a spike in the leaf axils of the season's new growth. The female flower is formed inside a cup of bract-like sepals, which later develops into the acorn's cap.

Fruit Oak trees are identified by their fruit, the acorns, which are nuts set in scaly caps. Acorns mature and fall from the trees during September and October.

Beneficial Properties

Edible Properties The staff of life of some Native Americans was acorns. The Native Americans usually gathered the acorns before they fell from the trees, storing up to 500 pounds per family for a year's supply.

Acorns are not eaten raw because the presence of tannin makes them very bitter. A number of methods have been devised to rid the acorns of this bitterness. One of the Native American practices was to bury the acorns in a swamp and return the following year. This removed the tannin and blackened the acorns. Sometimes shelled acorns were wrapped in a cloth container (such as a burlap bag) and submerged in a river overnight. The flowing water would leach the water-soluble tannin from the acorns by morning.

Some would shell and grind the raw acorns into meal. This meal was then put into a shallow depression tamped into a river's shady edge. Hot and cold water was poured over the meal for most of the day, washing the tannin out into the sand. The resultant acorn mush would then be carefully scooped from the sand and either dried or eaten as is.

Another method for removing the bitterness involved the use of a primitive leaching plant. It was a bowl made of twigs or pine needles, supported about two feet off the ground by vertical stakes. Cloth or burlap was placed over the bowl, and the ground acorns were put in. Water was poured into the acorn meal and allowed to filter through. The leaching time depended on the bitterness of the acorns, but a few hours was usually sufficient. The final product would then be boiled into a mush and was usually eaten cold. The acorn flour was usually baked into bread in crude ovens or used as a base for soup. Cornmeal was often mixed into the acorn meal.

Boiling is the quickest way for rendering acorns edible. Boil the shelled acorns continually, changing the water whenever it becomes brown. You know the acorns are done when you taste them and the bitterness is gone. Though this method may take only 45 minutes, it does result in a loss of oils and flavor.

A better method is to peel the acorns, place them in a container, and cover with water. Pour out the water after 24 hours and replace with fresh warm water. Three or four changes of water with this non-boiling method should be sufficient to leach out all of the tannic acid.

Once leached, the acorns must be ground into flour and then dried to insure a long storage life. If you have a meat grinder, you can coarsely grind the just-leached acorns while they are still wet and easy to grind. The coarse grind should be dried and then finely ground with a hand mill, stone grinder, or heavy-duty blender. If you're camping, the acorn meal can be ground between rocks.

The resulting flour is used in foods, such as bread, muffins, pancakes, grits, and soup, either alone or mixed with wheat or corn flour. Here's my favorite acorn bread recipe:

Christopher's Acorn Bread

1 cup acorn flour	3 tablespoons honey
¾ cup whole wheat flour	1 egg
¼ cup carob flour	1 cup raw milk
3 teaspoons baking powder	3 tablespoons oil
1 teaspoon sea salt (optional)	

Mix well and bake in greased bread pan for about 45 minutes (or longer) at 250° F.

I use this exact same recipe for making pancakes simply by adding more milk or water until the consistency is correct for pancake batter.

Ricardo Duarte-Heniger Dorame, of Gabrielino heritage, learned about using acorns from his grandmother. His grandmother preferred the acorns from the coast live oak (Q. agrifolia). These acorns are abundant in the lower mountain slopes and valleys of California. (Botanists generally divide the oaks into two major groups: the white oaks, which contain less tannic acid, and the black oaks, which tend to be more bitter due to the presence of more tannic acid.) I tasted an acorn of the coast live oak after talking to a kin of Mr. Dorame. Though smaller than the canyon live oak acorns I prefer to gather, this coast live oak acorn was sweeter and nearly palatable raw. I could easily understand why the Gabrielinos preferred this acorn.

Analysis of acorn meal has shown it to be 65 percent carbohydrates, 18 percent fat, and 6 percent protein.

In the wild, acorns are eaten by mallards, pintails, and other water-fowl, as well as by deer, elk, peccaries, and mountain sheep. Quail eat little acorns, and squirrels and chipmunks traditionally store them for winter.

Even in its death throes, the oak is useful in that it becomes a host for a myriad of other life forms. Gall wasps lay their eggs in the smaller oak branches, and, as the immature wasps develop, that section of the branch appears to sprout small green apples that slowly harden into brown balls. These balls are like miniature apartment houses for the young wasps. Oak rot fungus (Armillaria mellea), an edible fungus, appears at the base of dead and dying oak trees. The thick oak leaf mulch under the tree provides ideal growing conditions for the pored Boletus genus of mushrooms, many of which are edible. Countless edible termite larvae thrive on dead and fallen branches. The hollowed trunk becomes a home for bees, birds, snakes, and rats. What appears to the untrained eye to be death and decay, therefore is, in truth, part of the symbiotic relationship of plant and wildlife.

Medicinal Uses The bark is used medicinally to treat chronic diarrhea and as an internal astringent. Externally, an oak bark decoction is used for skin sores and as a sore throat gargle, according to Alma Hutchens, author of *Indian Herbology of North America*.

Other Uses Songs and poetry praise the stately oaks, which were considered sacred by the Druids, the Greeks, and the Romans. It has been honored in both war and love songs for the many benefits it furnishes besides food: the fallen leaves are used as a wilderness mattress stuffing; the bark is used for tanning buckskin; and excellent dyes of various colors are obtained from mixing the oak bark with other plants.

The oak tree has a very high transpiration rate. It returns (or recycles) up to 300 gallons of pure water a day, via transpiration through its leaves to the environment where it is planted.

Detrimental Properties

Livestock that have eaten large amounts of the young foliage and buds have become ill and in some cases died within a few days. Eating large amounts of the raw acorns can lead to toxicity due to the tannic acid.

Humans rarely eat toxic amounts of raw acorns because of the extreme bitterness. Those who have persisted in eating raw acorns have nearly always been stopped short of death because of the onset of frequent urination and constipation, abdominal pains, and extreme thirst. However, anyone with a normal sense of taste would find it nearly impossible to consume raw acorns in large amounts, unless they were either coerced into doing so or needed to do so to prevent starvation.

John Kingsbury, author of *Poisonous Plants in the United States and Canada*, included raw acorns on his list of poisonous plants. He stated that if large quantities were eaten over a long period of time, bloody stools and other symptoms would result. In an interview in the May 1972 *Mother Earth News*, Gibbons responded to Kingsbury's stand on acorns as follows:

> *Well, I wouldn't argue with him about that. If you ate raw acorns in large quantities—maybe a bushel every day for 10 years—you'd probably get something like that. But then Kingsbury ended up by saying something like, "The effect of even the smallest amount one time on a very young child is simply not known." You see what he's done? He's thrown a hell of a scare in there for every mother in the country. I could say exactly the same thing another way: "There's no evidence whatever that a small quantity of acorns taken only one time ever had any effect on a child." That's all he really said, but he said it in a way to make every woman grab her baby and run every time she sees an oak tree. I know 80-year-old Indians out West who've eaten acorns all their lives— every year. Whole cultures depended on them.*

Where Found

Oaks are native both to the temperate regions of the northern hemisphere and to the mountains of the tropics. Oak trees can be found in cities, mountains, deserts, valleys, and chaparral areas.

Growing Cycle

Acorns mature and fall from the trees during September and October.

Lore and Signature

At night, when man's prying faculties are not there to interfere, the stately mature oaks are said to converse in whispers with each other, while the young, more energetic oaks pull up their shallow roots and dance thunderously in the full moon. Thus, beware where you lay your camp if in an oak forest, and be careful under whose boughs you whisper secrets or hatch infernal plans—you never know who may be listening!

Passionflower (Passiflora caerulea and incarnata)

Passionflower Family (Passifloraceae)

Common Names P. caerulea: passionvine, granadilla. P. incarnata: maypop, apricot vine

passionfruit hanging from the vines

Most Prominent Characteristics

Overall Shape and Size

Passionflower is an herbaceous climbing tendriled vine becoming woody with age. These perennial, evergreen to semievergreen vines tend to climb over trees, shrubs, trellises, and fences, but rarely sprawl flat on the ground. The vines can reach 10 to 15 yards in length.

Stalks and Stems The stems of these hardy vines measure from 1/16 inch (young plants) to an inch in diameter in older vines. The older vines become increasingly ribbed or striate, and red veins appear as the vines mature. The very young stems are tender and easy to break, but they become increasingly fibrous and woody. Aggressive tendrils are found in the axils of each leaf.

Leaves P. incarnata and most other species of Passiflora have three segments or simple leaves. On P. caerulea, leaves are palmately shaped, and divided into five (sometimes seven) lobes. Each segment of the P. caerulea leaf is linear to elliptic in shape with a slightly wavy entire margin. The tip of each segment has a small bristle or awn. Each lobe measures approximately one inch to three inches in length. The leaf surface is glabrous (hairless), the upper surface being deep green, and the lower surface whitish green. The main veins visible on the lower side of the leaf are often red-stained. The petiole (leaf stalk) is from one inch to two inches long, sometimes with a red tint visible. The leaves are arranged alternately on the vine. P. caerulea is readily distinguishable from other species by its untypical five-lobed leaves.

Flowers The spectacular (almost otherworldly) flowers are present from May through August. The flower appears to have 10 white petals, but is actually composed of 5 petals and 5 identical-looking sepals.

The showy corona of P. incarnata is usually purple; in the case of P. caerulea, there is light purple on the outer fringe of the corona, a band of white, and deep purple on the inside of the corona. Five stamens develop on a column above the sepals and petals. The stamen's anther and filament are green, and the anther has a conspicuous margin of yellow pollen. Above the stamen is the pistil with three knoblike stigmas. The entire flower is usually two to three inches in diameter.

Fruit A superior ovary first develops into a green fruit, then ripens into a yellowish-orange to orange-red fruit (berry), approximately the size and shape of a medium egg. It measures up to two inches long and one inch wide in the middle. The fruit's flesh is approximately one centimeter thick. The inside is filled with mucilaginous, deep-red seeds, approximately one centimeter each in length. The withered sepals and petals usually persist and remain attached to the end of the fruit.

Roots The roots grow three or more feet in depth. The thickness is approximately the same as the thickness of the plant's stem. Interestingly, the root has an odor remarkably similar to that of ginseng root.

Beneficial Properties

Edible Properties P. incarnata is native to the eastern and southern United States, where it is considered a weed. Its fruit is yellow and egg shaped. John Muir described it as "the most delicious fruit I have ever eaten."

The fruits of P. caerulea, common in southern California, are not the best of the Passifloras, but they are certainly edible. They can be simply picked, sliced open, and the red, seedy insides eaten. Not only are they a welcome on-the-trail snack, but these sweet subtly flavored fruits can also be used in a variety of recipes. The pulp that surrounds each seed can be eaten pomegranate-style with no preparation whatsoever. Or you can strain the seeds through a colander to get the pure pulp, and add it to cold summer beverages, fruit salads, sherbets, and so forth. Although the orange skin and the thin layer of pulp on the inside of the skin are edible, they are bitter when raw. Cooking can reduce this bitterness. Although P. caerulea hasn't been tested nutritionally, a related species, P. edulis (also referred to as Purple Granadilla), contains 71 milligrams of vitamin C, 1,650 international units of vitamin A, 831 milligrams of potassium, 66 milligrams of sodium, 3.8 milligrams of iron, 151 milligrams of phosphorus, and 31 milligrams of calcium per pound of fruit.

Medicinal Uses The dried flowers and leaves are described as an anodyne, nerve sedative, diuretic, and antispasmodic. Passionflower tea is used for unrest, agitation, exhaustion, nervousness, and nervous headaches. Drinking a tea of the leaves relieves insomnia, soothes the nerves, and results in a more restful sleep and a feeling of being refreshed upon arising. Infuse ½ ounce of the dried leaves to two pints of water.

The Houma Native Americans added the pulverized root of P. incarnata to their water in the belief that it acted as a tonic for the entire body. An alkaloid called passiflorine is obtained from the root.

Other Uses Passionflower leaves are sometimes mixed into herbal cigarette blends for individuals attempting to quit smoking tobacco. Smoked by itself, the leaves act as a mild sedative. The leaves can be burned as a sweet-smelling incense. The odor has been compared to that of burning marijuana.

a close-up of a passion flower

The vine makes a fast-growing shade cover for patios, porches, and trellises. These vines also make excellent fiber for tying packages, securing shelters, or even for fishing in an emergency.

Detrimental Properties
Drinking the concentrated tea from the leaves or smoking the leaves (see Other Uses) in sufficient amounts causes a sedative effect coupled with narcosis. Although the burned leaves make a pleasant incense, its aromatic similarity to burning marijuana should give you reason to exercise discretion as to where and when to use it.

Once planted, this hardy plant will quickly spread, and will—if unchecked—engulf trees, bushes, hedges, and so forth.

Where Found
P. incarnata, the United States native species, is found throughout the southern and eastern United States from Virginia to Missouri and down to Florida.

P. caerulea, found throughout southern California, is a Brazilian native, and is also grown as an indoor vine in Europe. In southern California, it is found growing over fences, shrubs, walls, from the foothill chaparral region, throughout the cities, and to the ocean.

Growing Cycle
This is an evergreen or semi-evergreen vine. Fruits ripen in mid to late summer. The flowers appear in the spring.

Lore and Signature
The flower has often been used to tell the story of the passion of Jesus Christ, hence the name passionflower. The perianth segments (5 petals and 5 sepals) are all identical in size and color. These 10 parts are said to represent the 10 faithful apostles—only 10 instead of 12 because Peter denied and Judas betrayed. The purple corona is said to represent the

crown of thorns placed on the head of Jesus during his trial. The five out-stretched stamens represent the head and limbs of the outstretched body of Jesus as it was being nailed to the cross. The three stigmas of the pistil represent the three nails that were used to nail Jesus to the cross; one for the feet and one for each hand. The twining tendrils are said to represent the whips used by the Roman soldiers. The fact that the Native Americans relished the fruit of this plant was interpreted by the missionaries to mean that the Native Americans were "hungry for Christianity."

The Gulf Fritillary butterfly is a common host on the passionflower vine. Its minute eggs can be seen as small cups with red rims, supported by green projectiles. The caterpillars (or larvae) are often seen crawling and feeding on the plant. Both eggs and larvae are edible in an emergency, but they're quite small. The adult butterflies are usually visible in the vicinity of the vine. Their golden orange spotted top and silver spotted underside identify them. Because of the presence of butterflies on this vine, and due to the unique life cycle of butterflies, the Spanish missionaries would also use the passionflower plant as a medium for teaching about the Resurrection.

Pinyon Pine (Pinus edulis, P. monophylla, P. quadrifolia)

Pine Family (Pinaceae)

Common Names Nut pine

pinyon pine tree

Most Prominent Characteristics

Overall Shape and Size Pines are evergreen and vary from roundish bushes to towering pyramid-like Christmas trees. The pinyons range from 10 to 35 feet tall. The pinyon is drought resistant, requiring only 10 to 18 inches of rain annually.

Trunk Pinyon is a short-trunked low tree, with a trunk diameter of about two feet.

Leaves The pinyons, like all pines, have needlelike leaves when fully mature. The needles of all pines, whether born singly or in groups, have a paperlike fascicle (or sheath) at their base. Pinyon needles occur singly or in pairs, and they measure up to two inches long.

Flowers There are no flowers present in the gymnosperm group of plants, to which the pines belong. Rather than flowers, there are woody cones. The cones of the pinyon are almost globe shaped with thick scales. Each scale is raised into a broad-based pyramid with a slightly flattened summit, bearing a minute deciduous prickle.

Seeds The seeds (also called pine nuts or Indian nuts) are available in late August through October. The large, wingless seeds are oblong, thin shelled, and from ¾ inch to 1½ inches long. The red-brown to black shell is not difficult to crack between the teeth. The nut meat is flavorful and easily digested. Pinyon nuts are abundant in cycles, usually every four to seven years.

Beneficial Properties

Edible Properties Pinyon nuts provided one of the most important foods for many Southwest Native American tribes, such as the Apaches, Hopis, Navajo, Paiutes, and Zunis, but other pines with large nuts were also used, such as coulter pine (P. coulteri), digger pine (P. sabiniana), and sugar pine (P. lambertiana). The nuts were gathered on the ground, or sometimes limbs were shaken so that cones would fall. If the scales on the cone are still tightly closed, the seeds cannot be simply shaken out. In such cases, the cone must be pried apart to release the seeds.

Pinyon nuts are from the low-growing pinyon trees of the Southwest. Although all pine nuts are edible, few are as large and are therefore not as valuable as the pinyon. The nuts can be eaten raw or roasted, ground or chopped finely into a meal that can then be made into pine nut soup. Some Native American children whose mothers had died were often fed pine nut soup, apparently a close substitute for mother's milk.

USDA analysis of pine nuts reveals that 100 grams contain 635 calories, 12 grams of protein, 60.5 grams of fat, 20.5 grams of carbohydrates, 604 milligrams of phosphorus, 5.2 milligrams of iron, 1.28 milligrams of thiamine (or 14.6 percent protein, 61.1 percent fat, 17.3 percent carbohydrates, 2.8 percent ash, and 3,205 calories per pound).

Many birds and squirrels rely heavily on pine nuts. Other wildlife eat the buds, bark, needles, and wood. Needles of all the pines can be nibbled for their vitamin C or made into a flavorful tea, which has the aroma of Christmas.

The tree's cambium layer (the soft layer of growing tissue beneath the bark, or inner bark) is also edible. Although supposedly edible raw, it is improved if it is ground into powder and made into flour or cut into slices and cooked like spaghetti. Some Native Americans mashed the cambium into pulp and formed cakes, which were baked on the coals of the fire. Once dried, these cakes were trail rations, but needed to be broken into bits and boiled to make soft enough to eat. Although this cambium layer has been highly praised in some literature, it should be considered an extreme survival food due to the work involved in order to obtain a food which, at best, is still resinous, fibrous, and tough.

Medicinal Uses Chewing the fresh sap or gum of pinyon is said to be effective for coughs and sore throats and as a laxative. The heated sap may also be used externally on sores, cuts, bites, boils, and burns.

Mashed green needles make an antiseptic poultice for open wounds.

Other Uses Pine sap is useful as glue or pitch to waterproof baskets, boats, and shelters. The Yuki Native Americans chewed the sap as a gum (actually, you don't chew the sap as you'd chew gum; it's best described as rolling the sap in the mouth).

Pine oil (made from the needles) is used not only medicinally but also as an antiseptic (especially in cleaning bathrooms) and as an air freshener.

Detrimental Properties

The needles, scaly cones, and bark can be rough on the hands when collecting parts of the tree. For safety, wear gloves when gathering any part of this valuable plant. The fresh sap is so adhesive and durable that if you sit on it or get it on your clothing, it will stick with you for a long time.

Where Found

Photo by U.S. Forest Service

Claimed to be a native of the southwestern United States, various pinyon species can be found along many coastal mountain ranges and into the Mexican and Central American highlands. The pinyons are widespread in chaparral woodlands up to timberline. Pinyons are found from 3,000 feet to 8,500 feet in the southern ranges, often in association with juniper. Pinyon-juniper woodlands extend up to the base of the ponderosa pine zone and are the first coniferous zone up the

close-up of pinyon pine needles

mountains from the desert sagebrush. Pinyon is found in areas of 10 to 25 inches of annual rain, high winds, temperature extremes, and an evaporation rate, which is the highest of any forest type. Pinyon can be found in pure stands or with the juniper on desert slopes, dry rocky foothills, mesas, plateaus, and on the eastern slopes of the Sierras. Other pines are found throughout the United States.

Growing Cycle

Seeds mature in late August through October. The actual cycle for seed production begins in August when the first winter buds (that will become new cones) start to form. The buds mature by October, but then growth stops and resumes the next spring in May. Pollination occurs in June and cone growth continues only to stop again in August. Growth picks up again the following May, and finally in September the cones are mature and the nuts soon fall to the ground.

Lore and Signature

In his book *Rolling Thunder*, Doug Boyd discusses the destruction of the pinyon pine as well as the deep importance of this tree to the Native Americans.

The pine nut shape and name resemble the pineal gland, located between the eyes, about two inches back. This is the region called the "third eye." Thus, those who accept the Doctrine of Signatures (which, briefly, states that plants contain some signature that alludes to its useful properties) suggest that the ingestion of pine nuts stimulates and/or awakens the pineal gland.

Plantain (Plantago major and P. lanceolata)

Plantain Family
(Plantaginaceae)

Common Names English plantain, white man's foot, ribwort

broad leaf plantain growing along a stream

Most Prominent Characteristics

Overall Shape and Size P. major was named white man's foot by the Native Americans, since the plant closely followed the European advance of civilization in North America. P. major grew around all of the earliest frontier settlements. Today, plantain is as common a city weed as dandelion, although not as commonly known by name. If left alone, the entire plant can grow to about 1 foot across, with the seed stalks rising from 1½ to 2 feet tall. Typically, the plants hide in lawns, much like dandelion.

Leaves The plant's leaves all radiate from the base in a rosette fashion, with the basal leaves reaching from six inches to one foot. P. lanceolata's leaves are prominently ribbed with parallel veins, which converge at their bases into a broad petiole about two inches long. P. major has large glabrous leaves, up to six inches long, roundish or ovate shaped. P. lanceolata has erect lanceolate leaves covered with soft short hairs; they reach up to a foot long and taper at the base into a slender petiole.

Flowers The ⅛- to ¼-inch flowers are arranged in dense spikes on simple leafless stalks arising up to two feet. Each greenish flower is composed of four sepals, a small corolla, and four stamens (sometimes two). The flowers are covered by dry, scarious bracts.

Seeds Each flower matures into a two-celled seed capsule, and the flowers are formed in spikes. Each spike is about one to two inches long. The spikes arise on stalks up to two feet tall, but typically the stalks are about nine inches tall.

Beneficial Properties

Edible Properties The tough fibers of the leaves make them difficult to digest. The young tender leaves of spring are the best to eat; use in salads or as you would spinach. The leaves that have become more fibrous with age need longer cooking; they are best chopped finely or pureed and cooked in a cream sauce. The leaves have a mild laxative effect. One hundred grams of the leaf (about ½ cup) contain 184 milligrams of calcium, 52 milligrams of phosphorous, 277 milligrams of potassium, and 2,520 micrograms of beta carotene.

The seeds can be eaten once cleaned by winnowing. The seeds can be ground into flour and used as you would regular flour. They can also be soaked in water until soft and then cooked like rice. Once cooked, the seeds are slightly mucilaginous and bland. They can be eaten plain or flavored with honey, butter, or other seasoning. The seeds are eaten by birds and other small mammals in the wild. One hundred grams of the seed contain 339 milligrams of potassium and 305 milligrams of phosphorus.

Medicinal Uses Eating plantain is said to have a healing effect on ulcers. Cooked plantain leaves have been used as a direct poultice on boils. Plantain and poppy heads can be mixed together and applied on wounds to kill pain. Plantain is a vulnerary (promotes healing) and is noted for its styptic, antiseptic, and astringent qualities. Shoshoni Native Americans used the cooked leaves as a poultice for wounds.

Patricia Earl of Laurel Canyon, California, reports that her family has long used the plantain leaves for healing. Her great-grandmother, Wilhelmina, who was from Germany, moved into the Minnesota area and learned about plantain from the local Native Americans in the years just after the Civil War. Since then, the family has used plantain leaves numerous times with miraculous results. For example, an Uncle Jake had a circulatory problem, which resulted in skin sores. To heal the sores, he placed crushed plantain leaves directly on the wounds, and they healed. In another instance, Patricia's son, Michael, accidentally jumped onto a board with a 16 penny nail sticking straight up. He was about 9 or 10 years old at the time, and the nail went through his tennis shoe and all the way through his foot. Patricia's mother, who lived about 20 minutes away, immediately brought fresh plantain leaves over and applied them to the top and bottom of Michael's foot. They did not go to a hospital, though Michael's foot was beginning to swell and he had some pain. Six hours later there was no swelling and no pain. Patricia reports that they used primarily the broadleaf plantain.

Early American colonists used plantain on insect and venomous reptile bites and used the seeds for expelling worms.

Boerhaaue, an 18th-century European botanist, recommended binding plantain leaves to sore and tired feet to relieve the fatigue of long hikes.

Chewing the root is reported to stop toothaches. The green seeds boiled in milk or a tea of the dried leaves will stop diarrhea.

The husks of the seeds of a related plant, Plantago ovata, commonly called psyllium, are sold in some markets. They are supposed to cleanse the colon, although the labels of the psyllium husks rarely say this. One is advised to stir one to two tablespoons of the psyllium husks into a glass of water or fruit juice and to drink the mixture in the morning. Readers who consume psyllium husks may wish to experiment with the husks of the common wild plantain seeds.

Detrimental Properties
We'd appreciate authenticated reports from readers.

Where Found
This European native grows best in rich soil; it tends to stay small in poor soil. Plantain is found all over the United States in agricultural lands, along streams (P. major especially), along walkways, in gardens, lawns, and waste places.

Growing Cycle
Plantain is a perennial. New leaves are produced each spring, a flower stalk arises in early summer, and the seeds mature in mid to late summer.

POISON

Poison Hemlock (Conium maculatum)
Parsley Family (Umbelliferae)
Common Names Queen Anne's lace, spotted hemlock

Most Prominent Characteristics

Don Hoover looks at the flowers of poison hemlock. This plant is over seven feet tall.

Overall Shape and Size This ferny-looking plant gracefully rises up to 10 feet, but more typically from 4 to 7 feet. All parts of the plant are destitute of hairs. When rubbed or bruised, the plant emits a nauseous odor.

Stalks and Stems The hollow main stalk and stems, particularly the lower stalk, are covered with characteristic irregular purplish blotches and dots. The Latin species name, *maculatum*, refers to this spotted characteristic of the stem.

Leaves The leaves are decompound, or finely divided; that is, the primary divisions are also compoundly divided into smaller segments. Each leaf measures from one foot to two feet long. The ferny-looking leaves are hairless. Leaves have a musky aroma, which is often described as being similar to cat urine or a mouse aroma.

Flowers Dozens of flat-topped compound umbels appear on each plant in early summer. Each umbel measures about 1½ to 2½ inches across. Each small white flower measures about ¹⁄₁₆ inch across.

Fruits The grey-green compressed ovate fruits appear in midsummer.

Seeds The broadly ovate seeds, which are somewhat laterally flattened, have prominent ribs and are seen in late summer and fall.

Roots Its stout taproot resembles the parsnip, but don't be tempted to eat it.

Beneficial Properties

Edible Properties *Extremely poisonous!* if eaten. The result is nervousness, muscle weakness, trembling, coma, respiratory paralysis, and death. The roots are sometimes mistaken for parsnip, carrot, or cow parsnip and eaten, with death usually resulting.

The leaves are occasionally mistaken for an edible plant, such as parsley, and eaten by campers who are either misinformed or uninformed. In one case on March 17, 1976, James Kenny, 23, of Gainesville, Florida, and Douglas Clark, 18, of Santa Cruz, California, were camping in the mountains near Santa Cruz. Both Kenny and Clark had eaten the poisonous hemlock, but Clark, who had already become ill, managed to travel and call for help. Kenny was already dead when the rescuers reached the campsite. Convulsions usually start within half an hour of ingestion and death is quick to follow. Clark said that they had mistaken the fatal herb for watercress, an herb that bears no resemblance to hemlock.

This is the plant from which Socrates drank a tea (see Detrimental Properties). Curiously, the toxicity of the leaves varies with climate and the age of the plant. People have reportedly eaten young leaves with no ill effects, a practice I would strongly discourage.

Medicinal Uses   For a time, both methylconine and conine, the deadly alkaloids present in this plant, were used by United States physicians. Conine ($C_8H_{17}N$), a volatile, colorless, oily substance was extracted from the seeds and used in very small amounts as an antispasmodic, sedative, and pain reliever. It is rarely, if ever, used as such today.

An extract made from the green fruit is sold as a sedative, because the methylconine and conine are supplanted in the fruits by another, far less toxic, alkaloid, called conhydrine. It is often prescribed for chorea, incontinence, paralysis agitans, and as a vapor to relieve cough.

Used as a poultice on the solar plexus, the crushed flower umbels are said to chase away anxiety. As a poultice on top of the pectoral muscles, the umbels are said to reduce convulsive coughing and to relieve the panic of asthma attacks.

Other Uses   Although the strong, hollow stalk might tempt you to make a whistle, blowgun, or peashooter, *do not do it*! In the mid-1970s, a young boy in Seal Beach, California, made a whistle from a hollow dried segment of the stem. He felt sick later in the day, was hospitalized, and died before the day was over. (This incident was related by Dr. Leonid Enari during one of his Edible, Medicinal, and Poisonous Plants classes at the Los Angeles County Arboretum in Arcadia.)

Detrimental Properties

Very poisonous! Contains up to four alkaloids, all of which (to varying degrees) paralyze the central nervous system, especially the nerves controlling the respiratory organs. It effects paralysis of the peripheral endings of the motor nerves with only a slight effect on the nerves of sensation. Thus, Socrates was clear thinking after he drank the tea, yet his body and muscle use—especially his ability to breathe—quickly diminished.

Gasping for air and convulsions usually start within a half hour of ingestion of any part of the plant, but the degree of toxicity apparently varies with climate and the age of the plant.

Plato wrote an account of Socrates' death and physical reactions (from *Phaedo*) as follows:

> Crito made a sign to one of the attendants, who soon returned with a man
> bringing the poison in a drinking cup. Socrates said, "Tell me, my friend,

*what should I do?" "Only drink it, and then walk around until your legs
begin to feel heavy," he replied, handing the cup, "then lie down."*

*Socrates walked about until his legs began to feel heavy. Then he said
his legs felt heavy and he lay down on his back as he had been instructed.
The man who administered the poison kept his hand on Socrates and after
a short time examined his legs and feet. Then he pressed his foot hard,
and asked if he could feel anything. Socrates said he couldn't. After that,
the man did the same to Socrates' legs, and moving his hand up the body,
he showed us that Socrates was becoming cold and numb. Later the
attendant felt Socrates again and said that when the numbness reached
the heart, Socrates would die. It was already almost to his waist when
Socrates uncovered his face and spoke his last words.*

*"Crito, I owe a cock to the god who heals, Asclepius. See that my
debt is paid." "It shall be done," said Crito with complete understand-
ing. "Is there anything else?"*

*But Socrates made no reply to his question. After a little while
Socrates moved slightly, and the man uncovered him. His eyes had
become fixed. When Crito saw this, he closed Socrates' eyes and mouth.
"So ended the life of our dear friend," said Phaedo.*

Sometimes the common name of Queen Anne's Lace is used to
describe this plant. One problem with common names is that they are
sometimes used for other plants. Queen Anne's Lace is also commonly
used to describe at least two other plants that I'm aware of—one is wild
carrot (Daucus carota) and another is Eulophus bolanderi. All three are
related since they're all in the parsley family. Wild carrot roots and seeds
are edible. Thus, you'll likely encounter various books and people who
give you contradictory accounts, some saying that Queen Anne's Lace is
edible and some saying it's poisonous. Both are right, of course; they're
just talking about different plants.

Where Found
Generally considered a European native, poison hemlock also grows in
Britain and in some parts of Asia. It likes moist, sandy areas and is often
found near streams and riverbanks. It is common along the Pacific Coast,
often interspersed with fennel and cow parsnip, look-alikes to the beginning forager.

Growing Cycle
Poison hemlock is a biennial, producing its ferny leaves the first year (in
the spring) and flowering the second year (in the summer).

Lore and Signature
By using analogy, we can learn much from the world around us in a practical way. For example, note the beauty of poison hemlock and how its
beauty may seduce us into consuming it. What is outwardly "beautiful"
may be deadly inside.

Poison Oak (Rhus diversiloba)
Sumac Family
(Anacardiaceae)

poison oak vining up a tree

Most Prominent Characteristics

Overall Shape and Size Poison oak grows as a more or less erect shrub from four to eight feet high or as a vine with the stems climbing tree trunks.

Leaves The roundish, one- to two-inch long leaflets are glossy green, slightly toothed on the margins, and are clustered on their stems in threes (that is, each leaf is composed of three leaflets). The small, newly emerging leaves of spring are red. The leaves, which are deciduous, turn red in the fall.

Flowers The bunches of the small green flowers grow in the leaf axils.

Fruit The flowers later develop into poisonous yellow-white drupes (a fruit with a fleshy outside and a stony inside).

Beneficial Properties

Edible Properties An indirect food source from poison oak is honey, since the bees gather pollen from the poison oak flowers. The honey is reputedly completely safe and nontoxic, even to those who are easily susceptible to poison oak rash.

Many Native American tribes mixed the poison oak leaves into their acorn meal (and other mixtures) while cooking breads. The Native Americans were not naturally immune to poison oak. It was their regular contact with it that made them seemingly immune. Some of the Native Americans would eat the very young red leaves in spring to create an immunity in their bodies for the rest of the year. This generally worked because the antibodies that developed from the consumed poison oak leaves tended to prevent any future rash from occurring. However, this isn't a settled scientific practice, and thus cannot be unreservedly recommended. Bodies accustomed to a high white sugar and bleached flour diet seem to be extra sensitive to the plant.

I can testify that since eating the leaves, I've never gotten a rash from even prolonged skin contact with the mature adult plant. To underscore the practical survival value of developing this immunity, I once led a group of people along some unfamiliar trails during a wild food outing. One trail led directly to where we wanted to go, but a 15-foot section was

completely overgrown with a tangle of poison oak. Of the two choices—
go back the way we came or clear the trail—I chose the latter. With bare
hands, I broke off and bent back the tough poison oak stems that were
thickly covered with newly emerging glistening green leaves. During the
task, I ate more young leaves to ensure immunity.

In order to *really* test the immunity theory, I purposely avoided washing up at the end of the day. The trail clearing occurred on a Sunday; the
following Wednesday, I noticed a little line of small blisters on my arm
that I recognized as poison oak. I still did not treat it in any way. By
Friday, there were three small patches of pinhead blisters and one large
blister. I still did not treat it. By Monday it began to clear up; two days
later, it was gone. Thus my personal experience is that eating the poison
oak leaves prevents a full maturation of the rash, but doesn't necessarily
prevent all signs or outbreaks.

Thus, you're strongly advised to watch closely for poison oak; not
only will this watchfulness prevent misery, but it is also a beautiful plant
to the unprejudiced eye!

Medicinal Uses The Yukis and other Native Americans claim that the
juice of the young, tender poison oak stems is a wart cure. The wart top is
first cut or pricked open and the fresh poison oak juice applied directly
inside. This is repeated several times. I have tried this. Although I've
never seen it totally rid a wart, it does turn the wart a beautiful shade of
"midnight blue" for a few days. (See Lore.)

For rattlesnake bites, it was believed among the Yukis and others that
the fresh leaves, applied immediately to the bite, would counteract the
venom.

The closely related poison ivy (Rhus toxicodendron) was first used as
a medicine in Europe to treat difficult types of herpes infections.

Other Uses Poison oak is perhaps the most broadly disliked and/or
feared plant of all plants. But all plants have some beneficial effect upon
mankind, even if only to give us oxygen. It's up to us to discover and
understand plants' secrets, even those that induce fear and contempt.

Early Native Americans not only lived in harmony with poison oak,
but also had many uses for it, from food, to basket craft, to medicine.
Native American tribes used the slender stems of poison oak to weave
baskets, causing unsuspecting buyers—generally Caucasians—to break
out in the rash.

The Pomos used the fresh juice of poison oak to dye baskets, since it
turns dark quickly and leaves a fast stain.

Detrimental Properties

There are a number of ways that one can contract the rash of poison oak.
The most common way is direct skin contact with the oil that lightly coats
the leaves and even the leafless stalks in winter. However, the oil takes

time to penetrate the skin before doing any damage, so thorough washing after exposure may be all that is necessary to prevent the rash. Two of the best soaps for washing off the oil are Shaklee's Basic H and Fels Naptha laundry soap. Your clothes, if exposed to poison oak, should be washed before rewearing.

The smoke of burning poison oak transmits the infectious oils. Many firefighters, whose pores open from the fire's heat, receive serious infections from the plant's oil-laden smoke. This smoke can also cause serious eye damage; blindness can result from a sufficient concentration of smoke. Another transmitter of poison oak's oil is the coat of an animal that has been in contact with poison oak.

There are probably as many claimed cures and preventatives for poison oak as there are for the common cold. Talk to some of the old-timers and you'll probably hear some of the following suggestions:

1. The yellow juice of the aloe vera plant is the best natural cure for poison oak rash. While any of the aloes can be used, aloe vera seems to be best. To use, cut open a section of the succulent leaf, and apply the inner, wet side directly to the rash, which will result in an immediate cooling sensation and a subsequent rapid healing.
2. Other succulents, such as Chinese jade and ice plant, have been used with some success.
3. Rub mugwort leaves (Artemisia spp.) over the exposed parts of your body before entering poison oak areas to prevent the rash.
4. Use the fresh juice of crushed mugwort leaves directly on the rash.
5. Wash the infection with an infusion of wild buckwheat leaves (Eriogonum spp.).
6. Do the same with yerba santa leaves (Eriodictyon spp.).
7. Drink a tea of the leaves of chickweed (Stellaria media) for stopping the spread of the rash. Or you can apply the fresh leaves directly to the rash.

In the old days, mud or dirt would be spread on one's skin to prevent a rash. Interestingly, a manufacturer has produced a clay-based product for firefighters. It is spread on the skin before fire fighting in poison oak-infected areas to prevent the rash.

Another method is to quickly wash the contacted skin with anhydrous alcohol, which breaks down the urushiol, the active oil in poison oak. Afterwards, wash well with soap and water.

Other not so natural enthusiasts simply suggest that you see your doctor when you develop the infection. According to wilderness author George L. Herter, "Over nine million dollars a year is spent for hospitalization, doctors' fees, and drugs to cure and prevent poison ivy and poison oak." Yet, since the doctor will frequently prescribe hydrocortisone, a product that weakens the body's immune system over time, we feel that the safer and effective solutions, such as the aloe vera juice, as preferable.

Bathing in a hot (110° F to 115° F) tub, or washing with a top-quality biodegradable soap (such as Basic H) effectively removes poison oak oil from the skin after exposure.

Where Found
Poison oak is the most widespread shrub in southern California, often covering entire trees and hillsides. It is widely found throughout the western states.

Growing Cycle
Poison oak is a perennial shrub whose stalks are bare throughout the winter. Small red leaves appear in the early spring, which become a deep shade of green as they reach their full size in early summer. By the end of summer, the leaves turn red and fall off. At this time, the shrub is also full of clusters of yellow drupes.

Lore and Signature
Due to warts' characteristic of mysteriously appearing and disappearing, it may be that the Native American practice of applying poison oak juice and seeing the warts disappear was often a case of *post hoc ergo propter hoc*.

I believe we need to delve far deeper into the meaning of the phenomena of spontaneous appearance and disappearance of abnormal growths on (and in) our body—not, however, from the present viewpoint of cellular membranes, but of very specific body communications. In other words, we need to learn to read the sign language of these distressed body parts to see what they're trying to say to us, rather than be so quick to get rid of them.

Prickly Lettuce (Lactuca serriola)

Sunflower Family (Compositae)

Common Names compass plant, L. scariola, wild lettuce

Photo by Vickie Shufer

wild lettuce

Most Prominent Characteristics

Overall Shape and Size

Prickly lettuce stems vary from two to six feet tall, sometimes with one solitary stem, sometimes more. This plant is the mother of all cultivated lettuces.

Stalks and Stems The stiff gray-green stalk is sometimes smooth, but usually has ⅛- to ¼-inch spines. Milky latex drips out when the stalk is cut or broken.

Leaves The leaves are sessile or sagitate-clasping (the base of the leaves clasping the main stem). The leaves measure from two inches to eight inches long and about 1 inch to 1½ inches wide and are alternately arranged. The leaf shape is variable; it can be oblong, oblong-lanceolate, or divided into deep, pinnately lobed segments. When cut, the leaves exude a milky latex. A typical feature of the leaves is the row of short spines on the underside of the leaf midrib.

Flowers The small yellow, dandelion-like flowers, arranged in panicles, often close around noon. Each ray flower (or petal) has four or five teeth. There are about a dozen rays per head. The plant is in flower from June to October.

Seeds The flowers mature into small ⅛-inch long brown seeds attached to a cottony tuft, resembling a dandelion.

Roots The root is a somewhat fibrous taproot, several inches in length.

Beneficial Properties

Edible Properties Our modern-day common lettuces (L. sativa) are believed to be a cultigen evolved from prickly lettuce. The resemblance is still somewhat apparent in very young prickly lettuce leaves, both in texture and in flavor. The youngest leaves are good in salads, but the older leaves become extremely bitter, in some cases requiring a few boilings to render them palatable.

Samuel K. Miller of Laguna Hills, California, writes, "Prickly lettuce has become one of my staples because of its ready availability in vacant lots around here. I usually steam it with a wide variety of wild and domestic greens. Some tender leaves can even be found now [written August 17, 1980] on young plants as the plant seems to reseed even during these dry hot months."

The entire chicory tribe of the sunflower family contains no toxic members; most, therefore, can be eaten if they are not too tough or otherwise unpalatable. For more details, see Appendix 1 in the rear of this book.

Medicinal Uses When the mature stalks are cut, a white sap oozes out and can be gathered the next day when it dries and turns to a reddish-brown color. It apparently looks, smells, and tastes like opium, but it has a much weaker effect than opium. It is used for insomnia and to relieve coughing and diarrhea.

Other Uses At noon when in full sun, the edges of the leaves face north and south, and the faces of the leaves are turned east and west. It often appears as if the leaves were pressed in a book. The leaves grow in all directions in the shade. While I have observed the leaves flattened, the north/south orientation was not precise enough to be of any real help in orientation.

The dried sap from the root can be used as a gum.

Detrimental Properties
We'd appreciate authenticated reports from readers.

Where Found
This native of the United States is found all across the country, in gardens, vacant lots, moist soil, and fields. It is found in wilderness areas as well as urban areas.

Growing Cycle
This annual or biennial puts forth its new growth in the spring and flowers in the summer and fall.

Prickly Pear (Opuntia spp.)
Cactus Family (Cactaceae)

Photo by Timothy Snider

Christopher carefully collects prickly pear cactus fruits.

Most Prominent Characteristics

Overall Shape and Size Prickly pear grows in clusters with flat, broad, oval fleshy pads, which are its stems, and is covered with numerous spines, which are its leaves.

Flowers The many-petaled flowers are purple, yellow, orange, or red. The petals are somewhat fleshy. The corolla (petals united) is circular in outline or wheel-shaped from above. The sepals are thick and green or partly colored.

Fruit Throughout the summer and early fall, the mature purple, red, or yellow fruits grow from the tips of the pads. The fruits, which are full of seeds, are covered with small hairlike spines called glochids.

Beneficial Properties

Edible Properties All of the many varieties of Opuntia produce edible fruit and pads. The ripened fruits are succulent, somewhat sweet, and delicious. The fruits need to be twisted off (or cut from) the pads, then carefully peeled, and enjoyed fresh. Once chilled (in the refrigerator or in a stream), these fruits taste very much like melon. Even eaten unchilled along the trail, they'll satisfy both thirst and appetite. Drinks, pies, jams, ice creams, and so forth can also be made from this fine fruit. Juice can be made simply by pressing the peeled fruits and then pouring the pressed fruit through a colander to remove the pulp and seed. Ice cream can be made by replacing prickly pear pulp (with or without seeds) for the sugar and flavoring in an ice cream recipe. You can also flavor vanilla ice cream by substituting prickly pear pulp with soft vanilla ice cream, then refreezing before serving. Peeled fruits can also be sliced thin and dried (seeds left in). The flavor is sweet with somewhat of a burnt aftertaste.

The fruits are most abundant in late summer.

When you eat the fruits, you'll notice the abundance of small seeds. You can either eat them with the fruit, save them to grow new cactus, or follow the Native Americans' example of saving the seeds, drying them, and grinding them into flour. If you're processing a lot of cactus fruit, the seeds add up quickly, and you'll soon have enough for a few loaves of cactus seed bread.

For years when reading cactus fruit recipes, I saw the phrase "first remove seeds." Nowhere did I find details on how to easily remove these seeds. After several experiments during the summer of 1989, Nathaniel Schleimer and I discovered the easiest method: we blended the raw peeled fruit in a food processor until it was a watery pulp full of seeds. Then we poured the blend through a colander. Approximately 98 percent of the cactus pulp went right through the colander as a liquid, leaving behind a colander full of pure seeds.

The fresh young pads, called nopales, can be found for sale in many predominantly Mexican markets. When still small and glossy green, the nutritious pads will fry up into a delectable vegetable. Scrape, peel, and slice before frying. The texture is slimy like that of okra, but the flavor is good. These can be cooked alone, or with the other vegetables, such as onions, tomatoes, and bell peppers. Nopales are also good gently cooked, lightly baked like squash, or diced and mixed into egg omelettes. In all these recipes, onions mix well with the cactus.

Another popular use of the prickly pear is to pickle the peeled slices (or buy them pickled). These are generally served in much the same way you'd serve string beans.

John Watkins of Harbor City, California, suggests peeling and slicing the young pads into thin slices and letting them dry. "Use these interchangeably in recipes calling for 'leather britches,' which are dried string beans. You can also sauté these like zucchini sticks."

Raw, these pads have the flavor of slightly sour green peppers. The tender pads can be peeled, diced, and added to salads.

Since their water content is high, the pads and fruit can be literal lifesavers when water is scarce. Chewing the raw cactus (spines removed) may not quench your thirst in the same way that drinking a tall glass of iced tea would, but it will provide the body moisture necessary to save your life.

Medicinal Uses An elderly Mexican lady whom I met at the L.A. New Earth Exposition in 1978 told me that she was cured of diabetes by including raw and cooked prickly pear pads in her diet. Since then, I have met at least three people who claim to have stopped their insulin injections as a result of eating prickly pear cactus. Apparently, the nopales help the pancreas to do its job of producing insulin and there is more medical research demonstrating the beneficial value of prickly pear cactus for diabetics. I suggest that diabetics seek competent medical/nutritional advice before pursuing this as a form of treatment.

Separate research has shown that consuming the cactus fruits helps heal prostate infections.

Other Uses Small chunks of the peeled cactus can be mixed with a container of water; the resultant slimy water can be used as a hair rinse and conditioner as well as lathered into a soap.

The dried stalks of the older prickly pear plants consist of a network of coarse fiber. Sections of this stalk can be used as scouring pads for washing pots and pans or for making artistic designs on stationery.

Periodically, a white fuzz can be observed on the prickly pear pads. Within that fuzz is a tiny crimson cochineal beetle (Dactylopius coccus) that produces a red pigment when crushed. The pigment can be used as a paint, as a fabric dye, and as an entirely safe food coloring. According to the research of Sara E. Valdes-Martinez from the National Autonomous University of Mexico in Cuautitlan, the cochineal pigment produces a stable, long-lasting food coloring. Her research team found that the red hue remains stable for years, even at a temperature of 50° C. However, the pigment fades if the food's acidity increases or decreases sharply.

My associates and I have used the juice from the crushed beetles to produce an ink for painting. Mixing the extracted juice with oil produces the best results. We'd like to hear from readers who do further experiments with this red pigment.

Prickly pear cactus is the ideal drought-tolerant, low-maintenance fence. Planted on the perimeter of your property, it will keep out most unwanted intruders, while providing you with fruit and pad. It will serve as a firebreak as well. Grazing goats will also feed on the tender pads.

Detrimental Properties
You can't exercise too much caution when gathering the fruits and pads, for the small stickers are a days long irritation once they've worked their way into the skin. Scrape or peel off the entire skin surface of the fruit or pads with a knife, or burn off the stickers.

Where Found
Prickly pears are most often found in dry semiarid and arid regions. The plant grows best in the upper parts of alluvial plains near the base of mountains and coastal canyons.

Commonly associated with the southwestern United States, the prickly pears are found in city and desert alike. However, Opuntia is not restricted to the Southwest. Certain species are commonly found as far east as Nebraska, and one or two species are known to grow along the Atlantic Coast.

Growing Cycle
Prickly pear cactus is a perennial, which produces new pads each year, continuing to spread as the years progress. The new glossy green pads appear in the spring. The plant also flowers in the spring, and by the end of summer, the fruits are developed and ripe.

Purslane (Portulaca oleracea)
Purslane Family
(Portulacaceae)

Most Prominent Characteristics

Overall Shape and Size Purslane
is a low-growing fleshy herb,
whose outstretched, sprawling,
prostrate stems are from 3 to 12
inches long. The growing ends of
the stems are sometimes uplifted in
the lusher plants. The entire plant
seldom reaches over six inches tall.

purslane plant next to a pocketknife for size comparison

Stems The stems are tinted red, round shaped, and very succulent. The thick main stems of the plant radiate from the center root, and there are many lateral stems growing outward creating a matty appearance.

Leaves The succulent, glabrous (hairless and smooth) leaves, ½ to 1 inch long, are obovate (paddle shaped), flat, and alternately arranged.

Flowers The sessile, yellow flowers, about 3/16 inch across, open only in the sun. The floral parts include a two-cleft calyx, 5 (rarely 6) two-lobed petals, and 7 to 20 stamens.

Seeds The flowers mature into small seed capsules, with the upper top coming off like a hat to release many small black seeds. The seeds have a built-in survival mechanism that fastidious gardeners hate. This mechanism causes only half the seeds to germinate the first year, 40 percent the second year, and the remaining 10 percent the third year.

Beneficial Properties

Edible Properties Purslane is probably one of the most versatile and well-liked weeds commonly available. The plant can be eaten raw, lightly cooked, pickled, or fried; it can be added to soups and stews, and the seeds can be ground into flour.

In salads, use all the plant but the root. Wash it carefully to remove any grit adhering to this low-growing weed. Chop the leaves and stems for the salad. The leaves are mild tasting and slightly slimy. The thick, succulent stems are juicy and crunchy. A salad of purslane with seasoning and chopped onions is very acceptable fare. The stems are great to quench your thirst when hiking along a dusty trail.

Like spinach, the plant should be lightly cooked in a small amount of water, seasoned, and eaten. Gently fried, either alone or with onions, eggs, and so forth, it's a delicious entrée.

The chopped stem and leaves also mix well in soup, stews, and omelettes.

Ham and Purslane on Rye

Greg Kirshner of Fullerton, California, sent me this sandwich recipe. It's quite simple. Using toasted or untoasted rye bread, add a few slices of good quality ham. Instead of pickles, add a small handful of fresh purslane stems to the sandwich. Add a mixture of mustard and horseradish.

Verdolago con Queso

1 quart tender purslane, including stems
½ cup Monterey Jack cheese, shredded

Wash the purslane and then gently boil for about two minutes. Drain the water and chop the purslane into smaller pieces. Sauté the purslane and cheese in a skillet. Warm on a very low flame until the cheese is melted. Serves two.

Pickled Purslane

The thicker, more succulent stems can be pickled by following a basic pickle recipe, substituting purslane stems for cucumbers.

1 quart purslane stems and leaves, chopped into 1-inch pieces
3 cloves garlic, sliced
10 peppercorns
1 quart raw apple cider vinegar

Place chopped purslane in clean jars with tight-fitting lids. Add garlic and peppercorns. Pour vinegar over the purslane. (You can also use old pickle juice or jalapeño pepper juice.) Keep this in the refrigerator at least two weeks before serving.

Tropical Purslane

2 cups shredded coconut
1½ cups boiling water
6 cups purslane stems and leaves

Combine the coconut and water and let set for 10 minutes. Strain and reserve the coconut milk. Combine the coconut milk and the purslane greens and simmer gently until tender, for about 30 minutes. Add salt and pepper to taste. (From the *The Green Beret Gourmet*, by James Guttenberg, Guttenberg Press, Box 973, Rockledge, FL 32955.)

Purslane seeds are harvested by gathering the plant stems, placing them on a sheet of newspaper, and waiting a few days. The seed pods will continue to mature even after you've picked the plant. You'll be able to shake all the small black seeds out on to the newspaper. These seeds can be ground and used as you would flour or sprinkled on top of a fresh loaf of bread before cooking.

Dried purslane has been found to be about 30 percent protein and 35 percent carbohydrates. One hundred grams of purslane contains 2,500 international units of vitamin A when cooked; .10 milligrams of riboflavin raw and .06 cooked; 103 milligrams of calcium raw and 86 cooked; 25 milligrams of vitamin C raw and 12 milligrams cooked; 21 calories; and small amounts of phosphorus, niacin, and thiamine.

Medicinal Uses In 1986, purslane was identified as being the richest leafy-plant source of omega-3 fatty acids, a substance that helps reduce the body's cholesterol levels and reduces the risk of heart attack. This discovery was made by Norman Salem, Jr., a lipid biochemist with the National Institute on Alcohol Abuse and Alcoholism in Bethesda, Maryland.

Interestingly, rather than suggest that people include purslane in their diets, Salem and his collaborator, Artemis P. Simopoulos (of the American Association for World Health in Washington, D.C.), studied range-fed chickens that fed on wild purslane. The yolk from one large-sized egg from a purslane-fed chicken contained about 300 milligrams of omega-3 fatty acids (17.87 milligrams per gram), the same amount contained in a standard fish oil capsule and 10 times more than what is found in a typical supermarket egg (1.74 milligrams per gram). Salem and Simopoulos's findings about the eggs were published in the November 16, 1989 *New England Journal of Medicine*.

Other Uses We'd appreciate authenticated reports from readers.

Detrimental Properties
The only plant that is sometimes confused with purslane by the beginning naturalist is the mildly toxic prostrate spurge, which has a similar shape and growing pattern. However, prostrate spurge lacks yellow flowers, doesn't have thick red stems, and tends to be much less conspicuous. If in doubt, break a stem. The spurge immediately exudes a thick, white latex substance. Purslane has no such white sap.

Where Found
Introduced from tropical America, purslane was in the United States before colonial times. Purslane is believed to have originated from India, from which it gradually spread to southeast Asia, Europe, and throughout North America. It is common in gardens, flower pots, disturbed hillsides, rose gardens, and waste areas. In Iran (ancient Persia) and India,

purslane has been eaten for over 2,000 years. Today, purslane can be found nearly all over the world.

Growing Cycle

This annual begins appearing in late spring and is present into fall. Purslane is typically a weed that is picked throughout the summer. It is, therefore, available when most of the spring weeds have already begun dying back.

Lore and Signature

Henry David Thoreau was fond of this weed, and he used it frequently during his Walden Pond experiment. He wrote, "I learned that a man may use as simple a diet as the animals, and yet retain health and strength. I have made a satisfactory dinner off a dish of purslane which I gathered and boiled. Yet men have come to such a pass that they frequently starve, not from want of necessities, but for want of luxuries."

Rose (Rosa spp.)
Rose Family (Rosaceae)

Most Prominent Characteristics

Overall Shape and Size The rose can grow in the wild as a single, rambling vine or as a rose thicket. When cultivated, it can be in the familiar bush form or mass planted as a hedgerow or living fence. The rose family, which includes both the apple and the toyon trees, includes dozens of wild varieties, and literally thousands of hybrids. Roses are America's most widely planted home ornamental.

rose hips, the fruit of rose bushes

Stalks and Stems The stalks and stems of all but a few hybrids are notorious for their hard, sharp thorns. The thorns are usually tan, brown, or gray on a stalk that is light green (sometimes with a purplish glaucous cast). Generally, there are fewer (and weaker) thorns on plants growing in rich soil, and more (and harder) thorns on those plants growing in poor or depleted soil. Although older rose stems can measure several inches in diameter at their base, most newer stems measure about ½ inch thick.

Leaves The rose's odd-pinnate leaves are ovate to elliptical and finely toothed. At the base of each leaf are two conspicuous stipules, which point toward the tip of the leaf.

Flowers Their incomparable fragrance and breathtaking beauty seem to well justify the considerable effort and expense that is put into their care and feeding each year.

The petals come in nearly every primary color and scores of hues in between. Sometimes the flowers on a single bush have more than one distinct color. Nearly all wild roses contain five petals; cultivated roses contain numerous petals. There are five sepals, which are green, long, and pointed. The pistils are numerous. The stamens are also numerous, with the filaments often conspicuously golden colored.

Fruit The fruit, commonly referred to as a hip, is an orange to red globe that seldom grows over an inch in diameter. The fleshy outer layer of the fully ripe hip has an applelike consistency; the inside contains numerous fibrous seeds. The withered stamens and pistils can be seen at the top of the ripe hip, and sometimes the withered sepals remain also.

Beneficial Properties

Edible Properties Were you aware that the rose is a top-quality food source? The petals can be eaten in a variety of ways. Plucked when the flower bud is in the process of opening, their sweet, perfumed flavor and somewhat dry texture provide a colorful, tasty addition to a green salad.

Petals can be placed in the bottom of baking pans, waffle irons, and pancake griddles before pouring the batter. Minced, the petals add their subtle flavor to pancake batter, puddings, and muffins. Chopped petals can be mixed with marjoram into an omelette. Wines are rendered visually elegant when served with a rose petal in the glass.

To capture the full flavor, the petals are best gathered in the morning before the sun shines on them. Snip off the white base of each petal to avoid its bitterness (these are then called prepared petals). Here's a standard raw jelly recipe:

Raw Jelly

> 1 cup prepared petals
> ¾ cup warm spring water
> Juice of 1 lemon
> 2½ cups 70°–90° honey
> 1 packet powdered pectin
> ¾ cup water

Thoroughly blend prepared petals, warm spring water, and lemon juice (preferably at high speeds with an electric blender). Slowly add honey, blending until dissolved. In a separate pan (preferably stainless steel), add a packet of powdered pectin to ¾ cup of water. Heat until thick and add to the just-blended rose mixture. Blend together thoroughly and then pour into jars. Within six hours at room temperature, you should have a jelled product. Use this delicious food on toast, pancakes, and in tea.

If the flowers are allowed to stay on the growing stems until they dry, wither and fall off, the round green base of the flower becomes immediately visible. If allowed to grow, the green base enlarges and eventually ripens into a beautiful orange or red fruit, usually the size of a large marble. This fruit (or hip) of the rose is an incredibly rich source of vitamin C. One cup of the cleaned hips contains as much vitamin C as 12 dozen oranges (up to 7,000 milligrams of vitamin C per pound of raw pulp).

Hips are usually eaten only after the top and bottom have been cut off, the fruit split, and the fibrous seeds scraped out. The flavor has that delightful tart snap of wild mountain pippin apples, which many people prefer to the blandness of so many commercial apples. The texture is similar to a fibrous apple. As well as eaten raw, hips can be added to salads, used in making jam, sauces, soups, and teas. Even wine can be made from the hips.

Native Americans ate the fruit, flowers, and tender tips of newly emerging stems, and brewed the leaves into tea.

Medicinal Uses Askham's *Herbal* of 1550 states:

> *Some do put rose water in a glass and they put roses with dew thereto and they make it to boile in water, then they set it in the sune tyll it be readde and this water is beste. Also drye roses put to the nose to smell do comforte the braine and the harte and quencheth spirites.*

Another interesting use of the rose is described in Ram's *Little Dodoen* of 1606:

> *Take drie rose leaves, keep them close in a glasse which will keep them sweet, then take powder of mints, powder of cloves in a grosse powder. Put the same to the rose leaves, then put all these together in a bag, and take that to bed with you, and it will cause you to sleepe, and it is good to smell unto at other times.*

Rose water is used in various medicinal mixtures.

Other Uses Fragrant petals are also used as ingredients in sachets for drawers and closets. Rose water is used for bathing, perfume, baptisms, as an additive to drinks, for medicine, mouthwash, hand lotion, and many other uses.

Rose water is best made by distillation; however, if distillation is not possible, the petals can be steeped in a tightly covered container, or even just soaked for several days in room-temperature water.

For more information on the manifold uses of roses, consult

The Edible Ornamental Garden by John E. Bryan and Coralie Castle

Stalking the Healthful Herbs by Euell Gibbons

Folklore and Symbolism of Flowers, Plants, and Trees by Bacchus

Rose Recipes from Olden Times by Eleanour Sinclair Rohde

Western Gardening Book by Sunset editors

Detrimental Properties

The main precaution in using rose petals and hips for food is to be certain that the plant hasn't been sprayed with an insecticide during the present growing season. Once sure of this, you're free to compete with the aphids for this rare wild feast.

Where Found

Wild roses are found throughout the United States and Canada along streams and around springs and wherever the soil is sufficiently moist. The rose is the most common garden plant in the entire United States. Whether in the wilderness or city, you can be sure that a rose is not far away.

Growing Cycle

The rose plant begins new growth in early spring. Though some varieties have longer flowering periods, the plant is generally in flower throughout the summer. In the fall, the rose hips begin to mature. If not picked, many of them will remain on the plant throughout the winter.

Lore and Signature

Roses are perhaps America's best-known flower. Their symbolic associations are numerous and diverse. Ancient legends abound; societies have adopted the rose as

hips or fruits from a wild rose bush

their logo (such as the Rosicrucians); the loftiest of praises and most precious adorations have been bestowed upon it; and countless sayings, books, and tales have this lovely flower as their focal point.

Roses embody both masculine and feminine traits; the beautiful and aromatic flowers are balanced with the protective thorns. The flower is also a symbol of spiritual evolution: as each petal unfolds, the golden inner self is revealed.

Allowed to mature to fruition, one of the most nutritious fruits in all of nature is produced. Yet strangely, few people recognize the value of these fruits, possibly due to humankind's penchant for something easier. Most gardeners clip and discard the brilliant orange and red hips. Possibly this corresponds to a statement Godfrey Higgins made in *Anacalypsis* (to paraphrase):

> *The true Wise Ones are never recognized by the society at large. They come, they do their Work, and they pass on, the world barely knowing who and what was in their presence. Yet, the manqués and the charlatans and the spiritual babes-in-the-woods and the false gurus attract all the attention of a world more interested in instant gratification than in the hard Work of genuine spiritual evolution.*

Rosemary (Rosmarinus officinalis)

Mint Family (Labiatae)

rosemary

Most Prominent Characteristics

Overall Shape and Size

Rosemary is a perennial shrubby plant reaching from three to six feet tall.

Stalks and Stems
The older plants develop a woody base. The stems are squarish in their cross section.

Leaves
The evergreen leaves are narrow and needlelike, growing opposite each other on the stems. The leaves are resinous, glossy green on top, and light grayish-green underneath. Each leaf is from ½ to 1 inch long. The entire plant has a strong fragrance that is unmistakable once you learn to recognize it.

Flowers
In spring and summer, the plant is covered with small blue approximately ½-inch labiate flowers that strongly attract bees.

Beneficial Properties

Edible Properties
Rosemary's very useful leaves can be gathered year-round. Both the wild varieties and the common garden rosemary can be used for flavoring soups, stews, and omelettes. Rosemary is commonly used to flavor pork, rice dishes, and fish.

Medicinal Uses
A tea made from the dried leaves is excellent for headaches and nervousness and also aids digestion and circulation. Rinsing the inside of the mouth with the tea, hot or cold, is good for the gums and for eliminating bad breath.

Other Uses
Rosemary is useful in herbal baths and shampoos. A rosemary infusion added to your bathwater not only gives a pleasant fragrance, but also helps to calm your nerves. The leaves are said to repel moths. Rosemary can be grown as a good border or hedge plant.

Detrimental Properties

We'd appreciate authenticated reports from readers.

Where Found

In the foothills, and in drier regions, rosemary does quite well. In the city, it is a common hedge and ground cover for homes and business land-scapes. Rosemary is native to the Mediterranean region.

Growing Cycle

Rosemary is a perennial whose leaves can be gathered year-round.

Lore and Signature

Rosemary has been used as the symbol of enduring love, devotion, and memory. Thus, we have the well-known saying sang by Ophelia: "There's Rosemary, that's for remembrance; pray you love, remember."

A Christian legend attributes the odor of rosemary to a stop made by Joseph, Mary, and Jesus during their flight into Egypt. Mary spread Jesus' clothes over a bush to dry. The result, in the words of the poet John Oxenham, "that bush gives forth the faint, rare, sacred sweet of Him."

Carrying a sprig of rosemary is said to ward off evil and black magic.

Rock Cooking

Not long ago, I found a flat rock measuring about ½ inch thick and roughly 10 by 7 inches in size. I decided to use this rock to practice stone cooking.

My cooking surface was the side of the rock that was completely flat. I placed my flat rock on a fire, oiled it, and then let it warm up. Then I cooked some eggs. A rock that thick takes a lot longer to heat up than a standard kitchen skillet, but once warmed, it stays warm for a long time. The egg cooked slowly and evenly and didn't burn. It tasted as good as an egg cooked in a stainless steel or cast iron skillet. There was no sand or grit whatsoever.

I became interested in cooking without modern utensils many years ago when I learned how people cooked in the distant past. In the prehorse and premetal days some 500 or more years ago, Native Americans cooked on flat stones, directly on the ashes or coals of the fire, in specially carved stone bowls, on wooden grills suspended over the fire, or in wooden bowls into which hot rocks were dropped.

Native Americans would select a piece of sandstone and carefully shape it, sometimes taking as much as a month to make a family cooking stone. It would have to be completely smooth and of an even thickness. It would be oiled and slowly heated before it would actually be used. Such a rock was the frying pan of the old days.

Russian Thistle (Salsola kali)

Goosefoot Family
(Chenopodiaceae)
Common Names Tumbleweed

Russian thistle

Most Prominent Characteristics

Overall Shape and Size This bushy plant is formed in round clumps or balls up to three feet in diameter. The plant begins almost grasslike and forms the common tumbleweed, up to three feet tall.

Stalks and Stems The color of the young stalk is pale green—almost bluish at times—fading to a tan color when mature. The stalks and axils are sometimes tinged with red.

Leaves The leaves are 1 inch to 2½ inches long, spiny and needlelike, and roundish in the cross section. When young, the leaves have fine hairs and are very tender.

Flowers The small, approximately ⅛-inch-diameter flowers consist of papery sepals (no petals) sometimes tinged with red. They are formed singly in the upper axils of the mature plant.

Seeds In autumn, when the seeds are ripe and the leaves withered, the stems are broken off or uprooted in the wind and carried across open fields and along highways, scattering seeds as they roll. A single plant may produce from 50,000 to 200,000 winged seeds, which are distributed as the plant rolls and bounces over the countryside.

Roots There is a tremendous root system of rhizomes which build themselves into a mat, much like strawberries, and dominate the environment. However, the upper part of the root that actually anchors the plant in place readily rots from rain, releasing the plant, allowing the tumbleweed to travel with the wind.

Beneficial Properties

Edible Properties The youngest, newly emerging shoots, two to five inches tall, are excellent when steamed for about five minutes. The tender tips of a more mature plant can also be carefully picked and cooked. The leaves are not recommended raw, unless chopped very fine, since they can cause irritation in the throat. The seeds contain 3.9 calories per gram, but they are difficult to harvest.

Medicinal Uses We'd appreciate authenticated reports from readers.

Other Uses Ashes of this plant were once used in Europe for a carbonate of soda called barilla.

The tumbleweed has been researched as a practical energy source: tumblelogs. The tumbleweeds are collected and compressed into logs. These logs reportedly burn four times longer than ordinary firewood.

The presence of Russian thistle indicates a soil high in iron.

In a survival situation, the plant can be used as emergency fire fuel and (if crumbled finely) in place of pine needles for bedding and/or insulation.

I've seen large tumbleweeds made into western snowmen. Two or three large balls of tumbleweeds are piled up, snowman-fashion, and then the snowman is dressed with scarf, hat, cardboard eyes and nose, and pipe.

Detrimental Properties

Tumbleweeds are considered a great problem to farmers and ranchers.

Eating the young tumbleweed shoots raw can cause a prickly irritation in the throat. They often cause injury to animals who try to eat the maturing, tougher tumbleweeds when they've begun to dry out in late spring and summer.

The plant produces an auxin which subdues anything else growing near it.

Where Found

This plant is found in dry waste areas, in the plains, and along roadsides. The plant is most common in the western United States and seldom occurs above 8,500 feet in the mountains. The plant is native to central Asia and Eastern Russia. It came to the United States in 1874 to Scotland, South Dakota, in a flax shipment from Russia.

Growing Cycle

This annual's edible shoots can be collected in the spring and early summer. Once the plant matures, it is inedible, except the seeds, which are difficult to harvest.

Sea Rocket
(Cakile edentula)
Mustard Family (Cruciferae)

sea rocket in flower

Most Prominent
Characteristics

Overall Shape and Size Sea rocket grows in low, branched clumps or mounds in the upper sandy sections of the beaches on both the Pacific and Atlantic coasts. These mounds are generally no more than two feet tall, with the weak stems sprawled on the beach.

Stalks and Stems The stalks on the mature plant are about ⅛ inch thick and somewhat fibrous. The stalks and stems on the upper parts of the plant are less fibrous. The stalks are not rigid and upright, but flexible, reclined, and sprawling.

There is a purple coloration at each joint, or axil.

Leaves The alternately arranged, bluish-green leaves are hairless, succulent, and fleshy. The upper leaves are often simply lanceolate or linear, whereas the larger lower leaves are pinnately divided into linear segments. The tips of the leaves and leaf segments are rounded. Each leaf seems to fold inward lengthwise along its central midvein. The base of each leaf is often tinted purple where its meets the stem. The leaves measure up to three inches long, with lateral leaflets usually no more than one inch in length.

The fleshly leaves measure about 1/16 inch thick (or more), and the cross cut of any section of the leaf is a U-shape.

Flowers The lavender flowers measure about ⅜ inch across. As is the case with all members of the mustard family, the flowers are formed in racemes. Also, there are four lavender petals (in a cross shape), six stamens with yellow anthers (four tall, two short), one pistil (in the middle of the stamens), and four purplish-green sepals under each petal. The unopened flower buds on the top of the raceme resemble a small head of broccoli.

Seeds Possibly, the plump seed pods are the source of the name *rocket*. Each plump and succulent pod looks like a Native American's spear head, complete with the two small downward-turning projectiles. There is a seam along both sides of this pod.

Beneficial Properties

Edible Properties Sample a bit of the fresh leaf while hiking on the beach, and you'll enjoy the salty, horseradish flavor of the juicy, succulent leaf. A handful of the fresh, young leaves, chopped finely, makes a flavorful addition to most salads, such as lettuce or potato salad. Don't add too much, though. Add about ⅓ cup of the chopped leaves to an average dinner salad for four people. Like horseradish, a little is fine, but a lot can be miserable. Pick the larger leaves for your salad, and wash them before using to get rid of any sand.

Another way to enjoy this plant is to steam a pot of the freshly picked leaves. Cooking mellows the horseradish flavor. With older plants, cooking is essential since the leaves become bitter with age.

The chopped leaves and tender pods can be added to soups, chowder, cooked egg dishes, and stews. The tender stems and pods can also be pickled.

While hiking on the beach at Point Reyes National Seashore (north of San Francisco), my friends and I spotted an old, partially dried-up sea rocket plant from the previous season. The plant had already produced and dropped hundreds of seeds into the sand. Under the plant, we saw hundreds of tiny sea rocket sprouts, each no more than two inches long. We carefully collected a bag of the tender sprouts for our dinner. That evening, we washed all the sprouts to eliminate the sand. We used half of the sea rocket sprouts mixed with miner's lettuce for our salad. The rest of the sprouts we added to our clam chowder (made with fresh clams). These young sprouts were tender and delicious and not nearly as strongly flavored as the leaves on the mature plant. You probably won't find these sprouts year-round—only in the late winter and spring.

Medicinal Uses We'd appreciate authenticated reports from readers.

Other Uses We'd appreciate authenticated reports from readers.

Detrimental Properties
Be sure that you don't collect sea rocket on those beaches where sewers empty directly into the ocean, since this may affect the plant's safety.

Where Found
Sea rocket is found along the Pacific and Atlantic Coasts in the upper zones of sandy beaches where the soil is a bit more stable. It can be found a few hundred feet from the shore, on the cliffs overlooking the beach, in the coastal back bays, and even along the coastal rivers that feed into the ocean.

Growing Cycle
Sea rocket is an annual that produces seed in the fall when the plant dies. These seeds sprout in early winter and spring. The plant is available for picking throughout most of the spring and summer. In fact, there are usually some leaves to be found year-round, but not in large amounts during the off-season.

Seaweeds (All species)

Brown, Red, and Green Algae (Phaeo-, Rhodo-, and Chlorophyceae)

Most Prominent Characteristics

Musician Jon Sherman looks at Pacific Ocean kelp (seaweed).

Overall Shape and Size The marine algae, taken as a whole, constitute a vast array of shapes, sizes, and colors.

All algae are nonflowering plants, one of the two categories of thallophytes (the other category is fungi). Thallophytes, growing in both water and on land, are the simplest of all plants, which means that they're not differentiated into roots, stems, and leaves as in the higher (or more complex) plants.

Although all marine algae contain chlorophyll, they are distinctly colored by pigments. The variety of their coloration is so great that pigmentation plays an important role in marine algae classification.

Brown Algae

The color, which ranges from brown to muddy yellow, comes from the pigment fucoxanthin. Although this group includes some small, almost microscopic members, larger seaweeds with leathery textures predominate. The variety of shapes ranges from several-hundred-feet-long kelps, to whiplike fronds, to leaflike structures of one to three feet in diameter. All large brown algae (this includes several genera of kelp, plus rockweed, and sargassum) anchor themselves to rocks. This anchoring is accomplished by means of holdfasts, which are structures similar in appearance to roots of land plants. Their tough outer layer renders them relatively immune to being rubbed by fish and to the beating they receive when they're broken off and washed ashore. They're held upright by hundreds of air bladders. There are approximately 1,000 species of brown algae.

Red Algae

On the whole, the red algae are smaller than the browns. They're also more delicately shaped, often appearing as graceful, branching ferns in hues ranging from violet, to red, to purple, to pink. Some are lance shaped with wrinkly margins; others have wide elastic fronds, and look like sheer sheets of plastic with ruffled margins. Some grow as thin filaments or leaflike structures. The reds include Irish moss (Chondrus crispus), laver (Porphyra spp.), dulse (Rhodymenia palmata), and Grinnellia. There are approximately 2,500 species of red algae.

Green Algae

These also grow as filaments or branching fronds. The most commonly eaten seaweed in this group is sea lettuce (Ulva lactuca). Most green algae are found in fresh water. There are approximately 5,000 species of marine green algae.

Once washed ashore, seaweed seems to be nothing more than gooey, smelly, fly-infested garbage. However, as unpalatable as they might seem, seaweeds are, in fact, extremely important plants. They're not only nutritious eaten as is or lightly cooked; they're also usable for many nonfood aspects of survival, for example, in fertilizers, paper, binding pills together, and nutritional supplements.

Stems Seaweeds contain no stems in the botanical sense of the word. The section in seaweed that resembles land-plant stems is called the stipe.

Leaves Technically, seaweeds contain no leaves. However, to the layperson's eye, many seaweeds appear to be one large leaf, or expanded flat leaves or ribbons. Other seaweeds have the appearance of a head of lettuce. In the brown algae group, the part of the seaweed that resembles land-plant leaves is called the lamina. This is where photosynthesis occurs.

Roots Seaweeds contain no roots. However, many seaweeds have a specialized region that enables them to attach to rocks. These are called rhizomes, horizontal-growing stemlike growths, which acts much like the rhizomes of land plants, upon which grow rootlike tough fibers called holdfasts, which anchor the seaweed to rocks.

Reproduction Reproduction of seaweed occurs in one of three ways: 1) by the division of the whole body of the parent plant (vegetative reproduction); 2) sexual reproduction; or 3) asexual reproduction.

Beneficial Properties

Edible Properties Although the conspicuous red, brown, and green marine algae are, for the most part, a safe group to consume, botanists disagree as to exactly how safe. Some believe that seaweeds are completely nontoxic (which doesn't mean they are edible). Others point out that certain known macroscopic species of these three groups of marine algae are toxic to other marine life, and thus humans should exercise caution. Furthermore, the seaweeds have not all been studied adequately to simply recommend eating them unreservedly. Becoming more specifically acquainted with individual seaweeds certainly seems appropriate. Books that are useful in this regard are:

Stalking the Blue Eyed Scallop by Euell Gibbons

Seashores, a Golden Nature Guide

Seaweeds and Their Uses by Valentine J. Chapman

The Seavegetable Book by Judith Madlener

Some seaweeds are simply unpalatable due to their rubbery texture, and rigid structure, which can be overcome by drying and powdering or by various cooking methods. What works for one seaweed may not work for another. Only by experience will you be able to learn which seaweeds are more palatable than others. As you experiment, don't rely *only* on your taste buds' first reaction—try ingenious ways of using seaweeds.

Generally, seaweeds are used

1) for food directly (eaten raw, cooked into soup, and so forth);

2) as a seasoning and/or flavoring (due to their salt and minerals);

3) in any food product requiring thickening, smoothing, or jelling, such as candies, jellies, puddings, ice creams, and gravies; and

4) as a combination steaming/flavoring agent in clambakes. Some of the tastiest seaweeds are dulse, laver, sea lettuce, kelp, and Irish moss.

Those seaweeds that can be eaten raw can be either eaten fresh (from sea or beach) or dried first and then chewed like jerky. Boiling is preferred in some cases where the seaweeds are bone-dry. Others become more palatable after cooking (up to 30 minutes) in water; both the resulting broth and the seaweed will usually be very good. When the broth cools, it will normally gel, making it useful in various dessert items.

Dried and powdered/shredded seaweed is an excellent item to carry in your survival pack. Placed in a pot of water with other wild vegetables, seaweed makes the closest thing to instant soup that's available from the wild.

Most of the hollow stalks and air bladders of the brown algae can be eaten raw or pickled. I've tried the following recipe with the air bladders of the Pacific Coast kelp, and found it delicious! Pack approximately 100 raw air bladders (alone or with other pickling vegetables, such as cauliflower, onion, and sliced carrot) into clean quart jars. Add apple cider vinegar until the air bladders are nearly covered, and then add one to two tablespoons of cold-pressed olive oil. Sprinkle in your favorite pickling herbs (such as dill seed, tarragon, and celery powder), and add approximately 10 freshly sliced garlic cloves. Cap tightly and shake once or twice a day for a few days. These air bladders can then be eaten as is or as a side to Mexican dishes as a chili pepper substitute.

Many seaweeds can serve the same thickening function as okra does in soups. Tender seaweeds can be added directly to soups; the less tender seaweeds are better broken into bits, blended in an electric blender to a fine mush, then strained through a fine mesh or muslin cloth to remove the solids. Then bottle, label, and refrigerate. This liquid can then be used as the soup or gravy base, substituting for flour. The strained-out pulp also has many uses—it can be cooked into homemade ice cream as a smoother/stabilizer, can be used for compost, mulch, or earthworm food, or can be added to animal foods.

The algin that is used to smooth commercial ice cream is obtained from brown algae. Algin is also used as a thickener or smoother in many other foods, such as puddings, jellies, and candies. In packaged foods, the ingredients alginate, alginic acid, and carrageenin are all seaweed derivatives.

Seaweeds have long been used in clambakes. When heated, they give off a steam that adds flavor to other food being cooked near them. Thus, seaweed is thrown directly into large fire pits next to meat, seafood, potatoes, corn, and so on. Seaweeds can also flavor and help steam foods at home if you add a layer of them to both the bottom and top of any large pot or roasting pan containing meat or vegetables.

In 1958, wilderness expert George L. Herter wrote in his *Professional Guide Manual* about some of the fresh water green algae. Herter writes:

Pond scum or green algae is a wonderful food eaten either in liquid or dried form. Green algae, which makes up the scum, contains more than 50 percent easily digestible protein. This is more than potatoes or wheat. Dried green algae tastes like raw Lima beans or pumpkin. Pond scum soup or liquid green algae has a raw pumpkin-like taste. You can stay healthy and even put on weight on a diet of green algae. If the ponds are frozen over, simply chop out some of the frozen pond scum and melt it over a fire.

The Japanese, as I write this in 1958, are leading the world in producing food from algae. They are now mass producing an artificial food called chlorela. This food is made entirely of algae. Twenty five grams of chlorela powdered is equal in nutrition content to 1.5 bottles of milk, 1.2 eggs, or 25 grams of roast beef. Algae today are the world's most important single item. Algae are far more important to the world than atomic energy. Atomic energy can create power and heat but cannot produce food. Algae can create food in unlimited quantities and can go on creating it with no loss to the parent stock and with no raw materials except water and sunlight. The more impure the water, the faster algae grow and multiply. As for energy, algae can produce more usable energy than any substance in the world.

With ten dwellings to the acre, the whole population of the earth could be housed in an area the size of Kansas. By raising algae in the remaining area of the state, enough food could be produced to feed over ten times the people that now live in the whole world.

When people foolishly talk about food shortages in this world, just remind them of these proven facts.

George Herter wrote these words over 40 years ago, and the booming world population has undoubtedly altered his figures. Nevertheless, his message is an extremely important one.

I've eaten fresh green algae from mountain streams many times. The flavor is bland, with a somewhat crisp texture. On July 3, 1982, I tested some methods of preparing green algae. I collected fresh green algae from Eaton Canyon on Pasadena's east side, washed them, and then sautéed them in oil. The algae nearly liquified. The flavor was acceptable, though somewhat bland. John Watkins of Harbor City suggested that I first dry the green algae and then sauté it. The final product would be very similar to eggs.

Interestingly, a bottle of "Spirulina" pills sells for nearly $10. Spirulina is actually a blue-green algae. While spirulina is excellent nutritionally, so are most of the thousands of fresh water green algaes. Rather than give away my hard-earned dollars, I prefer my green algae fresh!

Medicinal Uses Most iodine is obtained from two sources: brown algae and red algae. Iodine, necessary for the proper functioning of the thyroid gland, has been used for the treatment of goiter for over 5,000 years. Goiter is an enlargement of the thyroid gland, visible as a swelling on the front of the neck.

In his book on nutrition, *Are You Confused?*, Paavo Airola lists kelp as 1 of the 10 plants that help the body's glands reach their peak of healthy activity. Many seaweeds—most commonly kelp—when powdered yield potassium chloride, a salt substitute. This is a godsend particularly for those who must restrict the amount of sodium chloride in their diet. By dry weight, kelp is about 30 percent potassium chloride.

Red algae is the source of agar (also called agar-agar), used for the laboratory culture of bacteria. Algin, from brown algae, is used in many medicines such as cough medicines and laxatives. The gelatinous material extracted by boiling seaweeds can also be used as a remedy for burns and bruises or as a hand lotion.

One hundred grams of dulse contain 3.2 grams of fat, 296 milligrams of calcium, 267 milligrams of phosphorus, 2,085 milligrams of sodium, and 8,060 milligrams of potassium. One hundred grams of Irish moss contains 1.8 grams of fat, 2.1 grams of fiber, 17.6 grams of ash, 885 milligrams of calcium, 157 milligrams of phosphorus, 8.9 milligrams of iron, 2,892 milligrams of sodium, and 2,844 milligrams of potassium. One hundred grams of kelp contain 1,093 milligrams of calcium, 240 milligrams of phosphorus, 3,000 milligrams of sodium, and 5,273 milligrams of potassium.

Other Uses Pacific seaweeds, mostly brown algae, have been used as a source of potassium for fertilizer. Ernest Hogeboom, formerly a professional gardener in Pasadena, California, once showed me his "secret" fertilizer. Into a 55-gallon drum he emptied several trash bags full of kelp, then filled the drum with fresh water and put on the lid. As the seaweed began to decompose, it colored the water dark brown. Within about two months, almost all of the seaweed liquified. This liquid was used as a fertilizer concentrate, which Ernest diluted with fresh water before using on customers' plants.

The liquid that is extracted by grinding seaweed in a blender and straining out the pulp can be used for a mineral bath. Diluted until there's no ocean odor left, it can be used as a water softener for doing the laundry, enabling you to cut back on soap about 30 to 40 percent.

The long flat stipes of some seaweeds, if treated with a leather softener such as Stock Slick, can be used as an interim lashing/binding material (preferably in places where they won't get wet). The long hollow stipes of some of the kelps have been used as fishing lines for deep-sea fishing by Native Americans in Alaska. These same stipes, along with any of the stringy segments of seaweeds, can, if the need arises, be woven into moccasins, mats, baskets, and pot holders, and even be used for short-term furniture and clothing repair.

Algin from brown algae is used as an additive to hand lotions, inks, and dyes. Thousands of tons of kelps are used annually in the chemical industries.

Detrimental Properties

Be certain that the seaweed you gather for food hasn't been sitting on the beach long enough to begin rotting. Seaweed that has already begun to decompose contains bacteria that will cause sickness if eaten.

Any seaweeds growing near a sewage effluent or by mouths of rivers, bays, or inlets where pollution is being dumped readily pick up the toxins in their bodies, and thus become "poisonous." Such seaweeds should not be eaten. Don't collect seaweeds for consumption after an oil spill.

Be sure to *thoroughly wash* your seaweed before consumption. This elminates any adhering sand and many harmful substances. A suggested method, especially if the purity of the ocean water is questionable, is to wash the seaweed in your bathtub or sink. First wash in hot water with a small amount of biodegradable soap, then drain. Repeat the wash and drain process three times in the hottest tap water possible. Finally, rinse at least once in unsoapy water. Then you can dry the seaweed or cook it into a variety of recipes.

Where Found

By definition, seaweeds are the brown, red, and green algae found in marine waters. Brown algae thrive on the east and west coasts of the United States and in many other oceans of the world. Red algae is most abundant on rocky coasts of warm water on both the east and west coasts. Green algae are more commonly found inhabiting fresh or brackish waters. The greens that are found in marine waters are found along both the east and west coasts, most abundantly in warm waters.

Growing Cycle

Many seaweeds are perennials. They are easiest to gather at low tides. Some are better quality in the spring; others are equally good gathered throughout the year. Often one can ask the locals which seaweeds are the best in the area, and when the best time is to gather them.

Ocean waters near any of the world's major population centers may indeed be toxic, but not because of the salt. Various forms of urban waste water routinely flow into oceans worldwide. Such wastewater can contain biological contaminants and dangerous chemicals. The water can be bad as much as two miles out to sea, especially during and immediately after rainstorms, when the water treatment systems are unable to handle the increased water flow. During such circumstances, all forms of waste flow directly into the ocean, untreated.

Is Salt Water Poisonous?

When we refer to ocean water as salt water, you would think we're talking about water with sodium chloride. In fact, ocean water contains 20 or more suspended minerals. The *toxic* quality of ocean water has more to do with the way people have consumed it during emergencies, rather than its inherent quality. Rapid drinking and gulping in order to quench one's thirst is often a culprit, since this way of consuming ocean water can lead to vomiting and a net loss of water.

On the other hand, virtually everyone who has survived a shipwreck or whose ship was stranded at sea has consumed ocean water. These survivors disciplined themselves to slowly sip and then chew—never gulp—the ocean water.

Shepherd's Purse (Capsella bursa-pastoris)

Mustard Family (Cruciferae)

Photo by Vickie Shufer

shepherd's purse with seeds

Most Prominent Characteristics

Overall Shape and Size This slender annual grows from 6 to 18 inches tall, appearing as an inconspicuous stalk with a minimum of leaves. When young, the plant is a low-growing rosette, often unseen in lawns or fields.

Stalks and Stems The branching slender green flower stalks rise usually no more than about 18 inches tall.

Leaves The toothed basal leaves are deeply incised with the terminal lobe the largest. The leaves which grow high on the flower stalks are arrowhead shaped, stalkless, and toothed on the margin but not generally incised. The leaves are sparsely covered with stiff bristlelike hairs. The basal leaves spread in a rosette at ground level.

Flowers The terminal clusters of small white flowers, often tinged with purple, are in the typical mustard family configuration (four green sepals, four petals, six stamens—four large and two small—and one pistil), occurring in elongated clusters (racemes).

Fruits Flat, heart-shaped green fruits or seed pods are *very* distinctive. They are borne along the flower stalks. These notched pods are almost identical in general configuration to a type of purse carried by the shepherds of southern Europe.

Seeds The small, orange-brown seeds can be easily collected from the mature plant and winnowed between the hands. Approximately 64,000 seeds are produced from one mature plant each season. Since the seeds can thrive in almost any soil, the plant's worldwide distribution is not surprising.

Roots The slender taproot is approximately the same size and shape as the main, above-ground stalk.

Beneficial Properties

Edible Properties Shepherd's purse leaves make a tasty salad, which even the most finicky people will find agreeable. The flavor is similar to that of mild watercress. The leaves can also be cooked, which is common throughout China.

An analysis of 100 grams (about ½ cup) of the leaves shows 208 milligrams of calcium, 86 milligrams of phosphorus, 40 milligrams of sodium, 394 milligrams of potassium, 36 milligrams of vitamin C, and 1,554 international units of vitamin A.

The seeds can be collected from the mature pods and eaten directly or ground into flour. Some Native Americans ground the seeds into pinole.

The seeds are often used in birdseed mixes.

Medicinal Uses   Cahuilla Native Americans reportedly used the leaves as a tea to treat dysentery. A decoction of the entire plant is used to stop internal or external bleeding. A cotton ball soaked in this tea is useful to stop a nosebleed.

Shepherd's purse was used medicinally by the ancient Greeks and Romans and was popular all over Europe into the Middle Ages. The entire plant is eaten raw or cooked, and the effect is astringent, diuretic, and antiscorbutic.

Other Uses   I've observed that the heart-shaped pods seem to be most abundant on the plants (around Valentine's Day). Due to this remarkable coincidence, clusters of the stalks with pods may make an ideal Valentine's Day gift for a loved one. As an added bonus, such a gift would provide the opportunity to introduce the loved one to the wild foods, that lie outside the doorway, in the yard, garden, and sidewalk cracks.

Detrimental Properties
We'd appreciate authenticated reports from readers.

Where Found
This Mediterranean native, which has naturalized throughout most of the world, is common throughout the United States.

Growing Cycle
This annual (sometimes acts as a biennial) begins its rosette of leaves in early spring and has usually matured and died by early summer.

Sow Thistle (Sonchus oleraceus)
Sunflower Family (Compositae)
Common Names Milkweed, tall dandelion

Photo by David Santana

Christopher examines a sow thistle plant.

Most Prominent Characteristics

Overall Shape and Size
Commonly mistaken for dandelion, sow thistle is an annual weed with a more or less erect leafy stem from one foot to four feet tall.

Leaves The young plant forms a rosette of large pinnately divided leaves, which are characterized by their almost triangular terminal lobe. The young sow thistle is distinguished from dandelion by its tender bluish-green leaves, which are coated with a type of powdery substance. The lower leaves on the mature plant are glaucous and pinnately divided. The upper leaves of the mature plant are more or less entire, and they clasp the stem. When a leaf is torn or the stem is cut, a white sap oozes out.

Flowers The yellow flower heads are clustered at the top of the plant. The flower heads closely resemble dandelion flowers except that the base of each sow thistle flower is somewhat swollen. Each flower head of sow thistle, like dandelion, is made up entirely of ray flowers. Sow thistle can be easily distinguished from dandelion since dandelion flowers appear singly on each flower stalk, whereas sow thistle flowers appear in groups on the stalk. Also, unlike sow thistle, dandelion flower stalks are leafless. The flowers of sow thistle mature into cottony heads that children love to blow away. Each seed has numerous soft hairs attached to it, which facilitate the seed's dispersal by the wind.

Beneficial Properties

Edible Properties Although raw sow thistle leaves are slightly bitter, many people still enjoy them in salads when mixed with other greens or covered with a light oil and vinegar dressing. The young cooked leaves make a mild dish similar to spinach popularly enjoyed the world over. Pinch off just the leaves for cooking, preferably the large lower ones. The upper leaves are also acceptable but tend to be more bitter and may require longer boiling. For an interesting dish, cook a pot of sow thistle leaves with onions, rice, chopped walnuts, and butter.

The stout stems of the just-beginning-to-flower plant are tasty eaten raw. They need to be first peeled of their thin (and slightly bitter) outer layer, which is usually tinged with red. These stems are good in salads and can be steamed or added to soups.

The roots can be used for a coffee substitute like the dandelion root, although the result is inferior to dandelion root coffee. The roots need to be dug, washed, dried, and then roasted dark brown. Then they are ground and percolated into your coffee.

Medicinal Uses The bitter white sap of the stems and leaves has been used to formulate an agent to combat opium addiction. The work involved to do this, however, hardly justifies the results.

Other Uses For children, sow thistle is a source of joy. They love to blow the mature seed clusters and watch the tiny seeds float away on their cottony tufts of hair.

Detrimental Properties
We'd appreciate authenticated reports from readers.

Where Found
This European native has now naturalized throughout much of the world. It is found in virtually all gardens and is vigorously pulled and discarded year after year. In most vacant lots, untended lawns, parks, and even in sidewalk cracks in downtown areas you can expect to find sow thistle. In the mountain areas, it is found mainly along the streams in sandy soil and occasionally in moist fields and meadows.

Growing Cycle
Sow thistle is an annual. The leaves and roots are best gathered in the spring before the plant has flowered.

Thistle (Cirsium spp.)
Sunflower Family (Compositae)

Most Prominent Characteristics

Overall Shape and Size There are
many species of thistle, all of which
resemble one another. Thistle normally reaches four to five feet at
maturity. They are either perennial
or biennial herbs.

Leaves Thistle has alternate leaves
that are prickly or spiny and generally toothed. They measure
approximately eight inches long,
depending on the age of the plant.

young thistle plant

Flowers The flowers, approximately ½ inch to 2 inches tall, are clustered
in heads that appear bristly and burlike. The flowers are crimson, purple,
pink, and, occasionally, white. The lower half of the flower heads are covered with spiny bracts. In fact, when you eat an artichoke, you're eating
the tender portions of the bracts of an unopened flower of a cultivated
thistle. Thus, wild thistle flowers resemble small artichokes.

Beneficial Properties

Edible Properties When thistle is young and the leaves are still in a basal
rosette, the roots are edible. The roots are starchy and by themselves make
a rather flat-tasting meal. As thistle begins to flower, the root becomes
steadily more fibrous, since the starch is used by the growing stalk.

The stalk of thistle baked, lightly cooked, or eaten raw is the best food
the plant produces. The stalk must be cut when the flower buds are forming, but not yet mature. (Stalks gathered when the flowers are mature are
generally fibrous and inedible.) Preparation is simple: peel or scrape off
the fibrous outer layer and enjoy! The flavor is similar to that of celery.

Being related to artichoke (all of you who've impaled a fingertip on
an artichoke bract can readily believe that artichoke is a thistle), some of
the thistle flowers have edible hearts. The heart is at the bottom of the
flower (where it meets the stem). Cook the entire flower; then remove the
flowers, and you're left with the edible heart. Do not expect a great deal of
food from this part of the plant. Some thistles, in fact, have so little edible
heart that they'd hardly be worth the trouble if they didn't taste so good
and weren't so packed with nutrition.

Medicinal Uses We'd appreciate authenticated reports from readers.

Other Uses We'd appreciate authenticated reports from readers.

Detrimental Properties

When handling or gathering parts of the thistle plant, protect your hands from the sharp spines with something, such as a pair of gloves, a rag, or a brown paper bag.

Where Found

Since there are so many types of thistle, one variety or another can be found growing in most any type of soil or environment, be it desert, mountain, forest, field, valley, swamp, riverside, or backyard. This European native is the floral emblem of Scotland.

Growing Cycle

Thistles are either perennial or biennial herbs. Roots are generally collected in the winter and spring, the tender stems, in the spring, and the flower heads, in the late summer and spring.

Toothwort
(Dentaria californica)
Mustard Family (Cruciferae)
Common Names Wild horse-radish, pepper-root, milk maids

flowering toothwort

Most Prominent Characteristics

Overall Shape and Size
Toothwort rises 8 to 12 inches from a stout, fleshy tuber. Due to its somewhat weak stem, it often crawls along the ground. In areas where the plant is abundant, hillsides and valleys are colored white in spring.

Stems The stems are generally not branched and are sparingly leafy.

Leaves The basal leaves are trifoliolate (having three leaflets), roundish, egg shaped, or kidney shaped. The stem leaves are tri- to quinquefoliolate (having three to five leaflets), lanceolate or linear. The leaves are glabrous (not hairy).

Flowers The white- to rose-tinted four-petaled flowers have the typical mustard family floral arrangement of four petals in a cross shape, four sepals, six stamens (four tall, two short), and one pistil. The flowers, approximately ½ inch across, are arranged in a raceme.

Roots Toothwort's characteristic features are the sharp mustard taste and odor of the tuber. The young tuber is white, roundish, and about ¼ inch in diameter; older tubers are tan, about two inches of knotty ½-inch diameter sections.

Beneficial Properties

Edible Properties Toothwort, a relative of true horseradish, is used more commonly for a flavoring or seasoning than as a staple. Its mustard flavor pleasantly spices salads and sandwiches, so long as the tubers are sliced thin before being added. The sliced or diced tubers can be cooked with meat or greens. Cooked, of course, the tubers become somewhat milder. You may even like to carry a few roots in your pocket while hiking to chew on when you're feeling tired. The brief stimulating effect may be the extra boost you need.

Medicinal Uses We'd appreciate authenticated reports from readers.

Other Uses We'd appreciate authenticated reports from readers.

Detrimental Properties
We'd appreciate authenticated reports from readers.

Where Found
Toothwort grows in woods, fields, and hillsides throughout California and Oregon. Other species of toothwort grow in the eastern United States.

Toothwort grows best on moist, shady hillsides where the leaf mulch is thick; in dry soil it grows poorly. If the stems are pulled, the tuber will stay in the ground; you must dig well into the soil in order to get the tuber. Thus, it is difficult, without sturdy tools, to get tubers where the soil is hard, but in the thick mulch that the plant prefers, it seems almost too easy to dig them out. We strongly urge you to pull up the tubers only when you really need to eat them. And even then, if you break or cut off two small sections and replant them, there'll be some for the next person who may be in an emergency situation.

Growing Cycle
Toothwort is a perennial. Its roots can be gathered year-round. The plant flowers in the spring, which is the time this plant is most noticeable.

Toyon (Heteromeles arbutifolia)

Rose Family (Rosaceae)

Common Names Christmas berry, California holly, native holly

toyon berries

Most Prominent Characteristics

Overall Shape and Size Toyon's greatest claim to fame is the fact that it is the plant after which Hollywood, California, is named. Many toyons still cover the hills in Hollywood's northern section. It is commonly called California Holly, although it is not a holly, botanically speaking. Toyon is found as both a shrub and as a small tree. It grows from 15 to 30 feet tall.

Leaves

The leaves are oblong (approximately three times longer than broad, tapering at each end from the wider middle), leathery, and evenly toothed. They vary from two to three inches long, are dark green on the top, and somewhat lighter green underneath.

Flowers The white, five-petaled, approximately ¼-inch broad flowers that form in terminal clusters appear in summer.

Fruit The flowers are followed by conspicuous ¼-inch red-orange fruits that resemble tiny apples.

Beneficial Properties

Edible Properties The berries are edible raw, but tend to be somewhat bitter, astringent, and dry tasting. For best results, the berries should be lightly baked, steamed or soaked in water, and then cooked. Cooked berries add an excellent dessert to any wild food meal, the taste varying from sour (lemony) to sweet. A tablespoon of honey greatly enhances the flavor of a pot of cooked toyon berries.

If you wish to eat the berries raw, their palatability is highly improved simply by soaking them in water. If you boil, crush, and sweeten the berries, you'll have a passable wild applesauce.

John Watkins of Harbor City, California, passes along a recipe that he got from an old Gabrielino woman. First you boil the toyon fruit. (At this stage, worms will often emerge.) Then you dry the fruit in the sun. Next, add some crystalized honey (or honey that has been boiled down) into a brown paper sack. As an option, you can add cinnamon. Put all the toyon berries into this sack, and then toast in your oven. Occasionally shake the sack. Soon the honey will melt and cover the berries. The resultant berries will be chewy and crispy—almost like raisins.

The berries can also be boiled and crushed, the pulp strained and sweetened to produce a delectable cider.

Linda Sheer, who was raised in rural Kentucky, makes a food called brickle from various wild berries, including toyon. Starting with ½ gallon of ripe toyon berries in a pot, she adds a little water and boils. She adds ½ cup of honey to the berries. She cooks the toyon berries for 15 minutes, stirring regularly. Reducing the heat to a simmer, she then drops small balls of biscuit dough into the berries. The mixture is cooked a little longer until the biscuit dough is done. The result is a rich, heavy dessert.

According to Sheer, this is one way leftovers were preserved in the old days. After the evening meal, all leftovers were added to the brickle pot, cooked, flour added, and then made into bricks. This brick would be set over the campfire to bake. Brickle would then be reconstituted the following night, with new berries added from that day's travels.

Another way to use toyon berries is to dry and powder them and then use them as you'd use flour.

Toyon is a versatile food, especially valuable since it provides fresh fruit in winter.

Medicinal Uses We'd appreciate authenticated reports from readers.

Other Uses John Linthurst from Altadena, California, uses toyon berries when fishing. "I pick the berries myself from the trees along the trail. When I spot a good-looking fish pond, I test it by throwing in some berries and watching for fish movement. Since the toyon berries sink slowly, they'll bring out the fish if there are any in the pool. This really saves on bait."

Detrimental Properties
Edson Johnson from La Canada, California, warns readers not to make tea from the toyon leaves since, like some other members of the rose family, they contain enough cyanide to cause cyanide poisoning.

Where Found
Generally, toyon grows in lower elevations in dry chaparral areas. Although it can often be found near streams, it is rarely found growing in stream banks, as is the case with trees such as willow, alder, and sycamore.

Growing Cycle
Toyon fruit is unique in that the greatest crop of ripe fruit is available during the winter when other wild fruit are out of season. Some early ripening berries will be found in the fall, and some can still be found well into spring. The toyon tree (or bush) is an evergreen.

POISON

Tree Tobacco
(Nicotiana glauca)
Nightshade Family
(Solanaceae)
Common Names Indian tobacco

Most Prominent
Characteristics

poisonous flowers of the tree tobacco

Overall Shape and Size Due to its relatively long petioles (leaf stalks) and the distance between the leaves, tree tobacco is often described as loosely branched. It is generally 6 to 9 feet tall, though it can reach as high as 12 feet in optimum conditions.

Stalks As the plant matures, it becomes almost treelike, but the narrow branches tend to arch over and droop with the weight of the fruit.

Leaves The ovoid leaves are entire (not toothed), glabrous (not hairy), bluish green, and alternately arranged. The leaves of the new young plant are extremely large, sometimes up to two feet in length. The average length of a leaf, however, is approximately six inches. As the plant matures, the leaves become much smaller—from one inch to three inches.

Flowers Bees and hummingbirds are attracted to the two-inch-long yellow, tubular flowers, which appear on the plant in terminal panicles.

Beneficial Properties

Edible Properties *Poisonous! Not for food!* This plant is one of our most poisonous. However, it often attracts hummingbirds, who collect nectar and eat the insects inside the tubular yellow flowers.

Medicinal Uses A poultice made from the leaves of this plant was occasionally used as a pain killer on cuts and was applied to a rattlesnake bite after an attempt had been made to suck out the venom. The leaves were also placed against the gums to relieve the pain of a toothache.

Other Uses The tree tobacco, closely related to commercial tobacco, has been used as a ceremonial smoke by Native Americans. This is a powerful smoke, with a much higher nicotine content than that of commercial cigarettes.

A dense tea brewed from the tree tobacco leaves can be used as an insect repellent and can be sprayed directly onto roses, vegetables, and animal pens and cages. Cook an ample concentration of fresh leaves in water in a big (covered) pot for an hour. Let cool, then strain and spray on your plants. The nicotine kills the bugs. You might wish to add a biodegradable detergent, such as Basic H by Shaklee, to the tobacco tea, so it will better adhere to the foliage once sprayed.

poisonous tree tobacco leaves

Detrimental Properties

When very young, tree tobacco resembles young pokeweed (Phytolacca americana) and is sometimes eaten by mistake. If tree tobacco is eaten, it can cause vomiting, stomach pains, diarrhea, general weakness, irregular pulse, shaking, convulsion of muscles, and even death. (Pokeweed, with its bright, glossy-green leaves, is uncommon in the southwestern and western United States where tree tobacco is found. The mature pokeweed's stalk turns bright violet, unlike that of the tree tobacco, which remains bluish-green.)

Where Found

This native of South America is now found along the flood beds of streams, along trails, and the least hospitable arid wasteland areas all over the southwestern and western United States. The plant's genus name, Nicotiana, is derived from the French diplomat Jean Nicot, who brought tobacco from Portugal into France.

Growing Cycle

Tree tobacco is a shrub. The new plants start to appear in late winter.

Watercress
(Nasturtium officinale)
Mustard Family (Cruciferae)

Photo by Doug Hajpt

Most Prominent Characteristics

Overall Shape and Size
Watercress can be found growing prostrate, floating in the water, or erect with its white roots often showing at the nodes of the floating stem.

Stalks and Stems The stalks of watercress are typically ⅛ to ¼

watercress flowers

inch in diameter, growing to a thickness of ½ inch in some older plants. The stalks are hollow and are often streaked with reddish pigment.

Leaves The hairless leaves are odd-pinnate (the leaflets are arranged opposite each other on a common stalk with a large single leaflet at the end).

Flowers The small, ¼-inch, four-petaled flowers are white.

Beneficial Properties

Edible Properties Wild watercress, the same plant that can be found in the more complete produce stores, can be eaten in salads or as lightly cooked or fried greens. An excellent source of vitamins and minerals, it includes a substantial portion of vitamin C and is one of the best sources of vitamin E (which helps the body use oxygen and increases physical endurance). Eaten raw in salads, it has an enjoyable peppery or mustardy flavor.

An analysis of 100 grams (about ½ cup) shows 151 milligrams of calcium, 54 milligrams of phosphorus, 52 milligrams of sodium, 282 milligrams of potassium, 4,900 international units of vitamin A, and 790 milligrams of vitamin C.

If you suspect that the water where you gather the green is polluted, soak the watercress in water in which the solution from iodine crystals has been added. On the other hand, cooking the greens makes this procedure unnecessary.

Watercress, steamed like spinach and seasoned, makes a tasty dish. Sautéing watercress with eggs and/or nopales (see Prickly Pear) and onions will produce an excellent meal. Season with soy sauce before serving. You'll have a healthful dish that'll be hard to refuse. For extra flavor, you can add edible wild tubers such as toothwort, chopped fine.

The watercress leaves can also be dried, powdered, and used as a seasoning to flavor foods.

Watercress soup is incredible. Here's a successful recipe:

Watercress Soup

4 cups milk
Dash salt (or powdered seaweed)
1 cup watercress
Paprika

Heat, but don't boil, three cups of milk in a pot. Add salt. Blend (or mince) watercress and add to hot milk. Cover and steep for five minutes. Add remaining cup of milk, cover, and heat again for five minutes, being careful that the mixture does not boil. Ladle into bowls and lightly sprinkle with paprika, garnish with a sprig of watercress, and enjoy a truly fine bowl of soup.

Medicinal Uses Watercress is used by herbalists as a diuretic, expectorant, for gout, and for stomach aches. Xenophon, an ancient Greek historian and general, and Xerxes, a Persian king, both observed that those who ate watercress invariably maintained better health. They thus recommended that their soldiers include watercress in their diets. The Greeks had a proverb that called watercress a wit-producing food.

Other Uses The stems of the large older plants are long and hollow. So, if being chased, grab a hollow watercress stalk, plunge your body entirely under water, and breathe through the stalk. And while you're lying there in that swamp water, you may even find a tadpole or a crawdad for dinner.

Detrimental Properties
Watercress will grow in almost any slow-moving water, and if the water is polluted, the plants may be covered with harmful substances (see Edible Properties).

Where Found
Watercress is a native to the Mediterranean region and Europe. It is found growing in slow streams, along riverbanks, in roadside ditches, and in swamps over the entire United States and throughout most of the world.

Growing Cycle
Watercress is a perennial herb. Under favorable conditions, watercress can be found and gathered year-round. Even in winter in some areas, one can break through the ice to find and collect watercress. Much of the older watercress in the streams gets washed away with the winter rains. By mid spring and early summer, the new plants will have re-established themselves along the slow-moving sections of the streams.

Water Hyacinth
(Eichhornia crassipes)
Pickerelweed Family
(Pontederiaceae)

water hyacinth

Most Prominent Characteristics

Overall Shape and Size Water hyacinth is a perennial that floats on water. The buoyant stalks support the broad leaves and flower spike, and rise erect from the leaf cluster from a few inches to two or more feet tall.

Stalks and Stems The leaf stalks are spongy and inflated, acting as buoys to float masses of the plants on the surface of the water. This clogs waterways and results in the plant's being referred to as a nuisance.

Leaves The erect, thick, fleshy bright-green leaves are borne in tufts directly up from the roots. Their shape is roundish to ovate, with a broadly acute apex. Each leaf stalk (petiole) is inflated like a spongy bladder, approximately four to five inches in diameter. The leaf blade is about five inches broad, tapering to the cylindrical stem and then swelling into the spongy float. The leaves form in matted rosettes.

Flowers The spikes of blue-violet to purple flowers are visible from June to August. Generally, eight flowers arise from each central stalk. The leafless flower stalk rises from 4 to 16 inches. Each flower consists of six perianth segments with indistinguishable petals and sepals. There are also six stamens and a three-celled ovary. The upper lobes of the flowers often have blue and yellow markings.

Roots The plants spread by means of stolons, horizontally spreading shoots, which are found just slightly below the water. The white, fibrous, almost feathery roots hang freely downward from the stolons in deep water, and in shallow water penetrate the soil beneath.

Beneficial Properties

Edible Properties Wild food foragers can use the stolons, leaves, swollen leaf stalks, flower stalks, and flower buds directly as food. Only the very youngest plant parts should be eaten raw, since a prickly irritation in the throat develops. All the parts must be thoroughly steamed or boiled before being eaten. Due to the plant's fiber content, the young plants are always preferred. The steamed stolons are the most tender and most desirable edible part of the plant, filling a place in the forager's

menu with a food similar in taste and texture to that of steamed asparagus. The leaves and leave stalks can also be sautéed. The flowers become
a bit gelatinous when boiled.

Water hyacinth researcher Godofredo Monsod, a native of the
Philippines, has developed a method of producing a protein concentrate
from the plant. Using special machinery, the withered leaves are crushed,
juiced, and put in a settling tank. This settled solid is air dried at 20° to
50° C for one to three days, then pulverized in a grinding machine so it
will pass through a 50- to 80-mesh sieve. The resultant flour is a rich
source of vitamins A (one capsule of it contains 5,000 international units
of vitamin A), B1, and B2, and niacin, protein, and chlorophyll. The flour
can be used to bake bread (add half corn or wheat flour). It can also be
used in noodles and in other recipes, such as in soups or fritters.

To produce a poultry, livestock, and fish food from this plant, the
roots and leaves are washed and then dried at 120° F. Grinding and filter-
ing (preferably in a classifier vibration screen No. 1, 80 to 100 mesh) is
done to produce water hyacinth meal. The meal is then used in percent-
ages of 20 to 90 percent with other feed, such as corn.

The leaves of water hyacinth are 18.7 percent protein, 2.07 percent calcium, .54 percent phosphorus, 3.2 percent fat, 17.1 percent fiber, and 36.6
percent carbohydrates. The roots are 11.8 percent protein, 1.03 percent calcium, .67 percent phosphorus, .5 percent fat, 7.9 percent fiber, and 41.6
percent carbohydrates.

Medicinal Uses We'd appreciate authenticated reports from readers.

Other Uses Fiber can be extracted from the water hyacinth stems, which
have a 16.08 percent tensile strength. The fiber length is 1.65 millimeters
and the width is 0.018 millimeters. This is categorized as a long fiber.
Long fibers (as opposed to short) are used for making fine papers, such as
documents, currency, and security paper.

Mature water hyacinth stems can be processed into paper pulp. The
stems are air dried for no more than 72 hours, until the stems begin to
decompose. The stems are shredded, and then mixed with water and a
solution of sodium hydroxide. The fully digested material, or pulped
product, is drained of the chemicals and washed with water. The cleaned
pulp can then be converted directly to paper or paperboard. It can also be
bleached if a higher quality paper is desired. The resultant paper has a
high burning and folding strength, and shrinkage is minimal.

The waste parenchyma resulting from defibering the stems (from the
above process) can be used to make multilayer particle board.

Water hyacinth can be introduced into polluted bodies of water to
cleanse the water of heavy metals. Water hyacinth can absorb lead, silver,
mercury, cadmium, cobalt, strontium, zinc, and aluminum. NASA has
developed water hyacinth water-purification ponds, in which polluted
water sits in a pond for awhile; then the water is sent to a series of

subsequent ponds. The water is purified by the time it passes out of the last pond. Furthermore, NASA has developed a means to recover significant amounts of precious metals (which had been in the water) from the harvested water hyacinth.

Another NASA project involves planting water hyacinths in long troughs in greenhouses. Into the troughs is fed all of a household's wastewater, including the toilet water. As the water is circulated through the series of water hyacinth trays, it becomes purified and made ready for reuse. The water hyacinth can then be periodically harvested and digested in a methane digester for the production of household biogas (for use in cooking or lighting).

Detrimental Properties
Because it has effectively blocked scores of once-navigable waterways and fishing spots, it is no small wonder the plant is despised.

The state of Florida spends up to $15 million annually to combat this enemy. Louisiana also spends several million dollars annually to wage its anti-hyacinth war. The United States officially declared war on the water hyacinth invader back in 1899, and has since fought it with dynamite, chemicals, flame throwers, pitchforks, and various cutting devices. Today, the battle is all but lost, since the plant has not only persisted but has spread over the globe.

All parts of the plants should be cooked before eating, or an irritating prickly sensation in the throat may develop. Even when the older plants are cooked, the prickly sensation may result, so it is best to always eat the youngest parts of the plant.

Where Found
The six known species are native primarily to tropical America. Before 1884, the species E. crassipes could only be found in Brazil. But the plant was on display at the New Orleans Centennial Exposition in 1884 and attracted much attention. Someone from Florida took a pailful of the plant in order to "beautify" the St. Johns River. A few other gardeners also took seedlings for their ponds and fountains. Little did they know that their seemingly innocent actions would have such far-reaching aftermath.

A flood hit Florida in the mid-1880s and carried the plant from Florida to Texas. Within seven years, the plant could be found in waterways north to Virginia and west to California. In 1895 the plant was found in Australia, from which it spread to Asia. A missionary introduced the plant in Africa in 1951. It was first growing in just a section of the Congo River a few miles from the town of Brazzaville, but it quickly spread more than a thousand miles into almost every tributary of the Congo, and then it spread into Ethiopia, Rhodesia, Sudan, and Uganda.

Today the water hyacinth can be found the world over. It thrives in major rivers, such as the Nile (it's choked the Aswan Dam), the

Mississippi, the Amazon, and the Mekong. I've observed it since 1977 in the Arroyo Seco Canyon on Pasadena, California's west side, just a few miles south of the Rose Bowl.

Growing Cycle

The water hyacinth is a perennial. It flowers during the months of May through August.

Mud Soup

In their *Professional Guide Manual*, George L. Herter and Jacques P. Herter wrote about the food value of mud.

> *The silt or mud on the bottom of lakes, ponds, and sloughs that have or have had some vegetation in them has a high food value for humans. Such silt or mud contains the accumulated organic food riches of thousands of years both from plants, insects, and in some cases from such things as clams, fish, and crayfish. The best way to eat such silt or mud is to make it into soup. It tastes surprisingly good. Laurel leaves, wild grape leaves, juniper berries, wild leeks, or dandelion will add to its flavor.*
>
> *If lost in the wilderness, mud soup alone will bring you through in fine shape.*
>
> *This is a proven scientific fact, not my personal opinion. The world famous scientist Robert Beauchamp, director of the East African Fisheries Research Organization, made a great many scientific tests on the food value of mud and silt from the bottoms of lakes. He found, for example, that the mud from the bottom of famous Lake Victoria in Africa was especially rich in food for humans. He proved the point by feeding himself and his family on the mud and in all cases the individuals gained weight.*

Western Black Nightshade (Solanum douglasii)

Nightshade Family
(Solanaceae)

Common Name White nightshade

Western black nightshade

Most Prominent Characteristics

Overall Shape and Size

Nightshade is a multibranched perennial that reaches up to four feet tall and spreads to three feet across.

Stalks and Stems The stalks of this plant are typically ⅙ inch in diameter, round, and covered with tiny white hairs which appear as a fine fuzz over the stalk's surface.

Leaves Its lightly pubescent dark green leaves are ovate with a pointed tip. The leaves grow approximately two to four inches long. The leaf margin can be either entire (not toothed) or sparingly and irregularly toothed. The leaves resemble those of lamb's quarter (Chenopodium album) except that they lack lamb's quarter's white mealiness and the characteristic red-veined stems on the old lamb's quarter plant.

Flowers The five-petaled ¼- to ½-inch-broad flowers are white to purple, with a conspicuous yellow center.

Fruit The new fruits (¼ inch in diameter berries) are green and ripen to a deep purple or black.

Beneficial Properties

Edible Properties The fully ripe berries are edible. They can be gathered most abundantly during the late summer; being related to tomatoes, raw, fully ripe nightshade berries have a flavor similar to tomatoes. The fully ripe berries contain little or no toxic substances and are safe to eat either raw or cooked into jam or pies. Cooking tends to further eliminate any possible remaining toxic substances.

The very young nightshade leaves are sometimes used as a potherb. Only the new growths, the tender young tips of the plant, should be used. They must be boiled, drained, and reboiled in a fresh pot of water. They then are safe for consumption; however, many foragers reject this food due to the potential inherent dangers.

Medicinal Uses There is one way that the nightshade's poison can be used to advantage: the fresh leaves can be crushed and applied externally to wounds as an anesthetic.

Other Uses We'd appreciate authenticated reports from readers.

Detrimental Properties
All parts of this plant, except the ripe berries, contain belladonna (atropine), solanine, and other alkaloids (although this is not the

some still-green nightshade fruits

plant from which belladonna is extracted for medicinal purposes). Eating the green berries or raw foliage in large amounts will cause convulsions, delirium, rapid pulse, cramps, and even death (although death is rare).

Always be cautious with any members of the nightshade family.

Where Found
Western black nightshade grows in dry wild areas, coastal regions, backyards, gardens, and in chaparral valleys and canyons.

Growing Cycle
This is a perennial, with the fruit beginning to ripen in late spring, and being most abundantly available in late summer.

Lore and Signature
Most members of the nightshade family seem to be steeped in some folklore. Though this plant is often mistakenly referred to as "deadly nightshade," it is not nearly as toxic as some other nightshades. Some reports suggest that this plant has been used in witchcraft ceremonies.

White Sage
(Salvia apiana)
Mint Family (Labiatae)

Most Prominent
Characteristics

Overall Shape and Size This close relative of ornamental garden sage grows from three to six feet tall and has conspicuous whitish-gray leaves.

Stalks and Stems The young stalks are yellowish white, and approximately ¼ inch thick and have a sticky surface.

close-up of white sage

Leaves The whitish-gray leaves are from one inch to four inches in length, and usually ⅓ as broad. The leaf margin may appear entire, but closer examination reveals that it is actually slightly toothed (subentire) with minute teeth. The fresh leaves are slightly sticky and have a distinct aroma. Once you are familiar with this odor you will be able to identify this plant with your nose alone.

Flowers The ½- to ¾-inch long, labiate-shaped white flowers are in loose clusters along stalks that reach to four feet. The seeds follow the flowers.

Beneficial Properties

Edible Properties Some Native American tribes of the Southwest gathered, ground, and utilized the white sage to make pinole, which they used for bread products. The tender tops of white sage were cooked and eaten by Native Americans who lived in what later became Las Vegas. These tops have a taste and texture similar to cabbage, but the sage flavor may be too strong for some palates. White sage can, like other related sages, be added to such dishes as stews, roasts, and soups for its subtle flavor. The fresh or dried leaves infused in boiling water makes a good-tasting tea.

Medicinal Uses Drinking sage tea is said to calm and strengthen the nerves. The tea has long been used as a digestion aid after heavy meals and also has the reputation of relieving headaches. Sage tastes good and freshens the breath. The sticky leaves are useful as a styptic.

The fresh leaves can be applied directly as a poultice to stop bleeding and to soothe insect bites, making it a valuable herb to carry when hiking.

Other Uses In her book, *Indian Herbology of North America*, Alma Hutchens writes, "The decoction [of sage] is used to cleanse old ulcers and wounds, and massaged into the scalp if troubled with dandruff, falling hair or loss of hair if the papilla [root] is dormant and not destroyed." Fresh (or dried) leaves create a pleasant aroma when added to bath water. Dried white sage leaves are commonly blended into tobacco mixes for use in various Native American ceremonies involving the calumet and the sweat lodge.

Donna Potter inspects white sage.

Detrimental Properties

We'd appreciate authenticated reports from readers.

Where Found

White sage is one of the Southwest's native plants, growing throughout the mountains and chaparral areas and reaching to the desert.

Growing Cycle

The useful leaves of this evergreen shrub can be gathered year-round. However, the best leaves are those gathered from the stalks that haven't yet flowered, generally winter through mid spring.

Lore and Signature

Some folklore lends to sage some mysterious overtones that suggest that we know very little, indeed, about its real values. One curiosity is the fact that wise men have long been called sage. Another stems from the Latin and Spanish root for sage being *salvia*, meaning to save. And lastly, an old saying of the Middle Ages states, "*Cur moriatur homo cui salvia crescit in hortis*," which means "why man would die, when sage grows in the garden."

White sage is regarded as a sacred herb and is often mixed in with the tobacco to be used in the Native American calumet. White sage is also rubbed on the body before entering the sweat lodges.

As clues to the signature of white sage, explore its whiteness, its sticky quality, its strong aroma, and its perennial nature.

Wild Asparagus
(Asparagus officinalis)
Lily Family (Liliaceae)

Gilbert Nyerges with a selection of asparagus spears or shoots. Wild asparagus shoots are identical to cultivated asparagus.

Most Prominent Characteristics

Overall Shape and Size The first growth of spring are the shoots, which are the edible parts. As the asparagus shoot continues to grow, numerous stems grow out of the main shoot. As these stems and their ferny leaves mature, the overall appearance of the plant begins to resemble a three- to five-foot-tall ferny bush.

Stalks and Stems Identical to the cultivated asparagus, the young shoots arise from the rootstock in spring. These shoots are stout and succulent when young and almost ¾ inch thick. The stems, which grow from the main stalk, are not as thick—generally from ¹⁄₁₆ to ¼ inch in diameter.

Leaves As the shoots grow (three to five feet), they become intricately branched, giving the entire plant a ferny appearance.

Flowers and Fruit The plant has ¼-inch-long, bell-like green flowers that are followed by small berries, dark green at first, then maturing to red.

Beneficial Properties

Edible Properties There is absolutely no difference between wild and cultivated asparagus (except that one was tended and cared for by a farmer or gardener); thus, the wild shoots may be eaten in the same variety of ways as the store-bought kind. A simple way to prepare asparagus in the wild is to bake, steam, or boil the shoots, season with herbs and butter (if you have any), and enjoy. At home, they can also be creamed, fried, made into soup, or eaten raw in salad. This is a truly fine vegetable to happen upon.

The plant is rich in vitamin A and is a fair source of calcium and vitamin C.

The plant is inedible once it has grown to the point of being highly branched.

Medicinal Uses We'd appreciate authenticated reports from readers.

Other Uses We'd appreciate authenticated reports from readers.

Detrimental Properties

Eating raw asparagus shoots and the small red berries causes a mild dermatitis reaction in some individuals.

Where Found

This European native prefers low valleys with moist, rich soil. However, it can also be found growing—though less abundantly—in semiarid areas that are shady. In the northwestern and eastern United States wild asparagus is a common inhabiter of roadside ditches.

Growing Cycle

Wild asparagus is a perennial. During the spring, the rootstock sends up the young shoots. Asparagus is an excellent garden plant, once established. The plant's underground rhizomes spread regularly, and one patch can produce edible shoots for up to 100 years.

Wild Buckwheat (Eriogonum fasciculatum)

Buckwheat Family
(Polygonaceae)
Common Names California
Buckwheat

Wild buckwheat flower heads that are mature and ready to harvest

Most Prominent Characteristics

Overall Shape and Size Wild buckwheat, one of southern California's most common chaparral plants, grows from a woody base, usually rising to a maximum of three feet. The overall appearance of the shrubs is green mounds with the round flower heads rising above the mounds.

Stalks and Stems The reddish-brown stalks are approximately 1⁄16 inch thick.

Leaves The nonaromatic leaves are linear with the margins rolled under, wooly white below, and green above. When not in flower, buckwheat resembles rosemary. Rosemary, however, has small blue flowers, glossy green leaves, and a very strong perfumelike odor, whereas buckwheat has no strong aroma.

Flowers The flower clusters form approximately one-inch diameter heads (round, spherical clusters) in groups of two or three. These heads are pinkish white and eventually turn reddish brown when they mature and dry out.

Beneficial Properties

Edible Properties The flowers begin blooming in spring; as they age, they become steadily more crumbly. The old flowers can be gathered easily, sifted, and used with half wheat flour and half corn flour to make dishes, such as pancakes and bread. Use the whole flower cluster, making sure to sift out stems and debris. Buckwheat used alone with no other flour is certainly edible but also gritty and bland. The young flowers do not grind easily, but they are worth the extra effort, since they add a sweet flavor to bread products. A mixture of about 1⁄3 of the young white flowers and 2⁄3 of the mature brown flowers is ideal.

Wild buckwheat is commonly used by bees to collect pollen and is thus an important plant for the bee industry (third most important after white sage and black sage).

Medicinal Uses A decoction of the leaves is said to alleviate stomach pains and headaches. The decoction used externally as a wash is claimed to cure poison oak rash.

Other Uses A tea made from the fresh flowers was used by some Native American tribes as an eye wash.

Detrimental Properties
We'd appreciate authenticated reports from readers.

Where Found
Native to southern California, wild buckwheat is found on canyon floors, rocky hillsides, dry slopes, and ridges. It is very common throughout the chaparral regions and much of the desert areas.

Growing Cycle
This woody-based shrub is found year-round. The flower heads begin their growth in later winter and early spring. The reddish-brown mature flower heads are mostly available in the summer and early fall.

Wild Cucumber (Marah spp.)

Gourd Family (Cucurbitaceae)

Common Names Manroot, chilicothe

wild cucumber fruits hanging from vines

Most Prominent Characteristics

Overall Shape and Size Wild cucumber can be found either as a trailing or climbing vine, generally reaching 15 to 30 feet. The plant's tendrils enable it to climb over and on top of other vegetation; thus it rambles over hillsides, twines through trees, and spreads over flat ground.

Leaves The light-green leaves are more or less heart shaped, with five to seven deep lobes. Arranged alternately on the vine, they are generally two to four inches broad and almost hairless.

Flowers The whitish-green flowers are approximately ½ inch broad and are found in racemes. The petals, united into a five- to seven-lobed corolla, are rotate (wheel shaped; spreading flat or horizontal and circular in outline).

Fruit The green fruits range from golf-ball to baseball size, are spherical to egg shaped, and very spiny. As they dry, the four large seed chambers become readily visible. The outer layer (which includes the spines) can be peeled away from the dried fruits.

Roots The root resembles a tan-colored carrot when young. However, it grows and grows and can actually get big enough to fill the back of a pickup truck.

Beneficial Properties

Edible Properties The entire plant has an extremely bitter taste. The root, though extremely bitter, is considered edible. However, it can also be poisonous in varying amounts to different people. Thus, the root is generally regarded as an unacceptable emergency food since long boilings and frequent water changes are required to leach out all the bitterness. I once boiled a baby root for an hour and it was still unacceptably bitter!

Still, the root was carried and eaten on long trips by some Native Americans. It would have been mostly a belly filler since the root is nearly all cellulose with little food value.

Medicinal Uses We'd appreciate authenticated reports from readers.

Other Uses When the fruits are mature and dry, a many-chambered oval is left (the outer layer of spines is easily peeled away). The inner, finely divided body of the fruit resembles the luffa—the dried insides of a gourd that is used as a scrubbing sponge. The luffa of the wild cucumber is superior to store-bought luffas (although about ⅒ the size) in its exfoliative and durability qualities. The insides of each fruit measure about three inches long by two inches across. These are excellent for scrubbing the skin during baths and will not fall apart even after many uses. A more intense use, such as pot scrubbing, will cause the dried cucumbers to fall apart more quickly.

According to Donald Gales, some Native American tribes tossed the mashed roots and fresh fruits into streams and pools to stun the fish, making them easy to capture.

Detrimental Properties

In South America, the wild cucumber roots are distilled into an alcoholic drink that produces LSD-type effects.

In the early 1960s, a few children in Ojai, California, were reportedly mildly poisoned by eating wild cucumber seeds.

Although I've occasionally read that these seeds can cause death, I've concluded that this is rare. I've yet to find a verified account of death from this plant or its seeds, and, due to the intense bitterness of the seeds, it seems unlikely that anyone would actually consume enough to cause death.

Where Found

Wild cucumber is commonly found in California in the upper sandy edges of valleys in both the coastal and chaparral areas. It grows on flat ground and climbs over hillsides, shrubs, and trees.

Growing Cycle

The plant is a perennial. The newly emerging vines begin their growth in winter; the green fruit are seen in the spring. The luffas from the dried fruits can be collected during the summer and fall.

Lore and Signature

When the 210 Freeway was being carved through the previously residential areas of Pasadena, California, some workers dug up a root that literally filled the back of their pickup truck. With great excitement, they drove it over to Dr. Enari at the nearby Los Angeles County Arboretum for identification, thinking they had found something rare. The root was certainly old, but not rare.

The root is sometimes shaped like a man. This provides one of the common names for this plant, manroot. Several other roots which take on a human form are known to be very good foods, unique medicines or drugs, or even poisons. Some examples of such roots are mandrake, ginseng, Jimsonweed, dandelion, carrots, and others. Perhaps there are still unknown uses of this manroot which we've not yet discovered.

Wild Onions
(Allium spp.)
Lily Family (Liliaceae)
Common Names Wild chives, wild leeks, ramps, wild garlic

Most Prominent Characteristics

Overall Shape and Size These perennial herbs are relatively inconspicuous plants when not in flower. They grow grass-like, to a height of generally under a foot.

Pat Fiedler holds a wild onion. The little flower is lilac colored.

Stalks and Stems The flower stalk is generally leafless, thin, hollow, and reed-like, growing a bit taller than the tallest leaves. It tends to be more fibrous than the leaves.

Leaves The leaves are hollow and round (in the cross section), with a distinctly oniony aroma when crushed. The leaves arise from the bulbs. Their appearance is nearly identical to that of a bundle of chives purchased in produce markets.

Flowers The petals and sepals (perianth segments) are indistinguishable from each other in appearance. Yet each is distinct from the other—the perianth segments are not fused or united into a basal tube. There are six perianth segments: three sepals and three petals, all the same color (most frequently a shade of purple). There are six stamens and one pistil per flower.

Seeds Seeds are flat, black, and usually wrinkled, with one or two seeds per cell.

Roots The perennial root is a bulb, sometimes a corm.

Beneficial Properties

Edible Properties All tender parts of wild onions are edible, above and below ground. Generally, the older flower stalks become fibrous and unpalatable. Otherwise, the bulbs and leaves are eaten raw or cooked.

Simply remove any outer fibrous layers of the plant, rinse, and then prepare as you would green onions or chives.

Wild onions can be added to salads, used as the base for a soup, cooked alone like spinach, chopped and mixed into eggs, cooked as a side to fish, and used to enhance countless other foods. Wild onions share many of the healthful benefits of garlic and improve any urban or wilderness meal. Backpackers who are relying on dried trail rations will certainly enjoy the sustenance of wild onions.

Many Native Americans heavily relied on wild onions and regarded them as staples, not just condiments.

Medicinal Uses Generally, when included in the diet, all members of the onion family provide us with the same benefits as garlic: lower cholesterol levels, prevent influenzas, and reduce high blood pressure. Used externally, the crushed green leaves can be applied directly to wounds to prevent infection.

Other Uses Some people report that they are less bothered by mosquitoes and other insects after consuming wild onions. In some cases, people have rubbed the fresh leaves on the exposed portions of their body to prevent insect bites. I have had only mediocre results at keeping the bugs away as a result of consuming wild onions (and all their relatives) and rubbing the leaves on my skin. (For the record, the best way to keep the bugs from biting is to include raw apple cider vinegar in your diet. Add about one tablespoon per cup of drinking water. See Mosquitoes sidebar on page 30 for more information on how to keep bugs at bay.)

Detrimental Properties
Eating excessive amounts of only wild onions can result in stomach and intestinal pain. In her book, *Know Your Poisonous Plants*, Wilma Roberts James states that wild onions are toxic when eaten in great quantities. Nevertheless, this is so rare that it's hardly worthy of comment. Eaten in normal amounts as part of a balanced diet, wild onions are an excellent nourishing food.

Never forget that many members of the lily family with bulbs are deadly poisonous when eaten. Be absolutely certain that you have correctly identified any wild onions that you intend to eat. Check the floral characteristics for the three sepals and three petals. Then, you must detect an obvious onion aroma. If there isn't one, don't eat the plant. (There are a few true onions that lack the onion aroma; nevertheless, it is imperative that you have absolutely identified those nonaromatic species as safe before you prepare them for your lunch.)

Where Found
Various species of wild onions can be found in every type of environment from coast to coast in the United States. Some are found in high elevations, some in meadows, swamps, ditches, and riversides, others in deserts, chaparral, and coastal areas, and still others in lawns, farmland, and fields.

Growing Cycle
Wild onions are perennials. The bulbs multiply every year, which results in an ever-expanding patch of wild onions. The new green shoots generally arise in the early spring. The wild onion flowers appear throughout the summer.

Willow (Salix spp.)
Willow Family (Salicaceae)

Most Prominent Characteristics

Overall Shape and Size The many species of willow are quite diverse in general appearance. Some are small and bushy, others are leggy shrubs, and others are tall trees.

willow in flower

Stalks and Stems Typically, the bark is smooth and though the coloration is most often gray, it can vary widely. Some species have nearly red bark. The bark can be readily peeled from the stems.

Leaves Willow leaves are nearly all thin and lance shaped, though the light-green coloration can vary significantly from species to species. Look for the small bud at the base of each leaf. The winter buds are covered with a single scale.

Flowers Willows produce both male (staminate) and female (pistillate) flowers. They form in catkins of various sizes. As these flowers mature, they produce a silky down that blows through the willow forest. If your timing is right (or wrong, depending on your point of view), the willow down will be everywhere in the air.

Beneficial Properties

Edible Properties Willow plants are also a source of food—sort of. For example, the inner bark of willows has often been described as an emergency food, which is another way of saying that you'd probably never eat willow bark unless you were literally starving. As a practical matter, it is difficult to scrape out the inner part of the bark, and you generally end up eating all of the bark. Cooking renders it a bit more palatable. If dried and ground into flour and then cooked, it is even more palatable, though still in the realm of emergency food. I have sampled this bark while backpacking with my brother and a friend. We rarely brought much food with us, preferring to catch fish and collect wild plants. We jokingly called our willow bark wild spaghetti, which is a disservice to spaghetti.

Euell Gibbons describes two species of arctic willows (S. alexensis and S. pulchra) whose tender young leaves can be eaten as a salad, or mixed into a salad. The flavor is said to be improved by cooking the leaves first. Though I have never tried these species, I have nibbled on the wild willows of southern California and would not include them in salads. They are a bit bitter, but are improved by steaming or boiling.

Medicinal Uses In general, you should think of willow as a medicine tree, not a food source. Every now and then during one of my walks, someone will tell me that they have a headache. I peel off two slivers of bark from the ubiquitous willow and hand it to them.

"Take two pieces of bark and call me in the morning," I tell them. Most people laugh when I say this, but some people don't get it because they aren't familiar with willow or its history. The inner bark of willow contains salicin and is the original aspirin. The bark of the younger shoots is strongest, and it is fairly easy to harvest. When steeped in water, willow tea is good for headaches, fevers, and even hay fever. Due to its strong antiseptic properties, the tea can also be used as a good mouthwash or used externally on wounds. A willow wash is said to work wonders for rheumatism sufferers.

Other Uses According to Dr. James Bauml at the Los Angeles County Arboretum in Arcadia, horticulturalists have noted that willow cuttings put in water add some unidentified substance to the water, which helps other cuttings develop roots. So if you want to root cuttings of various trees or vines, you can put them all in a bucket of water with willow cuttings. We have had good results with this method for rooting apples, roses, figs, jujube, and blackberries.

Willow is also one of the best sources of craft material. Whenever I collect willow, I go into the thickest patches and carefully cut only those branches I need with a sharp ratchet cutter. In all cases when I have returned to those areas, I find the best and healthiest growths of new willow where I had done my careful pruning.

I collect straight dead pieces of willow branches for use in the primitive bow and drill for fire making. Dried willow makes the best drill for fire making. It is also an ideal wood to use for the base plate—the flat piece of wood on which the drill is spun.

Willows make interesting-looking, lightweight walking sticks, and I have made many of these. Willow is a soft wood, so the walking sticks can be easily carved with either faces or your name or anything that your abilities allow.

Long straight willow stems are perhaps the single most useful plant in basket weaving. Willow is one of the most traditional materials used in baskets because it is light, easily worked, and flexible after being soaked in water for about five minutes. Always scrape off the bark before using willow in your basketry projects.

I have seen willow chairs and tables at craft fairs, and there are craftsmen all over the United States who commonly use willow in these backwoods furnishings. They are very attractive. Though the Plains Indians used no chairs in their tipis, they did make a chair of sorts out of willow. Using pencil-thick willow twigs, they lashed them horizontally onto two thicker vertical willow rods to create a backrest.

Because of willow's flexibility and common availability, I typically use willow whenever I make a sweat lodge frame. The sweat lodge frame is dome shaped. Once the perimeter of the sweat lodge is drawn in the dirt, I dig holes into which I secure the willow poles. Then I bend them down and lash them together at

Note the bud at the base of each leaf on this willow branch.

the top to create the desired dome shape. The sweat lodge is covered with tarps and very hot rocks are brought inside. Once everyone enters the lodge, it is closed up so that it is dark inside, and water is slowly poured onto the rocks, creating a high temperature sauna or steam bath. This was and still is a tradition among Native American peoples from North America through South America.

I have also used willow sticks for digging and for the framework for a primitive lean-to shelter. It is a good plant to become familiar with because it is so common and so versatile.

I have used the long dried willow stems as pipes, and—following in the tradition of Native Americans—I dry the bark of red willow and add it to my smoking mixture. I have sat outside my shelter made with a framework of willow, after sweating in my willow sweat lodge, and sat around the fire that was made with a willow drill, smoking some willow bark in my willow pipe. Indeed, willow is a good friend.

Detrimental Properties

Some people experience allergic reactions when they are walking through a willow thicket when the down from the catkins is blowing in the air.

Where Found

Willows are nearly always found along streams. I have seen them at sea level and higher than 8,000 feet. They are found throughout North America and much of the rest of the world. You might not have known offhand how to identify a willow, but I can assure you that you have driven by one or hiked by one whenever you were near a stream.

Growing Cycle

Willows can be bushes or tall trees. They are deciduous, so they lose their leaves in winter and produce their flowery catkins in the spring. Even when cut back, they seem to sprout back again and again.

Lore and Signature

Willow wands figure prominently in folklore and magic. Many dowsers claim they get the best results from a Y-shaped willow rod. Case in point was dowser Ralph Harris, who found all the water needed for General George S. Patton's troops in North Africa. Patton's geologists reported that there was no water to be found by drilling. Private Ralph Harris meekly told Patton that he could find water by dowsing but that he needed a willow twig. Patton had an entire willow tree flown in the next day. Ralph Harris then cut a Y-shaped piece of willow, dowsed, and told Patton where to drill. They found water at every site where Harris said to drill.

When I took a class in dowsing at Los Angeles City Class, taught by Ralph Harris and Legory O'Loughlin of the Dowsing Society, Harris claimed that everyone can learn to dowse if you can control your thinking and concentrate. Harris, who was a fourth-generation dowser, always provided documentation for every one of his dowsing successes. He said it was a gift from God. O'Loughlin often reminded his students that the light of dowsing shines brightest when helping humanity.

Uses of willow rods and staffs figure prominently in Wicca, in folklore, and in various religious and metaphysical traditions worldwide.

As always, I'd love to hear from readers who have unique data to share about willow, its lore, or uses.

Wood Sorrel (Oxalis spp.)

Wood Sorrel Family
(Oxalidaceae)
Common Names Oxalis,
Shamrock, Sour grass

wood sorrel

Most Prominent Characteristics

Overall Shape and Size This cloverlike, succulent plant has conspicuous long stems (up to about eight inches tall) and leaves that resemble clover. The plant is sometimes called clover, to which, however, it is not related.

Stalks and Stems The green flower stems are stout and succulent, more so even than the leaf stems. The stem's diameter is about ⅟₁₆ inch, with the leaf stems rising about eight inches and the flower stems rising a few inches higher.

Leaves The leaves are trifoliate (with three leaflets), each leaflet being heart shaped with a midrib or midfold. The leaves are borne on relatively long petioles or stalks. The leaflets spread out in the sunlight, and close, or fold back in cloudy weather and at night. The leaves are mostly basal, with long stems.

Flowers The flowers can be white, yellow, red, or pink, with 10 stamens, and with 5 sepals and 5 petals often united in a spiral twist. In some species, the flowers are purplish veined.

Fruits The narrow, linear, five-celled pod measures from ½ to 1 inch long, each of which opens with a valve. The coats of wood sorrel fruits shrink so violently that they split and send the seeds flying.

Beneficial Properties

Edible Properties The leaves, stems, and flowers can be used in salads to add a vinegary flavor. Don't add too much, though, as the leaves are quite sour. The leaves and stems can be fermented slightly to make a type of wild sauerkraut. Pioneers used the stems to make pies that resembled rhubarb pie in flavor. Several species are cultivated in Mexico and South America for their edible tuberous roots.

Medicinal Uses We'd appreciate authenticated reports from readers.

Other Uses Wood sorrel's oxalic acid has been used for removing ink stains and cleaning brass.

Detrimental Properties
The expressed juice of the plant's foliage contains a high percentage of oxalic acid and should not be eaten in large amounts if you're not accustomed to it. I can recall eating many handfuls when I was about 10 years old and vomiting it an hour later.

Where Found
Wood sorrel is found in shady, moist places in temperate North America and at the Cape of Good Hope. It grows in redwood forests along the Pacific Coast and in gardens.

Growing Cycle
The flowers appear from May until August. The leaves can be gathered year-round.

Lore and Signature
Wood sorrel is one of the three plants that has been interchangeably been designated as the shamrock (Irish national emblem). St. Patrick is said to have chosen this plant because it illustrates the doctrine of the Trinity. It has been occultly connected to a peculiarly Irish trait of sorrow (pronounced *sorra* in Gaelic dialect) that accentuates a penchant for bitterness that leads to revenge taking (as opposed to the "sorry" aspect of sorrow that leads to repentance).

Yarrow (Achillea millefolium)
Sunflower Family
(Compositae)

The yarrow plant has fernlike leaves.

Most Prominent Characteristics

Overall Shape and Size This strong-scented, erect perennial herb grows from 1 to 2½ feet tall.

Leaves The linear, aromatic leaves, alternately arranged on the stalk, are divided into many lateral segments, and each segment is again subdivided. Combined with the fact that the entire plant is covered with long, soft hairs, the net visual effect is an overall feathery appearance.

Flowers The very small white flowers, with four to five rays each, are in flat-topped or convex clusters.

Beneficial Properties

Edible Properties We'd appreciate authenticated reports from readers.

Medicinal Uses Tea from the dried leaves is a bitter but stimulating tonic. The tea is said to be useful for breaking up head colds and fevers. It is a strong diaphoretic (promotes perspiration). Although the taste may require some getting used to, many enjoy its aromatic bitterness with the first cup.

The cleaned, soft leaves pressed into an open wound have the ability to stop the bleeding and relieve some of the pain. This is due to yarrow's vulnerary, styptic, and anesthetic properties. When Napoleon's army tried to conquer Russia, they carried a good supply of yarrow to stop the bleeding from war injuries.

A cotton ball soaked in yarrow tea and put in a bloody nose effectively stops the bleeding.

It is said that balding can be prevented by regularly washing the head with a yarrow infusion.

Chewing the fresh leaves, or impacting a wad of them against a diseased tooth or gum area, is reputed to relieve toothache pain. We would appreciate the results of any experiments along these lines from our dentist-readers who are adventurous enough to give it a try—perhaps on a voluntary basis with patients. I once tried this when I had a bone-chilling toothache. I chewed a few yarrow leaves into a wad, and then packed that wad near the painful tooth. The pain subsided within about 10 minutes and was below the pain threshold within about 35 minutes.

Other Uses In areas where there are large stands of young yarrow, the uppermost tender parts of the plants can be snipped and stuffed into a pillow cover. The resulting pillow will be soft and aromatic and likely to promote wonderful dreams.

Detrimental Properties
Persons sensitive to ragweed and goldenrod may experience allergic reactions from drinking yarrow tea. These sensitive individuals should probably avoid sleeping on yarrow pillows.

Where Found
While it is a European native, yarrow is now common throughout much of North America. Though yarrow can be found in a variety of habitats, it prefers semiforested areas, sloping moist hillsides, and the edges of pine plantations.

Growing Cycle
Yarrow begins its annual growth cycle in the spring. For medicinal purposes, it can be gathered any time during the growing season. However, it is best gathered just before it flowers, which is generally late spring or early summer, depending on the location.

Yerba Santa (Eriodictyon spp.)
Phacelia Family
(Hydrophyllaceae)

the fragrant yerba santa in flower

Most Prominent Characteristics

Overall Shape and Size These erect, aromatic, evergreen shrubs grow from three to five feet tall.

Stalks and Stems The main stalks can be up to ¼ inch in diameter and are covered with a sticky resin.

Leaves The alternate, lanceolate leaves are rather thick, leathery, and irregularly toothed. The leaves' undersides are covered with small, dense, feltlike hairs; their upper surface is sticky and quite resinous on E. californicum, and densely tomentose (covered with soft wooly hairs) on E. crassifolium. On the resinous species, the sticky upper surface collects dust that gives the plant a dirty, wasted appearance. The leaves have a fine network of veins.

Flowers The funnel-shaped, red-to-purple flowers, approximately ½ inch long, grow in panicled, scorpoid cymes.

Beneficial Properties

Edible Properties Bees produce an amber-colored honey from yerba santa flowers, an indirect food source from this floral friend.

Medicinal Uses The leaves (fresh or dried) made into tea, are said to be excellent for laryngitis, sore throat, bronchitis, colds, stomachaches, vomiting, and diarrhea. The fresh leaves, made into a poultice, are said to speed the healing of and prevent infection in open wounds. The Native Americans used such poultices for themselves and their animals.

Yerba santa, meaning "holy weed" or "holy herb," was so named by early Spanish priests, who highly regarded the plant after learning of its virtues from the Native Americans.

Other Uses Chewing on a yerba santa leaf while hiking, though at first bitter, will gradually impart a eucalyptus-type sensation and will help keep the mouth moist. Yerba santa's odor is unique; once you learn it, you'll never confuse yerba santa with another plant. Yerba santa leaves can also be dried and smoked as a nonnicotine tobacco.

Detrimental Properties

We'd appreciate authenticated reports from readers.

Where Found

Yerba santa grows in dry, flat areas, dry slopes and ridges, and in chaparral. The aromatic leaves can be gathered year-round.

Growing Cycle

The plant is an evergreen shrub, whose leaves can be gathered year-round.

Yucca (Yucca spp.)

Agave Family (Agavaceae)

Common Names Spanish
bayonet, Spanish dagger, datil,
Lord's candle

yucca plant in full fruit

Most Prominent Characteristics

Overall Shape and Size This
shrub-like plant is shaped something like a large pin cushion,
since all the long, narrow leaves
radiate from a central point.

Leaves The plant has long, nar-
row, needlelike leaves that are rigid and sharp pointed. These leaves radiate from the center of the plant, appearing much like the coat of a porcu-
pine that is bristled for battle.

Flowers and Fruit The thick, single flower stalk arises from the center of
this needle fortress and shoots vertically up to 10 feet or more. Large
white flowers cluster around the upper 20 to 40 percent of the stalk, somewhat like a stick of cotton candy. The dying flowers are followed by fruits
resembling gourds or small bananas. After flowering and seeding, the
plant dies.

Beneficial Properties

Edible Properties The flowers and buds are edible raw, although light
cooking (such as steaming) improves their flavor. The raw fruits are likewise edible, but the flavor is improved by baking, boiling, or sun-drying.
The early Native Americans roasted or boiled the fruits of yucca and
worked them into a paste. This paste was formed into cakes and dried in
the sun for later use, either as is, boiled, or made into a beverage. The flat,
black seeds of the mature fruit can be ground and used as pastry flour or
cooked into an edible mush (the flavor and texture of which are unacceptable to some).

    The young, first-emerging stalk is also edible. This large, asparagus-like
shoot (five to eight inches in diameter and up to four feet in length) can be
cooked or baked. It is not altogether unpleasant raw so long as you peel
back all of the tough outer skin before eating. This part of the plant tastes
agreeable to nearly everyone who has commented on it. However, it is best
to eat the yucca only in emergency cases, since this stately beauty is rare.

Medicinal Uses Early southwestern Native Americans reportedly boiled
leaves for a snake-bite antidote. Do any readers have more information
about this?

Other Uses The fibers of the leaves were used by the southwestern Native Americans for sandals, mats, rope, and baskets. The green leaves were rubbed until only the fiber was left. Then the fiber was twined into rope or used for other products.

The old dried leaves, but preferably the leaves cut green and allowed to dry, are soaked and then woven into a great many products.

Many survival implements can be made from yucca if one has the basic knowledge of weaving techniques. An effective whisk broom can be made by fraying the bases of a large number of leaves (old dead leaves are best) and twining the sharp pointed ends together. A backwoods needle and thread can be made with a single green yucca leaf: pull off the outer fibers by grasping the leaf by the needle end with one hand and scraping with the thumbnail of the other hand. Do this until you're left with the sharp point and one or two attached fibers-remarkably efficient if properly made!

The root has a long reputation of being a good soap source. When chunks of the tough root are added to water and agitated, a thick lather results. This soap is said to be particularly beneficial to the hair and scalp. It is far easier to extract a usable soap from a fresh yucca leaf than it is from the root. Cut a few fresh yucca leaves, shred them a bit, wet, and then agitate between the hands. (Besides being much easier than extracting soap from the root, the plant need not be killed in order to make soap.) I've used this yucca leaf soap to wash off the fresh juice of agave leaf when it splashed on my skin (I was harvesting the agave). This juice quickly causes a rash like that caused by poison oak if not washed off quickly.

With all these uses of this valuable plant, yucca can truly be said to be a wilderness general store.

Detrimental Properties

Exercise caution when handling the leaves of yucca. Be careful not to cut your hand along the leaf's sharp margin or poke your body with the leaf's sharp tip.

Where Found

Yucca is found in desert areas and on dry chaparral slopes. Different species are found throughout the Southwest and a few throughout the United States.

Growing Cycle

Yucca is an evergreen shrub that dies once it flowers. Each plant lives up to 20 years before flowering. The thick asparagus-like flower shoot begins its growth in the early spring. By summer, one can usually see numerous yucca flower spikes dotting the hillsides.

Lore and Signature

Quality fiber plants were revered and respected in past ages when people made so much of what they used every day. We have lost sight of the value of fiber in our society since we have fasteners such as buttons, zippers, Velcro, hardware-store rope and twine, duct tape, glue, and epoxy. But in the age when plant fibers were utilized for weapons, fire making, clothes, shoes, hats, shelter, furniture, nets, carrying cases, and more, one appreciated fiber. As

close-up of a yucca fruit

one Paiute woman said, "In the past, fiber literally and figuratively tied our lives together." In addition to the many products from plant fibers, she was also referring to the old days when people would sit for hours and weave and work fibers. This was a time to meet, to talk, and to instill values into the youngsters.

Appendix 1

Safe Families

A Guide to the (Relatively) Easily Recognized Plant Families That Are Nontoxic and Primarily Edible

It isn't always essential that you know each particular plant species before you can consider it safe. There are several groups of plants that are either entirely nontoxic or mostly nontoxic with some qualifications.

Learning each and every plant you plan to consume is certainly the best way to proceed with the study of edible wild plants. Nevertheless, studying the edible families should not be considered a shortcut approach, since this method still necessitates careful observation of all the floral (and other) characteristics. Be absolutely certain that you've identified a given plant as a member of one of these families before sampling any part of it.

There are many other families of plants, which are for the most part safe to consume. We have included those that are the most abundant, widespread, easily recognized, and the most palatable.

Begin by reading the description of each family. Then try to actually observe the examples listed. By doing so, you'll begin to see and feel the similarities of all the members of each group listed. To expand your perspective, get a botany book of the flora for your particular area so you can read the botanist's description of each family. Also, in the book of flora, there should be a list of all the members of each particular family that are known to be found in your area. Call a botanist at a local college or arboretum to find which book of flora is used in your area. Another good reference in this regard is Thomas Elpel's *Botany in a Day*, published by HOPS, Box 691, Pony, MT 59747.

The examples we list here are by no means complete; we've simply listed a representative sampling of those plants most often recognized by name. Hopefully, you'll be able to observe as many of the examples listed as possible. We ask readers to share with us their comments, suggestions, and constructive criticisms to help expand this section in a future edition. I greatly appreciate and extend thanks to Dr. Leonid Enari who helped me prepare this section.

Amaranth Family
Amaranthaceae

These are annual herbaceous weeds or shrubs, with leaves that are simple and entire and either alternate or opposite. The small inconspicuous flowers are perfect or unisexual, and they are congested in terminal spikes or axillary clusters. Sepals are usually dry, thin, and membranous. No petals are present. The fruit can be a fleshy or membranous thin-walled, one-seed body that is either indehiscent, irregularly dehiscent, or circumscissile (which means that the top of the fruit separates in a circular line, much like the lid of a pillbox). The seeds are mostly black and shiny, and they mature about the time the spikes begin to fade and dry to a tan color. There are 40 genera and about 500 species worldwide.

Examples

forty knot (Achyranthes repens)

giant amaranth (Amaranthus hypochondriacus)

love-lies-bleeding (A. hybridus)

pigweed (A. retroflexus)

tumbleweed (A. albus)

pod of Amaranth
opening by a lid

Uses
The young leaves can be eaten raw or cooked. The older leaves should be cooked since they become bitter with age. The abundant seeds can be easily harvested, winnowed, and used as a flour substitute or extender.

Cautions
None.

Cactus Family
Cactaceae

Cactus plants are perennial succulents, herbaceous, or woody. There are believed to be as many as 2,000 species worldwide. The stems are columnar, globose, or flattened and are technically leafless in most varieties. (The pads are not considered leaves.) Branches, spines, and flowers develop in the raised areas on the stems called areoles. The flowers have both stamens and pistils, and the flowers are sessile (stalkless). The sepals and petals are numerous and intergrading with each other, overlapping in several rows, and the bases merge together. Stamens are numerous. There is one pistil with two or more stigmas. Seeds are numerous.

Examples

barrel cactus (Ferocactus spp.)

hedgehog cactus (Echninocactus spp.)

Mammillaria spp.

prickly pear cacti (Opuntia spp.) including beavertail, pancake pear, Indian fig

Saguaro (Carnegiea gigantea)

Uses

All the cactus flesh and fruits can be eaten if they are sufficiently tender, readily available, and palatable. Most of the young cactus pads, once peeled, can be eaten raw. Most cacti, assuming they are not too woody, can be eaten. In some cases, cooking will improve the flavor and texture, thereby improving the palatability. The fruits are edible raw or cooked, once peeled of their outer skin.

Cautions

Be very careful when collecting cactus. Take special precautions to protect your hands from both the spines and the tiny hairlike glochids at the base of each spine. Be sure to remove all the spines before consuming cactus. Woody parts are not used, and some parts may be very bitter, in which case cooking may improve the flavor. A small number of relatively scarce cacti, including peyote and desert rock, are extremely bitter and if eaten in sufficient amounts, can cause a narcotic or hallucinatory effect, often in addition to vomiting. Some Euphorbia spp., which resemble—but are not cacti—exude a thick milky juice when cut. *Do not eat* Euphorbias since they are poisonous.

Cattail Family
Typhaceae

The cattail family consists of just cattails. By some accounts, there are up to 15 species worldwide. They are all aquatic with the familiar hot dog on a stick flower spike.

(See the main text under Cattail for uses and cautions.)

Chicory Tribe of the Sunflower Family
Compositae

The sunflower family is characterized by the typical sunflower-like or daisy-like flower head (that is, having both ray and disk flowers on each head). They can be annual or perennial herbs. The sunflower family is one of the largest plant families, divided by botanists into 11 or 12 distinct groups called "tribes."

One of these tribes is the chicory tribe, characterized by being herbs with alternate or basal leaves and milky juice. The flowers, clustered in heads, are all perfect. Each ray flower is five-toothed at its apex, an easy-to-make observation.

Examples

chicory (Cichoreum spp.)

dandelion (Taraxacum officinale)

hawkweed (Hieracium spp.)

Malacothrix spp.

Mountain dandelion (Agoseris spp.)

sow thistle (Sonchus spp.)

wild and cultivated lettuce (Lactuca spp.)

Uses

When young, many of these herbs can be included in salads or used as the main salad ingredient. They quickly become bitter as they get older and are then best as cooked greens. The roots of some species are also worth digging up to use like parsnips or to dry, grind, and percolate into a noncaffeine beverage.

Cautions

Some members are quite bitter and some are too fibrous to eat when older.

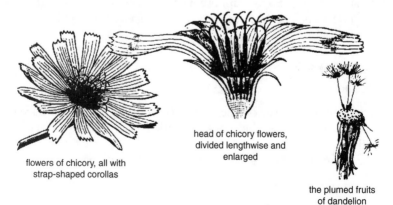

flowers of chicory, all with
strap-shaped corollas

head of chicory flowers,
divided lengthwise and
enlarged

the plumed fruits
of dandelion

Ferns
Filicae or Polypodiaceae

The fronds of ferns are often finely divided, borne on stalks arising from creeping rootstocks. The spore-bearing cases (called "sori") are found on the backs or margins of the leaves, commonly in lines or in dots. Worldwide, there are believed to be as many as 6,000 species divided into about 150 genera.

Examples
bracken (Pteridium spp.)

cliff brake (Pellaea spp.)

maidenhair (Adiantum spp.)

Uses
The young, uncurling growing tips are edible and taste nutty. They can be served steamed and covered with butter or mixed into various cooked vegetable dishes.

Cautions
It is best to cook all fiddleheads if you plan to eat any quantity of them, since some may be mildly toxic when raw. Also, don't eat any of the mature fern fronds; some are safe, but you'd need to know each fern's individual characteristics.

Certain reports have indicated that fiddleheads are carcinogenic, but this conclusion is based on statistical evidence; no direct link between cancer and fiddleheads has been found.

Goosefoot Family
Chenopodiaceae

These are herb or shrubs, often preferring saline soils. These succulent or scurfy plants are generally considered weeds. The leaves are simple, without stipules, alternately arranged (rarely opposite), and in some cases, reduced to scales. The small flowers, often inconspicuous, have a calyx of five or less sepals; the calyx is absent in the female flowers. There are usually as many stamens as sepals, but sometimes there are fewer. The ovary is superior, which means that the stamens are connected beneath the ovary. The one-celled ovary develops into a dry, one-seeded indehiscent fruit. There are 1,400 species worldwide.

Examples
glasswort, samphire, or pickleweed (Salicornia spp.)

lamb's quarters (Chenopodium album)

Russian thistle or tumbleweed (Salsola spp.)

Saltbush (Atriplex spp.) including redscale, arrowscale, crownscale, orach

garden or sugar beets (Beta vulgaris)

sea blite (Suaeda spp.)

winged pigweed (Cycloloma atriplicifolium)

Uses
The leaves of most can be eaten raw in salads. Older greens may need cooking to render them less bitter and more palatable. Seeds of most members can be harvested, winnowed, and used as a flour or flour extender.

Cautions
Some species become quite woody and fibrous when mature.

Grass
All species

There are about 10,000 species of the grasses worldwide (divided into about 600 genera). We find about 1,000 of those species in the United States.

(See the main text under Grass for the description, examples, uses, and cautions.)

Mallow Family
Malvaceae

These are herbs or soft-woody shrubs with mucilaginous juice, tough fibrous inner bark, and covered with small evenly scattered hairs. There are about 1,500 species of the mallow family worldwide, divided into 85 genera. The leaves are alternately arranged, simple, and palmately lobed. The flower has a five-lobed calyx and five petals that are twisted in the bud. There is an indefinite amount of stamens, which are joined together in a column or tube around the pistil, attached on the receptacle beneath the ovary. This pistil is composed of several carpels, each of which separates upon maturity.

Examples
checker bloom (Sidalceae malvaeflora)

desert mallow, globe mallow, or apricot mallow (Sphaeralcea ambigua)

Hollyhock (Althaea spp.)

mallow or cheeseweed (Malva spp.)

rose mallow (Hibiscus spp.)

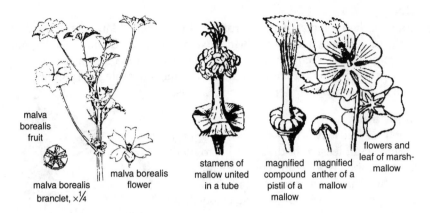

malva borealis fruit

malva borealis branclet, ×¼

malva borealis flower

stamens of mallow united in a tube

magnified compound pistil of a mallow

magnified anther of a mallow

flowers and leaf of marsh-mallow

Uses

The leaves of all these can be eaten raw in salads or cooked like spinach. The roots of some are tender enough to be used like parsnips. The flowers and fruits are edible raw or cooked.

Cautions

Some parts of some mallows, due to age or the particular species, may be too fibrous to eat.

Mint Family

Labiatae

This family includes mostly aromatic herbs or low-growing shrubs with square stems and leaves that are always simple and opposite. Worldwide, there are about 3,500 species of the mint family. Flowers are formed in dense sessile cymes, which have the appearance of globelike whorls encircling the stem. The sepals are more or less united, frequently two-lipped, usually five-lobed. The corolla has a distinct tube and is two-lipped, commonly with two lobes in the upper lip and three lobes in the lower lip; or the lips are almost equal and the lobes nearly regular.

Examples

horehound (Marrubium vulgare)

true mints (Mentha spp.) such as peppermint, spearmint, bergamont mint, pennyroyal

horsemint (Monarda spp.)

catnip (Nepeta cataria)

true sages (Salvia spp.) such as white sage, thistle sage, chia, black sage

Uses

Some of these plants are more aromatic than others. Many of the leaves are used for beverages or medicinal tea, particularly the mints, sages, and horehound. The seeds of many can be harvested and used in bread products, ground into flour, or used in tea. The most notable seed source is chia (Salvia columbariae) and other Salvias.

Cautions

Don't use the leaves for tea if the flavor or aroma is unpleasant or disagreeable to you. One member, wooly blue curls (Trichostema lanatum), has been used to stun fish in small pools of water. Do not use wooly blue curls for tea.

chia flower and seed cluster

Mustard Family
Cruciferae

All members of the mustard family are herbs with alternate leaves and flowers in terminal racemes. There are four distinct sepals and four (usually colorful) petals in a cross or x-form. There are six stamens, four long and two short. There is one pistil whose stigma is two-lobed or one-lobed. The fruit can be a two-celled silique or one-celled and indehiscent. The fruit (commonly called a "pod" or "capsule") can be long and narrow, short and roundish, or flattened. The herbage typically has the strong, pungent mustardlike juice. Worldwide there are 3,200 species divided into about 375 genera.

magnified stamens and pistil

Examples

bladderpod (Lesquerella spp.)

broccoli

common mustards (Brassica spp.)

silique of tooth-wort, opening

silique of shepherd's purse with one valve missing

silique of Shepherd's purse

flower of mustard

hedge mustard (Sisymbrium spp.)

pennycress (Thlaspi spp.)

peppergrass (Lepidium spp.)

sea rocket (Cakile edentula and maritima)

shepherd's purse (Capsella bursa-pastoris)

squaw cabbage (Caulanthus spp.)

sweet alyssum (Lobularia maritima)

tansy mustard (Descurainia spp.)

toothwort (Dentaria spp.)

turnip

wallflower (Erysimum spp.)

watercress (Nasturtium officinale)

wild radish (Raphanus sativus)

winter cress (Barbarea spp.)

Uses
Mustard leaves add a spicy flavor to salads and make a good steamed vegetable or spinach-type dish. The flowers, unopened flower buds, and many of the tender fruits can also be added to salads or cooked foods.

Cautions
Older mustard plants tend to be quite bitter, so they usually need to be cooked to be palatable. Also, you may encounter tough and woody specimens, which are thus inedible.

Oak Family (also called Beech Family)
Fagaceae

The oak family includes oak trees, beeches, chestnuts, and chinquapins. By some counts, there are about 900 species worldwide. Even children readily recognize oaks by their fruit, the acorn, with its scaly cap. Most members are trees, some are shrubs, and most have deciduous leaves. (See Oak Tree in the main text for a more detailed description.)

Examples
beechnuts

black oak

bur oak

chestnuts

live oak

scrub oak

spiny chinquapin

Uses

The nuts (such as acorns) are eaten. (See the main text for the processing of acorns.) In some cases, the bark and leaves may be used for medicinal and craft purposes.

Cautions

Though the acorns are a good food, you must leach out the bitter tannic acid before you use them. (See the main text for directions.)

Onions

Allium spp.

True onions belong to the Allium genus of the lily family (Amaryllidaceae). They are perennial herbs, with a leafless flower stalk arising from a bulb, and in some cases, a corm. All the basal leaves are grasslike, with a most typical oniony aroma when crushed. The petals and sepals (perianth segments) are indistinguishable from each other in appearance. Yet they are distinct from each other—they are not fused or united into a basal tube. There are six perianth segments: three sepals and three petals, all the same color. There are six stamens and one pistil per flower, and the seeds are black, flat, and wrinkled, with one or two seeds per cell.

Examples

chives

garlic

leek

shallot

swamp onion

Uses

Some Native American tribes subsisted almost entirely on onions during certain parts of the year. Onions are great added raw to salads, made into soup, or used as a flavoring for omelettes, vegetable dishes, fish, and meat. Use both the bulbs and the tender shoots.

A lily bulb. In the view at the right, the short stem and the overlapping scales are evident.

Cautions

Some members of the lily family are deadly poisonous if eaten. You must check for three sepals and three petals as well as the distinct onion aroma. There are some true onions that lack the onion aroma. Don't eat any nonaromatic species unless you have absolutely identified them as safe.

In *Know Your Poisonous Plants*, Wilma Roberts states that wild onions are toxic when eaten in great quantities. However, she neither defined the toxic element nor the amount that constituted "great quantities." Consumed in moderation, wild onions have been used for food for centuries.

Purslane Family
Portulacaceae

These are annual or perennial succulent herbs whose entire leaves can be alternately or oppositely arranged, or mostly basal. The flowers are perfect (contain both stamen and pistil). There are normally two sepals, up to eight sepals in one genus. There are commonly 5 petals, but there can be from 3 to 16. The flowers open in the sunshine and wither quickly. There are 3 to 20 stamens, sometimes more. Two to eight styles are born on the one-celled ovary. The fruit is a capsule. There are 580 species worldwide divided into about 19 genera.

miner's lettuce, flower view 1, ×3

miner's lettuce, dehiscing capsule set in calyx, ×3

Examples

bitterroot (Lewisia rediviva)

desert purslane (Calandrinia spp.)

miner's lettuce (Montia perfoliata)

purslane (Portulaca oleracea)

pussy paws (Calyptridium spp.)

miner's lettuce habit, ×⅓

miner's lettuce, flower view 2, ×3

Uses
The entire above-ground plant can usually be eaten raw; it may need to be steamed sometimes for improved palatability. The seeds can also be harvested and eaten.

Cautions
None.

Rose Family
Rosaceae

The rose family consists of herbs, shrubs, and trees, all with alternate leaves. The calyx is four- or five-lobed. There are five petals (although cultivated rose flowers contain many more petals). There can be 10 or numerous stamens; there is one to many simple pistils. Fruits are variable, ranging from a pod (follicle), an achene, a drupe (such as a plum), a cluster of drupelets (such as a blackberry), or a pome (such as an apple). Worldwide there are about 3,000 species divided into 100 genera.

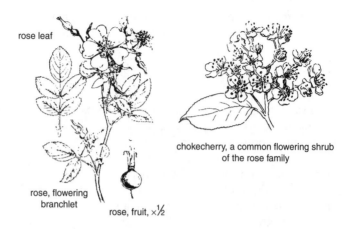

rose leaf

chokecherry, a common flowering shrub
of the rose family

rose, flowering
branchlet

rose, fruit, ×½

Examples

apples

blackberries and raspberries

cinquefoil (Potentilla spp.)

Cotoneaster pannosa

pears

serviceberry (Amelanchier spp.)

stone fruits (Prunus spp.) including peach, cherry, apricot,
almond, plum

all wild and cultivated roses (Rosa spp.)

strawberry (Fragaria spp.)

toyon (Heteromeles arbutifolia)

Uses

Many leaves of this group can be eaten, some raw, some when cooked.
However, the only valid general statement that can be made about this
group is that the petals can be eaten as well as the fruits, if fleshy and
palatable. This group contains most of the commonly recognized berries,
the bulk of cultivated fruits, all roses, and many wild plants. This is certainly a worthwhile group of plants to know.

Cautions

The leaves of some members of this group contain cyanide. An indicator
of this is the bitter-almond aroma that emanates when the leaves are
crushed. Do not make tea from such leaves, since a mild cyanide poisoning can result. Also, the seeds of many of the fruits (such as apple, cherry,
and apricot) contain cyanide. There is rarely a problem consuming these
seeds (or nuts) in small to moderate amounts, but poisonings have
occurred when eaten in larger amounts.

Seaweeds
Green, red, and brown marine algae

(See Seaweeds in the main text for the description, examples, uses, and cautions.)

Walnut Family
Juglandaceae

Worldwide there are about 60 species in this family, most of which are walnuts. These are deciduous trees with pinnately compound leaves. The male flowers are catkins. The fruit is a two-lobed, hard-shelled nut enclosed in a sheath.

Examples
bitternut

black walnut

butternut

English walnut

hickorynut

pecan

Uses
The nuts of all can be eaten, though in many cases a rock or hammer is required to break the thick, hard shell. The husks of the walnuts and some of the others are used as a black dye.

Cautions
Only eat mature nuts. Also, when collecting the freshly fallen walnuts, the husks can stain hands and clothing, so wear gloves.

Appendix 2

Why Eat Wild Food?

Dolores Lynn Nyerges[1]

"Live light upon the land if you would not be earthbound."
—Shining Bear

For years I thought, "Wild food would get me through an emergency, so I'm glad I'm familiar with the local wild plants." Though I used wild food somewhat frequently, this context lurked, unacknowledged, as one of my major motivations for using wild food. It was only after marketing Wild Salad (a mix of wild greens) through the local certified farmers' markets that I began to appreciate the broader opportunity that my knowledge affords. I was listening to our sales pitch:

These greens are fresh picked every morning. Many of them are more nutritious than regular produce. They have never been fertilized, waxed, or treated with pesticides, herbicides, or fungicides. They've not been genetically engineered. We wash our hands before we pick them and then use tongs or gloves for any subsequent handling. And your dollars don't support greedy "agribiz."

As I considered the deeper meaning and ramifications of these words, I saw my knowledge of wild food in quite a different way, and realized that there were several very good reasons to use wild food on a daily basis. And, from that process within myself, this appendix sprang to life.

218   WHY EAT WILD FOOD?

Freshness

Studies have shown that fruits and vegetables tend to lose both vitamins and minerals as they age. When one knows and uses local wild foods, genuine freshness is assured. By harvesting your own food, you can also know for certain that the plants are at their peak of readiness.

It's hard to tell how fresh grocery store produce is. We know that most produce comes from far away and thus must be *at least* a few days old. Irradiation, refrigeration, fungicide, and wax prolong the appearance of freshness long after an item would have normally begun showing signs of deterioration.

In agribusiness, salability takes priority over real freshness. Produce is hybridized specifically to make it more marketing hardy (such as more durable in transport, longer shelf life), and many fruits and vegetables are picked before they are ready in order to minimize spoilage and bruising during the trip from farm to store. Many farmers pick the whole crop at once and then preserve it for the selling season. Apples, stone fruit, and grapes may be weeks or months old due to cold storage. Many objectionable things are done to produce to make it appear fresh.

Until I actually worked in the certified farmers' markets, I had generally assumed that the produce available there was fresh and that asking the merchants was a reliable way to get information about the produce for sale (such as whether it was sprayed). I hasten to interject that I've concluded that the certified farmers' markets are the best commercial source of produce available to people fortunate enough to have access to them, but even at these stores, shoppers need to buy with discretion. Always ask each farmer/merchant about his or her produce and know that not everyone sees the value of honesty. (A fruit merchant lied to me for a couple of seasons, saying his fruit was unsprayed. Discovering this was a lie shocked me and woke me up to the need to be careful.)

Hybridization and Genetic Engineering

Wild edibles have the opportunity to be naturally strong, healthy, and adaptable. Survival of the fittest is the unspoken motto of wild food. Without the unwise intervention of Mammon-focused[2] humans, the unfit plants simply don't survive. But, we don't advocate just letting all the plants grow wild.

The nurturing of flora is a crucial part of humanity's spiritual development. Such nurturing might properly include Luther Burbank's[3] work. Some of Burbank's creations—testimonials to his loving efforts toward the exercise of dominion in the world of flora—live on today. Both agriculture and horticulture must have begun this way, but gradually fell to ignorance, pragmatism, and greed.

In agribusiness, plants destined for the table are hybridized—to look better and last longer—with salability as the main goal. Nutritional value, flavor, and other important qualities are given less consideration.

Hybridization is a controversial subject, and some research suggests that agribusiness hybridization is an unsound practice. Many hybrids couldn't survive without the intense agribusiness farming processes. Consider, for example, the seedless grape and watermelon—how would they propagate in the wild?

Genetic engineering, another practice in agribusiness, is yet another way to achieve the goal of maximum salability. Avoiding such creations will probably be challenging, in the foreseeable future, even if laws require that such products be identified on the grocers' shelves. Produce created through genetic engineering techniques end up in many food products (such as on a frozen pizza). The manufacturer of these food products, in turn, may not know about the origin of the produce they purchase and, therefore, neither do we unless manufacturers are required by law to disclose such information.

Our ability to choose what we eat is seriously threatened. If, for example, one opts for a vegetarian diet on moral grounds, it is becoming more and more difficult not to eat something objectionable (such as animal fat used to make produce shiny and attractive).

Commercial Fertilizer

Wild flora grow where conditions favor them, and such flora will continue to survive, even thrive, without applications of commercial fertilizer. Nature fertilizes flora in many ways—with animal droppings, earthworm castings, and decaying organic matter, such as fallen leaves. This natural plant food is delivered in balanced, appropriate amounts. There isn't a need for the commercial fertilizers of agribusiness, which today are nearly always from petrochemical sources and have the effect of creating flora addicts whereby such plants become unable to live naturally.

There are many other recognized objections to the use of commercial fertilizers. *One Straw Revolution* by Masanobu Fukuoka is an excellent source for more information on this topic.

Pesticides, Herbicides, and Fungicides

By now, most of us are aware that food, including produce, is treated to a wide range of potentially hazardous chemicals—pesticides, herbicides, and fungicides—all to enhance salability.

Soil, seeds, seedlings, both growing and mature plants, fruits, and even packaging and storage facilities may receive doses of poison for one reason or another.

Wild plants are, for the most part, free of chemical treatments of any kind. Those of us who choose to avoid chemical additions to our food have a great resource in the wild flora. There are, of course, ways that wild flora can be contaminated. Some cities and counties use pesticides, herbicides, and fungicides in areas under their jurisdiction. Select your wild food picking areas carefully. Call your state's department of agriculture, the Environmental Protection Agency, state extension service, or a local conservation group to get information on chemicals sprayed in your area.

An acquaintance of mine who operated a nonorganic garden service became severely ill and spent weeks in the hospital with a perplexing disease of the immune system. He told me one day that he felt certain his problems were the result of years of handling the pesticides and herbicides he routinely used in his garden service. And I was convinced he was right.

There are many articles and books that detail the myriad chemical applications used on and in commercially produced food and the many detrimental health effects that such use can cause. We highly recommend that you read the books listed in our bibliography for further study.

Wax

It's fairly common knowledge that many items of grocery produce are coated with a so-called food-grade wax in order to retard spoilage and enhance appearance. What many people don't know is how widespread this practice is. Would you believe chili peppers? Eggplant? Did you know that grocers are not required to list the pesticides and fungicides that are added to the wax, nor must they explain to you that lac resin (a standard wax ingredient) is excreta from the insect Laccifer lacca, the source of shellac. Wild flora is not coated with any such possibly toxic and unappetizing substance. Any bug poop or other organic matter can be washed off easily.

Irradiation

I believe that spices are the main food item that gets irradiated at this time. We can be certain that no wild foods have been irradiated. And there are many wonderful spices growing indigenously about. Near our home, we are fortunate to have many spices growing wild, including bay leaf, fennel, California pepper, and several types of sage.

For further discussion on irradiation, see Chapter 13 of *Diet for a Poisoned Planet: How to Choose Safe Foods for You and Your Family* by David Steinman.

Purity

In recent years we've heard more and more about food-borne disease. E. coli and salmonella are bacteria that can cause illness and death if consumed. Human hands transmit the bacteria to food. We associate these illnesses with undercooked meat or chicken, but E. coli in particular can be easily spread via any food (like salad) that has been handled and not subsequently well cooked or at least washed in very hot water.

Many types of produce can easily deliver dozens of socially transmissible diseases directly to our plates, simply because much produce is used raw and is too delicate for washing in water hot enough to kill any bacteria or viruses that may be present.

The fact is that hands pass on not only E. coli, but also many cold and flu types of illnesses. Tuberculosis is passed fairly easily by various social interactions.

The next time you visit your grocery store, ask the management who picks the produce you buy and if these people can (and do) frequently wash their hands with hot water and soap throughout the workday. Is the produce shielded from sneezes and coughs? How? And, then, what about the employees at the central market where the produce goes between farm and grocery store? Next, think about everyone who might handle produce in the grocery store, including perhaps dozens of customers each day. As you consider all the hands that touch the produce you buy, you might decide to turn to wild foods. Chances are only you and/or your family will handle the wild foods you pick and consume.

Some Moral and Spiritual Considerations
One needs to exercise choice for the better at every opportunity. Learning about and harvesting those wild foods available to us is one way to remove dollar support from, at least, the agribusiness part of the food industry. We all bear the responsibility for what we have supported with our dollars. It's neither possible nor wise to utterly isolate oneself from the "evil world," but the food industry, particularly that of North America, is fraught with unconscionable practices that we ought not to support. Learning to identify and use the wild flora around us will help us replace as much purchased produce as possible.

Harmless Harvesting
To put it plainly, many commercial produce items are killed plants. The head of lettuce, the bunch of spinach, the root crops like carrots, the celery—all plants destroyed in the picking. Wise stewardship involves gentle nurturing of the flora that sustain us. Killing for food (either floral or faunal) is not necessary in order to live.

Wherever possible, it is best to leave at least ½ of the plant so that it may continue to live. A great teacher of ours, Shining Bear, pinched the little tips, buds, and flowers and collected the seeds of his wild food sources. He never, to my knowledge, destroyed these floral friends.

Other Health Benefits
We have all heard of the damaging health effects of worry and stress. Preparedness and the ability to be self-reliant can contribute to a general sense of well being. The fresh air and exercise available through active food foraging can also be beneficial. Simply being in a meadow of wild flora can promote joy.

Try this experiment: find a commercial field of produce and just stand in it.

Note what you feel and what thoughts you have. Then spend some time in a field of wild flora. Take note of how you feel here. (I feel quite uplifted in the midst of a golden expanse of flowering wild mustard.)

Conclusion

We've considered a number of reasons why it's a good idea to be able to identify and use wild plants for food. Wild food often has superior nutritional qualities, whether eaten cooked or raw. Such foraging is a great way to avoid the drawbacks of agribusiness produce, such as hybridization, genetic engineering, commercial fertilizers, pesticides, herbicides, lack of freshness, fungicides, wax, and socially transmissible diseases. Foraging also allows us to withdraw our dollar support for agribusiness. It's also good for us to get out in the fresh air, get some exercise, spend time with truly happy flora, and to nurture and harvest the useful ones in a loving manner.

Endnotes

1. I'd like to thank Shining Bear for unique guidance and training, Susan Robbins and Chris Mitchell of the Vegetarian Forum on CompuServe, and Johnny Lynch, teacher of the Vegetarian No-Cooking Class.

2. Mammon-focused means valuing earthly riches over the riches of the spirit. See New Testament passages: Matt. 6:24 and Luke 16:9, 11.

3. Luther Burbank (1849–1926), American botanist and horticulturist who developed hundreds of new plant varieties, including the Burbank potato, the thornless Opuntia cactus, and the plumcot, a cross between the plum and the apricot. One of Burbank's objectives was to manipulate the characteristics of plants and thereby increase the world's food supply.

Glossary

The numbers within parentheses refer to the illustrations in the margin.

Air Bladder A sac containing air and/or water.

Alimentary Canal A musculo-membranous tube, extending from the mouth to the anus. It functions in digestion, absorption of food, and the elimination of residual waste. The parts of the alimentary canal are the mouth, pharynx, esophagus, stomach, and the small and large intestines.

Alluvial Fan A flat, fan-shaped deposit such as sand, silt, and clay made by rainwater falling on hills and/or mountains, washing off exposed dirt surfaces, and carrying dislodged particles down gullies.

Alternate Having only one leaf or branch protruding from each node. (1)

Anesthetic That which produces loss of sensation with or without loss of consciousness.

1

alternate

Annual Completing the life cycle in one growing season; flowering, fruiting, and dying all in the same year.

Anthelmintic Expelling or destroying parasitic worms, especially of the intestines.

Anther The part of the stamen that contains the pollen. (2)

Antiflatulent Dissipating gas in the stomach or intestines.

Antiseptic Something that prevents or arrests the growth or action of microorganisms (such as on living tissue).

2

anther

Apex The tip of the leaf.

Aromatic Having a strong, distinctive odor.

Astringent Something that draws together soft organic tissues. A styptic herb or puckery unripe fruit can be described as astringent.

Axil The angle between the upperside of a leaf or branch, and the stem or branch from which it grows. (3)

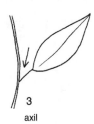

3

axil

Axillary Pertaining to, or growing from the axil (in other words, a flower or leaf).

Axis The central, longitudinal support on which a plant's parts or organs are arranged; the stem and root considered as a single unit.

Basal At, or forming at, the base of a stem or at ground level.

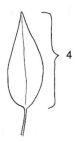

Berry A fleshy, indehiscent fruit containing several seeds (see Indehiscent).

Biennial Taking two years or seasons to flower, fruit, and die.

blade

Blade The flat, expanded portion of a leaf, distinct from the petiole. (4)

Bract A leaf situated at the base of a flower or its stalk. Ordinarily bracts are smaller than foliage leaves but are occasionally large and showy, simulating petals (see Stipule).

Branch Any woody protrusion growing from the trunk, main stem, or bough of a tree, bush, or shrub.

Bronchitis An inflammation, acute or chronic, of the mucus lining of the bronchial tubes.

Bud A small swelling or projection on a branch from which a shoot, cluster of leaves, or flower develops.

Bulb Cluster of fleshy storage leaves gathered tightly together on a short stem axis, forming what is called an "underground organ"; an onion is an example. (5)

bulb

Calyx The outer whorl (usually green) of a flower consisting of sepals.

Capsule Any dehiscent fruit made up of more than one carpel (see Dehiscence). (6)

Carminative Expelling gas from the alimentary canal.

capsule

Carpel A simple pistil or a single member of a compound pistil.

Catkin A tassel-like (usually pendulous) cluster of small unisexual flowers without petals, either staminate or pistillate. (7)

Caudex The persistent, often woody base of an herbaceous perennial; also refers to the axis of a plant (including both stem and root).

catkin

Cell 1. A small compartment or cavity, as in a honeycomb. 2. A small microscopic mass of protoplasm capable alone, or interacting with others, of performing all fundamental life functions; the smallest structural entity capable of functioning independently.

Chaff Threshed or winnowed husks of grain (thin, dry scales or bracts).

Chaparral Colony of thorny or rigid shrubs growing in dry soil or on rocky ridges and slopes. Chiefly characterized by great thickening of the epidermis, condensation of the plant body, and/or reduction of the leaf surface.

Cinereous Grayish.

Cleft With sharp lobes, usually near the middle. (8)

Compound (leaf) Having the blade divided to the midrib and forming two or more leaflets on a common axis. (9)

Corm Modified underground stem base, fleshy and globose, bearing scaly leaves and bulbs.

Corolla The part of a flower that comprises the circle of petals, found within the calyx and outside the stamens.

Corona An appendage or series of united appendages, on the inner side of the corolla in some flowers, such as the passionflower and milkweed.

Corymb A flat-topped or convex flower cluster, in which outer stems are long and those toward the center are shorter. (10)

Crenate Having a notched or scalloped leaf margin forming small, rounded teeth. (11)

Cutigen A cultivated organism of species for which a wild ancestor is unknown.

Cyme A flower cluster, often flat-topped or convex, in which the central or terminal flower blooms the earliest. (12)

Deciduous Not persistent or evergreen, as with trees and shrubs whose leaves fall off in autumn.

Decoction An extract obtained by boiling the plant or herb in water.

Decumbent Having stems that lie flat on the ground but whose ends rise above the ground.

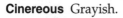

8

cleft

9

compound

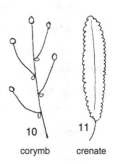

10   11

corymb   crenate

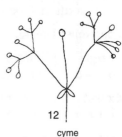

12

cyme

Decurrent Having leaves whose bases extend down the stem below the place of connection (as with thistle). (13)

Degenerate Having leaves, flowers, fruits, and other plant parts that are scrawny, inconspicuous, or simply vestiges of fully developed parts. Although the word degenerate implies something that has declined from its ancestors, it remains speculative that any given plant species has actually degenerated from a "higher" form.

13
decurrent

Dehiscence The natural bursting or splitting open of capsules, fruits, and anthers for the discharge of their contents.

Demulcent Something that soothes or protects by coating with a substance such as oil.

Diaphoretic Any substance that, after being consumed, promotes perspiration (usually drunk as a tea).

Diffuse Widely spreading; not concentrated or localized.

Dioecious Having stamens and pistils in separate flowers on different parts of the same species.

Diphtheria An acute infectious disease characterized by weakness, high fever, and the formation in the air passages of a false membrane that interferes with breathing.

Diuretic Increases the flow of urine.

Drupe An indehiscent fleshy fruit, such as a peach, cherry, or plum, containing one stony seed inside.

14
elliptical

Elliptical (leaf) Widest in the center with the two ends tapering equally, generally about 1½ times as long as broad. (14)

Emollient Something that softens and/or soothes, particularly the skin.

Entire Having a leaf margin that is smooth and uniform (in other words, not toothed, crenate, or indented). (15)

Epidermis The thin outer layer of all seed plants and ferns.

Evergreen Having green leaves throughout the year (as opposed to deciduous).

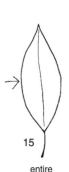
15
entire

Expectorant Something that causes mucus to be discharged from the throat or lungs by coughing or hacking and spitting.

Family A group of related plants or animals forming a category ranking above a genus and below an order and usually comprising several to many genera.

Fibers Part of the plant tissue that can be separated into threads or thread-like structures for weaving.

Fibrous Composed of or resembling fibres.

Filament The stalklike part of the stamen that supports the anther. (16)

Flatulent Affected with gas in the stomach or intestines.

Frond A large leaf usually with many divisions.

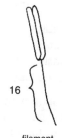

16

filament

Fruit The matured or ripened ovary, together with any other parts that develop with it, containing one or more seeds.

Genus A category of biological classification ranking between the family and the species, comprising structurally or phylogenetically related species or an isolated species exhibiting unusual differentiation, and being designated by a Latin or latinized capitalized single noun.

Glabrous Having no hair and smooth to the touch.

Globose Globular; having the shape of a globe or globule.

Glochid A barbed hair; a bristle; commonly used in reference to the minute bristles at the base of each spine of the Opuntia genus.

Head A globose cluster of sessile flowers, collected at the same point of the peduncle.

Herbaceous Not woody.

Husk The dry outer covering of various fruits and seeds.

Imbrication An overlapping of similar pieces or segments (somewhat like roof shingles); can be either vertical or lateral, such as the bracts at the base of many flowers in the sunflower family (Compositae).

17

incised

Imperfect Having stamens or pistils but not both.

Incised Having a leaf margin that is deeply and sharply notched. (17)

Indehiscent Remaining closed at maturity; not dehiscent.

Inflorescence 1. The mode of arrangement of flowers on an axis; a floral axis with its appendages; also a flower cluster. 2. The budding and unfolding of blossoms; flowering.

Infusion The liquid that results from pouring boiling water over herbs that are gathered into a vessel and letting them steep in order to extract their water-soluble particles.

Internode The section of a stem between the nodes. (18)

Labiate Refers to the mint family's (Labiatae) "lipped" petals. The tubular corolla is divided into two irregular parts, commonly with two lobes in the upper lip and three lobes in the lower lip.

Lanceolate Having a leaf that is three to four times longer than broad, generally widest below the center, and tapering to a point at the apex and base; so named because the leaf resembles the head of a lance. (19)

18

internode

Laxative Promotes bowel action or purgation.

Leaflet One of the divisions of a compound leaf.

Legume Characteristic of the Leguminosae family; usually a dehiscent fruit formed by one carpel with two dehiscent sutures; any plant with this type of fruit.

Linear Having a narrow leaf, four to five times as long as wide, with more or less parallel sides. (20)

19

lanceolate

Lobe A division of an organ; a segment of a palmately or pinnately lobed, cleft, or parted leaf.

Lyrate Pinnately lobed with the terminal segment round and large, and the lower lobes smaller. (21)

Margin The perimeter, or edge, of a leaf structure.

Monoecious Having stamens and pistils in separate flowers on the same plant.

Mucilaginous Sticky, viscid.

Naturalized Having adapted to an environment other than the native environment.

20   21

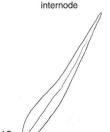

linear   lyrate

Nerve A simple or unbranched vein or slender rib. Most commonly refers to a leaf.

Neuralgia Severe pain along the course of one or more nerves.

Node A joint on a stem where a leaf, leaves, or branches originate. (22)

Nut An indehiscent, dry, one-seeded fruit with a hard, firm wall.

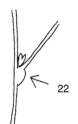

22

node

Oblong Two to four times longer than wide, with sides parallel or nearly so. (23)

Obovate Paddle shaped; narrowest at the bottom.

Opposite Having two leaves protruding from each node, and from opposing sides of the stem. (24)

Ovary The enlarged lower part of the pistil containing the ovules, or young seeds.

Ovate Egg shaped; widest below the middle. (25)

Ovoid Same as ovate.

Oxalate Acid A colorless, poisonous, crystalline acid $(COOH)_2$ found in oxalis and other plants.

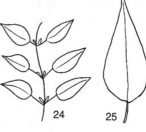

23

oblong

Palmate With the leaflets all borne at the apex of the common petiole or, a leaf with three or more divisions (or leaflet) arising from a common point.

Panicle A compound raceme. (27)

Pedicel The small stalk or stem of an individual flower of an inflorescence. (28)

24   25

opposite   ovate

Peduncle The stalk of a solitary flower, or the stalk which leads to an inflorescence (see Rachis). (29)

Perennial Having a life cycle that lasts more than two years.

Perfect Having functional stamens and pistil(s) in the same flower.

Perianth The floral structure consisting of the calyx and corolla. This term is used mostly when the calyx and corolla are either identical in physical appearance or not readily distinguishable from each other.

26

palmate

Petal One of the parts of the corolla, usually colored.

Petiolate Having a stalk or petiole.

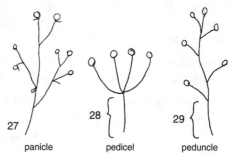

27

28

29

panicle   pedicel   peduncle

Petiole The stalk of a leaf. (30)

Pinnate With the leaflets arranged along each side of a common rachis. Can either be odd-pinnate (31a) or even-pinnate (31b).

Pistil The female organ of the flower, composed of ovary, style, and stigma. Once fertilized, it develops the fruit.

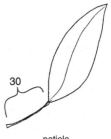

petiole

Pith The tissue in the middle of a plant's stem or branch.

Pod Any dry dehiscent seed vessel or fruit, usually a legume (but sometimes a silique or follicle).

Pollen A mass of microspores in a seed plant, appearing usually as a fine dust.

Pollination The transfer of pollen from an anther to a stigma.

Potherb A usually leafy herb that is cooked for use as greens.

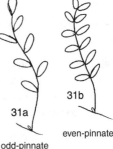

31b
even-pinnate

31a
odd-pinnate

Poultice A preparation of heated herbs, which are usually mashed, then spread on a cloth and applied to parts of the skin (such as sores or inflamed body parts) to soothe, heal, or act as an antiseptic or counterirritant.

Prophylactic Something that guards from or prevents disease.

Prostrate Trailing on the ground; flat; procumbent.

Pubescent Covered with hairs, usually short, soft and down-like (not matted).

32

Punk Wood or leaves so decayed and/or dry, that it is useful for tinder.

raceme

Quinquefoliolate A compound leaf composed of five leaflets.

Raceme A flower cluster in which the flowers are borne along the rachis on pedicels of nearly equal length, with the lower flowers blossoming before the upper ones. (32)

Rachis The central elongated axis of a compound leaf or inflorescence (such as in a raceme). Not to be confused with pedicel, peduncle, or petiole.

Ray 1. In the sunflower family: the ligulate, or strap-shaped, marginal flowers on the head, as opposed to the central regular flowers. 2. In the parsley family: one of the primary branches of an umbel or similar inflorescence.

Rhizome An elongated (usually horizontal) underground stem, producing shoots above and roots below; distinguished from a true root because of its buds, nodes, and usually scale-like leaves. (33)

Rosette A dense basal cluster of leaves arranged in a circular fashion like the petals of a rose.

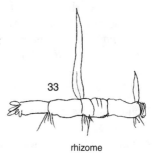

33

rhizome

Rotate Having the parts flat and spreading or radiating like the spokes of a wheel.

Rugose With wrinkled or creased surface.

Rugulose Minutely rugose.

Rush A genus of tall perennial herbs resembling grasses. They grow in wet places and have unbranched round stems; narrow, flat grassy leaves; and small clusters of greenish or brown flowers.

Salve Any medical ointment applied to wounds, skin irritations, or burns for the purpose of soothing and promoting healing.

Sap The juice or fluid contents of a plant.

Scale A thin, dry, membranous body, commonly glabrous, resembling the scales of a fish or reptile.

Scapose A leafless, flower-bearing peduncle, arising directly from the ground.

Scarious Thin, dry, and no longer green (if formerly green).

Scorpoid A one-sided inflorescence that is coiled at the tip like the tail of a scorpion.

Sepal One of the parts comprising the calyx of a flower.

Sessile Having leaves or flowers that are directly attached by their base (in other words, lacking a petiole) to the stem. (34)

34

sessile

Shoot A new growth, such as a sprout or twig.

Shrubs Woody, bushy plants of various sizes usually developing several main branches instead of one trunk.

Simple Consisting of only one part; not completely divided into separate segments.

Species All the plants of one kind having common attributes and the potential for interbreeding. In a plant's Latin name, such as *Chenopodium album*, the species is designated by the second term, which is almost always uncapitalized-in this case, album. Many related species constitute a genus. Within a species, there may be several natural or horticultural varieties.

Spike A flower cluster in which the flowers are sessile and densely arranged along a common rachis. The lower flowers blossom before the upper. (35)

35
spike

Sprout A new growth from a bud, rootstock, germinating seed, and more.

Stalk The main stem of an herbaceous plant; any part of a plant (such as petiole or peduncle) that supports another part, such as leaf or flower.

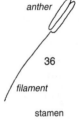

anther

Stamen The male organ of the flower, composed of an anther and a filament. (36)

36

filament

Stem The main trunk of a tree or plant; any part of a plant (such as a branch or a petiole) that supports another part, such as a leaf or flower.

stamen

Stigma The flat, outer end part of the pistil of the flower that receives the pollen grains and on which they germinate.

Stipule Either of a pair of appendages found at the base of the petiole (see Bract). (37)

Striate Marked with fine, longitudinal lines, grooves, furrows, or streaks.

37
stipule

Styptic A substance that will slow or stop bleeding. Most styptics work as astringents, contracting the surrounding tissues, and halting the flow of blood.

Succulent Fleshy and full of juice.

Symbiosis The intimate living together of two dissimilar organisms in a mutually beneficial relationship.

Taproot A single large, strong root that descends nearly perpendicular into the soil.

Tea A beverage or medicine made by infusing or decocting the dried and prepared leaves of specially grown or wild plants such as shrubs, herbs, flowers, and roots.

Tendril A slender, spirally coiling organ emanating from either the peduncle or pedicel, which serves to attach a climbing plant to its support. (38)

Terminal Anything such as a bud, flower, or flower cluster growing at the apex of a stem, branch, or shoot.

Tomentose Covered with densely matted hairs.

38

tendril

Tonic A medicinal or psychological remedy that is invigorating, strengthening, or toning to an organ or to the body as a whole.

Toothed Having leaf margins that are notched or indented with small, sharp lobes. (39)

Transpire To give off or exude watery vapor from the surface of leaves.

Trifoliate Having three leaves.

Tuber A thickened fleshy outgrowth of an underground stem bearing numerous minute leaves with bulbs ("eyes") in their axils, from which new plants may arise. An example is the potato.

39

Umbel A flat-topped or slightly convex flower cluster

toothed

in which a number of flower stalks of nearly equal length arise from the same center point.

Valve One of the parts into which a dehiscent fruit splits.

Variety A plant that has minor but noticeable differences from the others of the same species, such as in a horticultural variety; any natural variation that does not constitute a separate species. Within a species, there may be several varieties (see Species).

Vulneraries Herbs or other remedies that are used in the healing of wounds.

Whorl Arrangement of similar anatomical parts, such as leaves or flowers, in a circle around a point on an axis. (40)

Winnow To separate the chaff from grain or seed by wind or a forced current of air; eliminating the dry covering and other substances that are not desired in food.

40

whorled

Bibliography

Agricultural Research Service. *Composition of Foods, Agricultural Handbook No. 8.* Washington, D.C.: United States Department of Agriculture, 1963.

Ainge, Inez. "Native Chia." *Desert Magazine.* 1967.

Airola, Paavo. *Are You Confused? De-confusion Book on Nutrition and Health, with the Latest Scientific Research and Authoritative Answers to the Most Controversial Questions.* Phoenix, Ariz.: Health Plus, 1972.

Boyd, Doug. *Rolling Thunder: A Personal Exploration into the Secret Healing Powers of an American Indian Medicine Man.* New York: Random House, 1974.

Bramwell, Martin, ed. *The International Book of Wood.* New York: Crescent Books, 1985.

Bryan, John E., and Coralie Castle. *The Edible Ornamental Garden.* San Francisco: 101 Productions, 1974.

Castaneda, Carlos. *The Teachings of Don Juan: A Yaqui Way of Knowledge.* Berkeley, Calif.: University of California Press, 1968.

Cerney, J. C. *Acupressure—Acupuncture Without Needles.* Englewood Cliffs, N.J.: Parker Publishing Company, 1983.

Doyle, Harrison. *Golden Chia: Ancient Indian Energy Food.* Vista, Calif.: Hillside Press, 1976.

Duke, James A., and Alan A. Atchley. *CRC Handbook of Proximate Analysis Tables of Plants.* Boca Raton, Fla.: CRC Press, 1986.

Elpel, Thomas. *Botany in a Day: Thomas J. Elpel's Herbal Field Guide to Plant Families.* Third edition. Pony, Mont.: HOPS, 1998.

The Findhorn Community. *The Findhorn Garden.* New York: Harper Collins, 1976.

Fukuoka, Masanobu. *One Straw Revolution.* Emmaus, Penn.: Rodale Press, 1968.

Gail, Peter. *Dandelion Celebration.* Cleveland, Ohio: Goosefoot Acres Press, 1994.

Gibbons, Euell. *Stalking the Blue Eyed Scallop.* New York: David McKay Company, Inc., 1964.

—. *Stalking the Healthful Herbs.* New York: David McKay Company, Inc., 1966.

Guttenberg, James. *The Green Beret Gourmet*. Rockledge, Fla.: Guttenberg Press.

Herter, George L., and Jacques P. Herter. *Professional Guide Manual*. Waseca, Minn.: Herter's, Inc., 1960.

Hutchens, Alma R. *Indian Herbology of North America*. Windsor, Ontario: Merco, 1973.

James, Wilma Roberts. *Know Your Poisonous Plants: Poisonous Plants Found in Field and Garden*. Healdsburg, Calif.: Naturegraph Publishers, 1973.

Kingsburg, John M. *Poisonous Plants in the United States and Canada*. Englewood Cliffs, N.J.: Prentice Hall, 1964.

Krieger, Louis, C. C. *The Mushroom Handbook*. New York: Dover Publications, 1967.

Lehner, Ernst, and Johanna Lehner. *Folklore and Symbolism of Flowers, Plants, and Trees*. Detroit, Mich.: Omnigraphics, Inc., 1990.

Madlener, Judith. *The Seavegetable Book*. Culver City, Calif.: Peace Press, 1979.

Miller, Orson K. *Mushrooms of North America*. New York: E. P. Dutton, 1972.

Moore, Michael. *Medicinal Plants of the Mountain West*. Santa Fe, N.M.: Museum of New Mexico Press, 1979.

McIlvaine, Charles. *Toadstools, Mushrooms, Fungi, Edible and Poisonous; One Thousand American Fungi; How to Select and Cook the Edible; How to Distinguish and Avoid the Poisonous, with Full Botanic Descriptions*. Indianapolis, Ind.: The Bobbs-Merrill Company, 1912.

National Wildlife Federation. National Wildlife Federation study, Spring, 1984.

Nyerges, Christopher. "Passive Agriculture." *The Wild Foods Forum* 9, no. 1 (1998): 6–7.

Olsen, Larry Dean. *Outdoor Survival Skills*. Chicago: Chicago Review Press, 1990.

Plato. *The Apology, Phaedo and Crito of Plato*. Danbury, Conn.: Grolier Enterprises, 1980.

"The Plow Boy Interview with Euell Gibbons." *Mother Earth News*, (May 1972): 6–14.

Robbins, John. *Diet for a New America*. Walpole, N.H.: Stillpoint Publishing, 1987.

Rohde, Eleanour Sinclair. *Rose Recipes from Olden Times*. New York: Dover Publications, 1973.

R. W. "Once a Problem, Cattails Become a Solution." *Christian Science Monitor* (1997): 4.

Salem, Norman, and Artemis P. Simopoulos. *Science Weekly*. (1989).

Seddon, Marian. "Carob." *Desert Magazine*. (1976).

Smith, Alexander. *A Field Guide to Western Mushrooms*. Ann Arbor, Mich.: University of Michigan Press, 1975.

Steinman, David. *Diet for a Poisoned Planet: How to Choose Safe Foods for You and Your Family*. New York: Harmony Books, 1990.

Stoner, Carol Hupping. *Stocking Up: The All-New Edition of America's Classic Preserving Guide*. Emmaus, Penn.: Rodale Press, 1986.

Sunset editors. *Western Gardening Book*. New York: Leisure Arts, 1995.

Superweed, Mary Jane. *Herbal Highs*. San Francisco: Stone Kingdom, 1970.

Tobe, John. *Natural History of the Bible*. St. Catherine's, Ontario: Provoker Press, 1968.

United States Pharmacopoeia. Mack Publishing Co., 1986.

University of California, Berkeley Wellness Letter. New York: Health Letter Associates, 1990.

Walters, Charles, Jr. *Acres, U.S.A.: The Journal of Organic Farming*. December 1979/January 1980.

Wiekens, Carol. *Prevention magazine*. (1973).

Wood, Horatio Charles. *Dispensatory of the United States of America*. Philadelphia, Penn.: Lippincott, 1955.

Zim, Herbert Spencer, and Lester Ingle. *Seashores: A Guide to Animals and Plants along the Beaches*. New York: Golden Press, 1955.

About the Author

Christopher Nyerges grew up in Pasadena, California, near the Angeles National Forest where he spent much time hiking and studying wild plants. He studied botany in high school and college, with a special interest in ethnobotany. He joined the Los Angeles Mycological Association while still in high school. In 1974, he began leading wild food outings with WTI, Inc. Today he continues to lead wild food and survival-skills hikes on most weekends. Thousands of adults and children have learned these skills with Nyerges's help.

Christopher Nyerges strips a yucca leaf into fibers.

Christopher and his wife, Dolores, are the co-directors of the School of Self-Reliance where they regularly conduct survival classes, wild food cooking classes, and wild food outings. You can contact them via their Web site at www.self-reliance.net.

Nyerges has written three syndicated newspaper columns and written for hundreds of magazines and newspapers including the *Los Angeles Times*, *The Christian Science Monitor*, *American Survival Guide*, *Mother Earth News*, and *The Wild Foods Forum*. He is the author of *Urban Wilderness*, *Enter the Forest*, *Wild Greens and Salads: A Cookbook*, and *Testing Your Outdoor Survival Skills*.

Related Titles from
Chicago Review Press

High Trail Cookery
*All-Natural, Home-Dried, Palate-Pleasing Meals for the Backpacker
Revised edition*
Linda Frederick Yaffe

Simple, easy-to-follow recipes explain how to dehydrate food at home, store it, and pack it along on your next camping trip.

238 pages, 9 x 6
30 illustrations
ISBN 1-55652-313-0
paper, $12.95

Outdoor Survival Skills
**Larry Dean Olsen
Foreword by Robert Redford**

"The author has devoted a lifetime to learning and mastering the ways of the wilderness. . . . His concepts have been proven by the more than 10,000 students who have participated in his wilderness laboratories."—*Booklist*

272 pages, 6 x 9
96 color photos, 200 b & w photos, 10 line drawings
ISBN 1-55652-323-8
paper, $14.95

Survival Skills of the North American Indians

Second edition

Peter Goodchild

"This is the most comprehensive skills book I've found."

—*Tamarack Song, wilderness skills teacher and author of* Journey to the Ancestral Self

This comprehensive review of Native American life skills covers collecting and preparing plant foods and medicines; hunting animals; creating and transporting fire; and crafting tools, shelter, clothing, utensils, and other devices.

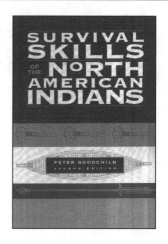

248 pages, 7 x 10
10 b & w photos, 145 line drawings
1-55652-345-9
paper, $16.95

The Well-Organized Camper

Linda Frederick Yaffe

Full of time-saving planning tips, this guide gets campers prepared for outdoor adventure by offering helpful advice on what to pack, how to organize gear, what to eat, how to plan a route, how to stay safe, and much more. Whether you're planning a backpacking, car camping, paddle, winter camping, or international trip or traveling with children, this book will be indispensable. A menu plan including home-dried one-pot meals makes eating on the trail fast and hearty.

240 pages, 6 x 9
128 b & w illustrations
1-55652-343-2
paper, $12.95